SET UP FOR FAILURE

WHY PUBLIC EDUCATION IN THE UNITED STATES IS FAILING,

AND WHAT WE CAN DO TO SAVE IT

by Sherli Leonard

VOX PRO DISCANDO PRESS

Set Up for Failure

Copyright © 2004 by Sherli Leonard
All rights reserved

Published by
Vox Pro Discando Communications: Sherli Leonard Publisher
1310 Knoll Road, Redlands, California, 92373
sherli@voxprodiscando.com

Printed on Demand by
Lightning Source Inc.
1246 Heil Quaker Blvd.
La Vergne, TN USA 37086
(615)213-5815

Printed in the United States of America

ISBN 0-9725002-1-9
Library of Congress Control Number:
2003109313

I dedicate this book to
all the children of the future:
may their public education
educate them well.

Set Up for Failure

Acknowledgments

Notions cannot grow in a vacuum. My notions about public education took root during my first year of teaching, and evolved in a rich mélange of equal parts of systemic idiocy and the passionate debates with my brilliant colleagues. Filled with the certainty of youth, my colleagues and I commiserated with each other about the apparent dead-end of the public education system. At least in our animated exchanges, we solved the problems of the schools.

Ah, youth. It passes, and with its passing goes the sense of invincibility. Life gets in the way of right.

We never realized our dreams to forge the perfect school, one where young people could learn again to love learning, could exponentially expand their curiosity, and could explore the nooks and crannies of their own minds and possibilities. But always, every one of us remained dedicated to do our small part to make our students' lives palatable, at least in our classes.

To this small band of pedagogical soldiers, I owe my clarity of thought: they challenged me as I challenged them, and in the process, we saw more clearly. Karen Juchau, Elaine Skeete, Ken Stacey, Ted Zimmermann, Tony Silva, and I spent many a long, enlightening evening planning and plotting how to improve the public schools.

I say thank you to my long-time friend and fellow Learning Facilitator, Cindy Gray Totten, for proofreading manuscripts, and for continuing to amaze me with her willingness to keep trying.

I say thank you to another long-time friend, fellow musician, fellow educator, and fellow horse-enthusiast, Jan Gudgell, for proofreading and for being the solid sounding board for my occasionally challenging ideas.

I say thank you to my colleagues of twenty years in the Social Studies Department at Moreno Valley High School in

Set Up for Failure

Moreno Valley, California, for their dogged determination to make a difference for their students: Berneice Cunningham, Judy Horrigan, John Ewens, Vic Kezer, and Bill Payne.

I say thank you to James Bowers, friend, fellow educator, and people-hugger, for stirring the stew of ideas, constantly tossing in fresh ones to help create a powerful concoction.

Thank you to all of my thousands of students over twenty-four years in the public school classroom—your responses and reactions to the system that chained you for most of your young lives made me ache for reason, for a logical, rational approach to preparing you to be thriving and thoughtful adults.

TABLE OF CONTENTS

Preface . . . .

PART I: PROOF OF FAILURE

Chapter 1: What does the public want and expect vs. what does it get 1

PART II: REASONS FOR FAILURE

Introduction: Why? 9

Section A: The Curriculum

Prelude 22

Chapter 2: Stuff they don't want to know + Stuff they don't need to know = Stuff they don't learn . . . 26

Section B: The System

Prelude 49

Chapter 3: The system's assembly-line model assumes everyone is identical 55

Chapter 4: Teaching strategies ignore what we know about how people learn 61

Chapter 5: The system's schedule ignores what we know about how people learn 83

Chapter 6: Class size: More is only more . . . 90

Chapter 7: Letter grades de-grade learning . . . 95

Chapter 8: Misplaced priorities say learning isn't important 100

Chapter 9: Lopsided budgets for education's corporate structure spell F-A-I-L-U-R-E. 110

Chapter 10: The media interferes 133

PART III: STOP THE FAILURE

Prelude 141

Chapter 11: Develop effective teachers 145

Chapter 12: Create meaningful, relevant standards, and test for achievement 160

Chapter 13: Create small schools 168

Chapter 14: Create rational, research-backed school structures and curriculum 193

Chapter 15: Create every opportunity to learn . 217

Chapter 16: Eviscerate standardized testing . . .232

EPILOGUE 252

PART IV: RESOURCES AND REFERENCES

RESOURCE LIST OF EDUCATION REFORM
ORGANIZATIONS 258

REFERENCES 261

Set Up for Failure

Preface

Jefferson turned quickly to face the escort. "Hasn't anyone taught them to think?" he implored, clearly distraught. "They can't tell a fact from an opinion, they don't ask questions, they can't even explain their reasons for their own ideas."

The escort stared down at his own clasped hands.

"When I asked them to identify the fallacy in an argument," Jefferson went on, whispering intensely, "they thought I was making a remark about sex, for God's sake. I queried them about how to resolve a boundary dispute between neighbors, and they said the 'dudes' should take it to court. When I asked them what they would do if no courts were nearby, they replied that lawyers were everywhere: someone would take care of them." Thomas Jefferson was dumbfounded.

"Well, sir," began the escort cautiously, "things have changed a little since you were here."

In an unexplainable happening, Thomas Jefferson had been transported to early 21st century United States to observe the nation he had guided 200 years earlier.

"The language certainly has changed," said Jefferson in disgust as he strode impatiently out of the room where the recent high school graduates had met him for the interview. "Like, well ah'm all, yuh know'. . . what kind of a sentence start is that? Hasn't anyone shown them how to talk?"

"No, not exactly," replied the escort. "The schools don't require them to use traditional speech patterns."

"The schools? Don't their parents teach them?" Jefferson asked, his face twisted in disbelief.

"Well," the escort attempted to explain, "The schools are the main source . . . in many cases, the only source . . . of formal education. More than half the homes with children have no books in them, so the children. . . ."

"No books in the homes?" Jefferson stared at the escort.

"Well, many of the schools have libraries."

"Many? Does that mean there are schools without libraries?" Jefferson was beside himself. "How will the people learn about the great ideas, the failures and successes and progress of civilizations? How will they know a good argument from a bad one? How will they know what to believe?"

"Sir, you have to understand," said the escort patiently. "Schools at the start of the twenty-first century have an enormous task. They are expected to provide food, psychological counseling, entertainment and socialization, job training, and a basic education. Frankly, they don't have the time, money, or expertise to teach the young people to . . . ya know, think critically."

Jefferson leaned in toward the escort and grabbed him by the arm.

"My young man, what will happen to democracy?" he whispered harshly. "If these students are not taught to make intelligent decisions—informed and reasoned decisions—how will they be able to protect and exercise their inalienable rights? How will they know when they are being lied to? How will they ever solve their own problems? How will they make their case for their ideas?" He hesitated. "How will they even have ideas? My, God; how long can this nation last since the people have become so, so. . . ." Jefferson could not finish. He turned in despair, and vanished.

While life in general and schools in particular during Thomas Jefferson's day were significantly different from those of today, the need to protect the democracy of the United States with the development of an informed, thoughtful electorate remains unchanged. If Jefferson were to visit the United States today, he might perceive that the problem in the intellectual fiber of this nation is a dearth of thinking, reasoning, questioning

Preface

young people who can solve their own problems, who accept responsibility for their own actions and for the well-being of their communities, who can readily communicate their thoughts in written and oral language, and who consequently make thoughtful decisions about their own lives and about their government.

This problem looms huge for the United States. Evidence abounds. Those who love numbers and charts and standardized tests can find proof of the problem in test scores that show high school and college students capable of recalling some facts, but woefully inadequate at reasoning an argument, defending their points of view, solving problems, making predictions—all higher-level thinking skills—, and clearly expressing all of the above in writing.

Those who prefer to look at the big picture can find proof in the gridlock of civil litigations in the courts, of plaintiffs and respondents seeking to prove someone else is at fault, and hiring someone else to argue for them.

The plethora of insulting advertisements offers more proof as they ply the consumers with half-truths and misleading claims. (If these didn't work, i.e., make money, marketing gurus wouldn't bother to use them.)

The rash of logic-defying violent acts offers still more proof: too many people cannot solve problems with anything but their fists or that substitute penis, the gun, neither of which, of course, actually solves the problem.

Has this dearth always existed in the United States, or is this something new? Jefferson's peer, Alexander Hamilton, argued that the general population of the United States—at that time, mostly farmers—was cognitively challenged and incapable of making intelligent decisions. Jefferson, however, held great faith in the capabilities of the common man, especially if that farmer or inn-keeper or store-owner could be educated and informed. For the purpose of creating an educated, informed agrarian society, he would have extended the benefits of education to all. Ultimately, if he had had to make a choice between having a government or a newspaper, he would have taken the latter, apparently in order to keep the people apprised of the goings-on of the former.

Theorists today might argue that the un-thinking, mindless, intellectually illiterate population is a monster of the last half of the twentieth century. Certainly, the nation-scape oozes with possible guilty parties. Lazy irresponsible parents, self-important legislators, irrational adjudicators, greedy business-owners, self-serving media and entertainment-mongers, and deliberately ignorant educators—they all need to raise their hands to accept some of the blame. Curiously, almost every blame-bearer is itself a product of the public school system in the United States.

Are the schools, then—including teachers, administrators, school boards, curriculum writers—the real perpetrators of this terrible threat to democracy?

Yes. And, no. Public education is one of the perpetrators; and it is the one which could be the salvation of a democratic society in the United States. As a mandated institution, it reaches—and affects—almost every young person, for better or for worse.

This book cries in the wilderness—where the United States public education has wandered these hundred-plus years—for reason, for a logical assessment of what we truly want from our graduates, and for a careful approach for getting where we want to go.

It presents proof of the failure of public education—what we get from our graduates digresses almost 180 degrees from what we say we want.

It defines the reasons for the failings, reasons that hark back to the early twentieth century and the advent of the assembly-line education system. It shows why the schools are set up for failure, why they cannot succeed.

Preface

Finally, it offers ideas for a logical, rational public education system that could truly deliver an informed, capable, and enthusiastic electorate.

Set Up for Failure

Chapter 1

Part I:
Proof of Failure

Chapter 1

What does the public want and expect vs. What does the public get

Promises, promises, promises. They woo the heart and tease the mind. They lift us with hope and tempt us to try.

The promise of a free public education shines as a glorious beacon on the tortuous path of life. Free public education promises to burst the barriers to race, income, religious preferences, physical challenges, and sex. It assures all parents that their children may have a chance of success in any field they choose. It promises to be the great equalizer.

The people of the United States expect education to be free and excellent. Some go so far as to say it is a Constitutional right, although the United States Constitution makes no reference to education of any kind.

Set Up for Failure

In general terms, we expect our young people, after their harrowing journey through the public schools, to have a general knowledge about how and why things function as they do. In most idealistic terms, an educated person knows how and where to find information, and can combine ideas into creative solutions for the self or the group. Through understanding and knowledge, the educated person tolerates, respects, and even enjoys differences amongst groups. We expect the graduate to be able to make thoughtful and critical decisions about what is best for the community and for oneself.

We would like to believe that the graduate can write an expository essay which thoroughly explains and defends a point of view; can tell the difference between "sine" and "cosine"; can recite all the dates of the military involvements of the United States; can tell the difference between a tadpole and a frog; can explain the rules for a few team sports played in the United States; can name most of the nations in Central America; can define "macro-" and "micro-economics; and can describe the plots of most of the major American literary works of the past three centuries.

In realistic terms, however, an "educated" person in the United States holds a diploma which signifies he or she has put butt to chair for a minimum, specified number of hours. The high school diploma makes no more and no less a guarantee than time spent in class. What the public actually gets from the free public education system bears little resemblance to what it wants and expects.

Measured by several different criteria, results do not meet expectations. The high school completion rate ranges from 95% of the students who entered high school (Maine) to as low as only 74% (Arizona), the latter statistic meaning that 26% of the students who entered high school in Arizona never graduated nor earned a GED.

Income and race figures into the picture: In Arizona, 87% of white young adults have a high school or GED diploma while

Chapter 1

only 59% of young adults of all other races can make the same claim. Ninety-eight percent of the young adults from high-income families in Georgia have a high school or GED diploma compared with 61% of young adults from low-income families.
    Graduation rate aside, a more telling criteria might be how well the students achieve on standardized tests. Connecticut eighth graders scored at or above proficiency on national assessments of writing at a 44% rate, and only 11% of the Mississippi eighth graders could claim proficiency. Math proved more problematic: 34% of Connecticut's eighth graders demonstrated proficiency on national math assessments, but only 7% of the low-income eighth graders could do the same thing. (Statistics from Measuring Up 2002: The State-by-State Report Card for Higher Education, The National Center for Public Policy and Higher Education)
    Math performances measured by the National Assessment of Educational Progress (NAEP) indicated in 1996 that 100% of all the twelfth graders could manage simple arithmetic facts; 91 % of African Americans, 92% of Latinos, and 99% of whites could conduct numerical operations and beginning problem solving situations; 31% of African-Americans, 40% of Latinos, and 69% of whites could do moderately complex procedures and reasoning; and only 1% of African-Americans, 2% of Latinos, and 9% of whites could successfully handle multi-step problem solving and algebra. Remember that these are students who have graduated from high school.
    Graduates fared only slightly better on reading assessments. One hundred percent of all students succeeded at simple, discrete reading tasks; 67% of African-Americans, 64% of Latinos, and 87% of whites could interrelate and make generalizations; 18% of African-Americans, 20 of Latinos, and 45% of whites could understand complicated information; and only 2% of African-Americans, 2% of Latinos, and 8% of whites can learn from specialized reading materials such as technical manuals.

Set Up for Failure

In practical terms, 35% of students graduating from a four-year college can write a brief letter explaining an error on a credit card bill, and can read a news article and identify a sentence that provides interpretation. However, that same group cannot state in writing the main argument made in a lengthy newspaper article, cannot contrast views in two editorials on technologies available to make fuel-efficient cars, and cannot compare two metaphors used in a poem. (The Education Trust State and National Data Book, Vol. II, Education Watch 1998)

Of every 100 children of each group that enter kindergarten in the public schools of the United States, an average of 86 African Americans, 61 Latinos, 58 Native Americans, and 93 Whites finish high school; 48 African Americans, 31 Latinos, and 62 whites complete one year of college; and 15 African Americans, 10 Latinos, 7 Native Americans, and 29 whites obtain at least a Bachelor's Degree. Young people from high-income families earn a college degree at a 48% rate while only 7% of those from low-income families finish college. (The Education Trust State and National Data Book, Vol. II, Education Watch, 1998)

Every available statistic reporting on student achievement indicates that students learn simple, basic concepts and skills, yet few master complex thinking processes. Clearly, the public does not get what it expects from its public education. We also expect something from the system that delivers the curriculum to our students. Our public schools, we think, will treat each student with care and compassion. We believe they should model tolerance and acceptance of differences, whether cultural, physical, cognitive, or social. They must, if they serve our needs, inspire and empower our students and drive them to lead considerate and thoughtful lives. We want the schools to offer a variety of learning experiences to enable the young people to sample life after school and, hence, eventually make informed choices.

Chapter 1

When we vote for one or another candidate to serve on the school board, we rightly hope they will monitor and direct the management of the school district with wisdom and character. We expect the elected representatives of the people to consider the people's mandate for protecting our children's rights to a legitimate, valuable education and protecting them from harassment and persecution. We anticipate that they will make decisions with fairness and equity. In reality, schools seldom model tolerance and acceptance. For proof, consider this truth. Researchers have identified at least twenty-three different ways that people learn. In any given classroom, a teacher will be facing students who learn in a variety of ways. Each way of learning requires a slightly different presentation of information. If you were to observe every classroom in the public schools of the United States, however, you would find that 80% of the time, lessons are presented in such a way that only two types of learners can easily understand. The other learners are left out and left behind. This is not tolerance or acceptance of differences.

While schools say they value each individual learner, they clearly demonstrate that they really want all students to be alike—the teacher-pleasers who sit quietly in their seats, ask few questions, do their homework regularly, and study hard for all their tests.

They say they want American kids to be ready to participate in a democracy; yet, when students do as the Founding Fathers did and question and challenge the authorities, including its board of education, they are ignored, condescended to, or punished.

We expect schools to encourage and inspire our young people, yet we find that a young person's self-esteem—the positive and confident feelings a person has about himself—actually declines during their years at school. Research reported by Jack Canfield, international consultant on self-esteem, revealed that 80% of five-year-olds entering school had good

Set Up for Failure

feelings about themselves. By age 12, the percentage dropped to 20. By graduation, only 5% of the students had a positive self-image. Of course, teen-age years, those years when young people are neither child nor adult, brim full of questions and confusions. And surely, the questionable parenting of half the kids contributes to this statistic. But for 95% of young people to have a poor self-image when they graduate from high school staggers the mind.

Do you know what people with poor self-esteem do and become? They become drug users, alcoholics, child-abusers, criminals, unemployed, unhealthy—all conditions that severely drain the social, political, and economic energies and resources of our society.

The schools, themselves, do not value education. Examine the priorities of the school system. Do you know if your local high school has a team for the Academic Decathlon? Does it have a debate or speech team? How well do those teams do in competition? Does that same school have a football team? How well did that team do this year? Chances are, you easily can answer the question about the football team, but not about the Academic Decathlon team. The first gets the publicity, the second does not.

Ask your local school board to tell you how much it spends on busses for its athletic teams, and compare that expenditure to the amount spent on text books.

If education in the basics truly ranks as the priority of the schools, why are athletic events scheduled so early in the afternoon that kids must miss all their afternoon classes at least once, sometimes twice a week in order to play their games?

No, this is not a case of bashing high school athletics. It is, however, proof of where, in the scheme of things, the school system places education of the intellect. Constant interruptions of class-time by intercoms and messengers, and punishing truants by suspending them provide other indications.

Chapter 1

How can students be expected to place a high value on education if the system, itself, does not?

College students usually come from the top 10% to 25% of any high school graduating class. When 13% of the college freshmen must take remedial classes in reading, 17% in writing, and 24% in math before they can continue their college education—as is the case today--, we know that the public education system fails to give the public what it wants and expects. (Education Watch, 1998)

What was conceived as a means to prepare every young person to intelligently participate in a democracy has become an extremely expensive baby-sitting institution that dulls the mind and numbs the senses. The system we expect to charge young minds with curiosity and finely tune the intellect accomplishes neither for the large majority of its clients.

Still, a significant number of young people who go through the system do succeed; they do learn to think critically and thoughtfully, to process multi-step mathematical problems, to pose provocative questions, and to take charge and solve problems. Many of them conceive and create highly successful businesses, and many others voluntarily take leading roles in the management of the government. For every two students who can't meet the minimum proficiency levels, at least one can. How can some students achieve in this educational wasteland while the majority can not?

Perhaps the schools are not the only ones who fail to live up to expectations. Perhaps the students themselves should bear some of the responsibility for their own failure. After all, who is it that makes the decision to try or not to try, to be polite or rude, to care or not to care, to do their best or nothing at all?

Why do some students make the effort and most do not?

Why can't teachers, after at least two years of specialized training for teaching, ensure the success of more if not all of their students?

Set Up for Failure

Why do school systems, with billions of dollars in the budget, fail to deliver on the wants and expectations of the public they serve?

For the students, the teachers, and the schools, failure is inevitable. They are set up for failure by a system conceived more than a century ago.

Part II: Introduction

Part II:
Reasons for Failure

Introduction:

Why?

Never try to teach a pig to sing:
it doesn't work, and it makes the pig mad.

Farmer Peterson squinted his weathered eyes at the ground, and propped his right foot on the fence's equally weathered bottom rail. He deliberately picked at the stained bottom tooth with his left hand, and rested his gnarled right elbow on the top rail.

"Young man," he drawled, lingering on each word, "I've heard tell that no one should ever [pause] try to teach a pig to sing." He paused, and still picking at his tooth, lifted his eyes to the lanky, suited black man in front of him.

Sky, roiling dark with angry clouds; air, rich with dusty rain-scent; breeze, waiting and breathless—even the environment predicted doom. Peterson's farm, like a nation with ill-educated children, lay trapped and helpless in the path of impending disaster.

The suited black man cocked his head, trails of sweat dripping past his chin. With a sparkling white handkerchief, he dabbed uselessly at his sticky neck.

Peterson pursed his lips, peering intently into the suited black man's face.

"It wastes your time," he explained softly, spitting out the "esses", "and it makes the pig mad."

Suited black man nodded his head up, then down, then up, then down—he jutted his chin toward Peterson, saying without saying, "Huh?"

Peterson stopped picking at his tooth. The left side of his lips curled into a patient smile.

"Why are you folks wantin' my son to graph an equation?" he asked softly. "Why do you want him to dee-ci-fur a poem? Why should he know the insides of a frog? I can see why he should know his own insides, but a frog's? How will that help him with figurin' out what to eat?"

The suited black man drew back a little, straightening himself. His face clouded up, then opened with a hint of understanding.

"Mr. Walker," Peterson began with great deliberation. "Now, my son ain't no pig, and graphing an equation ain't singin'. But it's just as useless to him as singin' is to that pig." He waited. Intensely, fiercely, spitting out the "esses" again, he said, "And it makes him mad. That's why he hates going to that school." He stopped, put his right foot squarely on the ground under him, extended his right index finger toward Walker's chest, and said, "And that's why he's not goin' back."

Walker stiffened, then stuffed his handkerchief in his left pants pocket. He looked away, then caught himself up, and began his standard lecture.

Part II: Introduction

"Peterson, every American should know these things. That's what makes them educated. That's what separates them from poverty, from being ignorant about life. Having an educated society is the foundation of a successful democracy. When we know these things, we can make better decisions about what to do and what to believe. It protects us from being taken over by some political despot. Why, our free public education opens the doors to every opportunity for young people. Your son should have that opportunity, too."

"Stop," Peterson commanded softly but emphatically. "There you go, shouldin' on everyone. You and all those administrators-crats and degreed folks have been tellin' the American people for more than a hundred years what we should know. Maybe you think we should know it because you know it. I can't figure that out. Nor can I figure out why you think we should know most of what is taught in the schools. Why should my son know the difference between "sine" and "cosine", or the rules for some of the team sports—he's not going to be a professional athlete. Why should he be able to define macro- and micro-economics to balance his checkbook? How will knowin' what the instructor thinks is the meanin' of Romeo and Juliet help him decide who should be the mother of his children? If he can diagram a complex sentence, will that help him know when to plant his crops?

"Besides all that, what about all those folks that do live in poverty? Didn't most of them get this education you think we all should have? That truck driver that just delivered that hay—do you think he remembers the difference between 'lay' and 'lie'? The proprietor of that little café up the highway—do you think she uses exponents to run her business? That insurance broker in town—do you think he knows where Turkmenistan is? Do you think he cares? Do you think it makes him stupid?

"Now, Mr. Walker, all those people went through the public education system, they all graduated, and I'll wager this farm that they can't remember 90% of what they heard and did

Set Up for Failure

for at least half of those twelve years they attended schools. Yet, there they are, still makin' it, still stayin' off the welfare roles, still raisin' their families and just doin' their deal. Now, if they can do all that without rememberin' their education, why did we—you—put them and me and 85% of the American people through a bunch of classes that only those kids goin' on to college will ever have any use for? Tell me, why?"

Walker shifted his weight to his left leg. "All I know is, if I hadn't been able to get an education, I would have been relegated to banging nails at a construction site or loading boxes on a truck or flipping burgers. I never would have been able to get to college and make something of myself."

"And that's good for you," Peterson observed. "But the construction worker or the loader or the restaurant worker didn't need that stuff. They didn't need to be able to sing. They didn't need to sing and what's more, they didn't want to sing. And they're still makin' their way, makin' something of themselves in their own way. Or are you sayin' that everyone should be an administrator like you? Is that the only way to be successful? Are you suggestin' that I'm a failure because I've only got this 160 acre family farm?"

Peterson waited, staring curiously at Walker's perplexed expression.

"No, of course not; you're not a failure." Walker looked at Peterson, proclaiming triumphantly, "And you went through the public schools, didn't you."

"That I did. And I can't tell you a damn thing about anything I was 'taught' for the last five or six years I went to school. I still can't sing, and I have no use for singin'." Peterson picked up the hay hooks he laid on the ground when Walker had driven up to talk to him about his son's absences.

"Yes, sir," he said, adjusting his cap with a gesture of finality, "I served my time. I put in my hours at those desks. And I wasted precious years I could have been doin' somethin' productive, somethin' the school wasn't teaching me. And my

Part II: Introduction

son told me he's sick of wastin' his time, sick of hearin' the same things over and over again, louder and slower."

He turned his back to Walker and strode toward the hay barn. After twenty feet, he stopped, and turned. "But, Walker, when that school promises to teach him somethin' he actually needs to know, he'll be back. I promise."

At five years of age, Farmer Peterson's son, Rocky, bounced and skipped and leapt his way to the bus stop, towing his mother by the hand. He was bound for his first day of school. Filled with wonder and anticipation, he seemed to expect great things that day, certain that nothing could disappoint or discourage him.

His enthusiasm never dimmed that first year, nor the second, nor the third. He continued to bounce to and from the school bus. He dragged books and papers and pictures home to show his mom and dad, and he carefully, precariously carried completed projects and models to school for his teacher's approval. Hardly a day went by that he didn't have some amazing story to tell about what happened in class. And he received decent grades.

When he was eight, in third grade, he stopped bringing home books.

"Where's your homework," his dad would ask.

"Oh, I finished it at school," he would reply before he went outside to start his farm chores.

His amazing stories stopped, the number of papers he brought home trickled to nothing, and his skipping and bouncing turned to plodding and shuffling. His grades actually improved.

The next year, he carried home stacks of books, seemingly enough to fill a small library. He went to work on

Set Up for Failure

homework as soon as he got home, and he came out of his room long enough to help with only a few chores. He never talked about his class, except to say he didn't think he was doing very well. His grades dropped. That was fourth grade.

Fifth and sixth grades went about the same as third grade—not much homework, not much class work, not much interest, but good grades.

The idea of seventh grade stirred the old excitement in Rocky. Six different teachers, six different subjects, taught just like at the high school and the college in the next town. This was going to be neat.

"Mom," he began with obvious irritation one rainy afternoon in November. Rocky had just sloshed in from the bus stop. "I hate that school," he exclaimed, slamming his books down on the kitchen table.

Mom turned quickly from her computer and stared at her son. "What? That can't be. You've always liked school. What's happened?"

"No, I haven't always like school," he corrected her. "Oh, I guess I liked it OK when I first went, but, gees! It's the same old thing, the same stuff I learned in third grade and fourth grade. The books are bigger, but the work's just as easy. Even easier, I guess, because I already know most of the stuff."

"You're kidding," his mom said incredulously. "You already know everything?"

"Well, almost. Well, I mean, there's some stuff that's new, but it's just stupid. I mean, why do I have to know poetry or write a creative story? Or, why do I have to tell what a preposition is? Now, science, that's fun. I really like knowing about how water percolates. I can see how that might help me with the farming. And I love to do those experiments; Mr. Howser never tells us the answer, but he shows us how to find out for ourselves. It's like a constant discovery. But, man, that other stuff. That's just stupid and boring."

Part II: Introduction

It took Rocky only two more years of hearing about the "stupid" stuff to get turned off completely. At age 14, he started to arrive too late at the bus stop, so he came back to the farm and helped his dad. He missed a lot of school. His grades, of course, dropped.

"He hasn't turned in any homework," his English I teacher told Peterson.

"How did he do on his tests?" Peterson asked.

"Well, he got a 'B' on all of his tests, but he still has to turn in the homework," the teacher explained patiently.

"Why?" Peterson asked simply. "Isn't the point to get him to learn something? And when he gets 'Bs" on the tests, doesn't that tell you that he learned something?"

"He has to do the assigned work in order to get the credit, and he hasn't turned in very much," the teacher said adamantly.

Peterson agreed to make certain Rocky wasn't late to the school bus, but his own memories nagged him, memories of years of writing pointless papers, reading meaningless books, completing assignments he never thought about once they were turned in. He sensed Rocky's restlessness.

Mom and Dad Peterson sat down with their son to tell him in no uncertain terms that he simply had to go to school. Rocky said nothing; he had said it all already. He went back to school, dutifully completing homework and class assignments. His grades hovered at barely average, except in science.

Rocky signed up to be Mr. Howser's student teaching assistant, and, whenever he could, he talked his way out of other classes to help Mr. Howser set up experiments or do research on the computer. He discovered some new information about economical, viable, and safe pesticides which his dad might be able to use on his crops, so he put together a project which included comparison data about new and old pesticides. The project won second prize at the county Science Fair, and caught the attention of a local newspaper which asked Rocky to write an article about his findings.

Set Up for Failure

While preparing his article, Rocky asked Mr. Howser for help, but Mr. Howser suggested Rocky ask Mr. Morinski, his English teacher, for help. So Rocky showed Mr. Morinski what he was doing.

"Rocky," Morinski began with some irritation in his voice, "shouldn't you be spending your time on your term paper for this class before you write something that won't help you?"

Rocky took his draft back to Mr. Howser, and, together, they used computer assistance and writing style books to complete an almost perfect paper. At the end of the article, Rocky thanked Mr. Howser for his help. After the article was published, the town council wrote both of them letters of commendation.

Rocky stopped attending the English class, and he failed it. He almost failed advanced algebra, but he earned straight "As" in both the science classes he enrolled in and as a TA. He also did well in drawing class. Learning how to draw with pencil and pen, he drew illustrations of the growth stages of the crops his father planted, and he illustrated crop damage by different kinds of pests. Although the assigned drawings asked for human figures, the teacher, Ms. Ellowitz, accepted Rocky's drawings and showed him ways to shade and texture the illustrations to look more accurate.

During the following summer, Mr. Howser's wife suffered a depilating stroke, so Mr. Howser took an early retirement. Ms. Ellowitz was reassigned to another school. Rocky quit going to school.

"Dad," he said, speaking confidently and clearly, "there's nothin' there for me. Without Mr. Howser or Ms. Ellowitz, that school can't do a thing for me. I know how to write—thanks to my sixth grade teacher and Mr. Howser and the computer--, and I know how to balance the books—you showed me that, and I can read any contract, or at least I can tell what questions I need to ask. I want to spend my time helping you and doing more research on the computer. Why, I've already linked up with the

Part II: Introduction

state university to get all kinds of information about the pests that have been buggin'—no pun intended—us for the past few years. One of the professors has asked me to help him with his project."

He looked up at the trees lufting in the late August afternoon breeze. Together, he and his dad had just finished putting away the equipment. They were pleasantly tired from a day's hard work.

"I'll get my GED, and maybe go over to the community college, but that depends on how much I can help here. Who knows: maybe I'll go on to the university and do some prize-winning research." He looked at his dad and smiled wryly. "Wouldn't that rattle Mr. Morinski's cage?"

Peterson chuckled. He put out his right hand to his son. Rocky grasped it hard, with both hands, and looked deep into his father's eyes.

"Just keep on studying life, son," Peterson said quietly. "That's where you learn about it. I know. I wish I could have left school when I was your age, even earlier." He put his arm around Rocky's shoulder and they walked to the house. "I can't say it hurt me to stay in school, but it sure didn't help."

They stopped, and Peterson looked at Rocky again.

"You know more about learnin' than most of those teachers, I think, so I expect you'll do just fine." They walked again. "But I suspect I'll be hearing from one of those administrator-crats pretty soon." They went in the house for dinner around the kitchen table.

The Petersons aren't real, but their story is. What happened to Rocky happens to hundreds of thousands of young people all the time. Maybe it happened to you.

Set Up for Failure

Children start out with a joy, a passion for learning, constantly seeking and questioning, often much to the annoyance of their significant adults. Well before they finish school, they all-but-hate it, preferring to do almost anything else—get a job, pass notes, watch videos, disrupt class, fight—to break the monotony. Those that finish the race—74.5 percent of those that started--, (Education Watch, 1998, p. 6) celebrate, throw their mortar-boards, throw parties, and never look back. Many get work, many go on to college. But most, like Peterson, forget almost everything they "learned" during the last five or six years in the public school.

Even so, they manage to make their ways through life, being relatively productive. They make a living, they buy homes, they raise children, they join clubs, they read magazines, they buy cars, they go to church, they pay taxes.

Could most people do better? Could they have a better quality of life? Could they think more carefully about whom to vote for, or what appliance to buy, or what religion to believe? Could they be more gentle in raising their children, giving more selfless guidance and subtle encouragement? Maybe. Maybe not.

Could public education, as it is structured now, teach them these things? No. It hasn't, it won't, and it can't.

In the early 1900s, secondary schools in the form of the four-year high school had only recently developed. Evolving from the formal and mostly private Academies of the 1800s, the high school served both college preparatory and "terminal" students, those finishing formal education with high school. In 1892, the Committee of Ten, a group of educational leaders sponsored by the National Education Association, made two resounding recommendations. First, many of the subjects taught in high school should be taught even earlier to give students a more solid background. Hence, the six-year high school—and eventually, the junior high school and high school systems—developed. Second, they encouraged the uniform teaching of

Part II: Introduction

subjects for both college and terminal students. Hence, the basic comprehensive curriculum developed which all students should receive. (Ornstein, 1997, p. 151)

By 1918, thirty states had passed compulsory attendance laws. Students were required to attend school full-time until age 16. Also by the turn of the twentieth century, the number of Americans living in the urban areas surpassed the number living in the rural areas. America's cities faced a tremendous challenge: how to fulfill compulsory education laws for rapidly increasing numbers of students for a longer time period?

The leaders looked to industry and found their holy grail: the assembly line.

Educators and manufacturers shared the same dilemma: how to process/produce masses of students/manufactured items in the most cost-effective, efficient manner. Manufacturers, following the "Taylor System", specialized each worker's assignment so he had to be an expert in only one activity. They put the worker in one spot and moved the manufactured item along a belt, allowing it to stop in front of each worker for a specific act. That done, it was moved on down the line to the next worker.

The system further provided for one manager-type person to over-see and make certain the workers were attentive and productive. This person also made any and all decisions about what happened in the factory; the worker merely did his one job and did it well. With this system, no worker, except the manager, had to be expert at more than one task. The worker, therefore, presumably became extremely efficient and productive.

Inherent in the system was a planning department which designed the work, several layers of manager and superintendents to coordinate it, and a cadre of clerks to keep the records as evidence of the efficiency. (Darling-Hammond, 1997, p. 40)

Set Up for Failure

The system applied amazingly well to schools, they thought. First, leaders decided to build enormous "plants", maintaining that schools that housed 4,000 students would cost significantly less per pupil than those with only 2,500 students. Fewer schools would require fewer expensive buildings such as the gymnasium, science buildings, home-economics classrooms, and theaters. (Darling-Hammond, 1997, p. 41) By 1910, high schools had become comprehensive in nature, teaching all things to all students, at least in theory.

The assembly line concept went further. Teachers—the workers—were to learn one subject well, and teach that subject only. Students—the manufactured items—were to move from one teacher to the next throughout the day, stopping at each one for a brief period so the teacher could "teach" them that specific subject. The principal—the manager—watched, observed, directed, and planned so the teachers only had to follow his orders. The administrative staff—the planning departments—organized the curriculum, scheduled the students, handled the staffing, ordered all the supplies, kept the efficiency records (attendance, receipts, expenditures). This "platoon" system, developed by William Wirt in 1908, intended to minimize wasted space and maximize teacher efficacy. (Darling-Hammond,1997,p.41)

Does this system seem familiar? If you attended the American public high school, did you not follow this system? Were you not one of the thousands of students on the same public education assembly line?

And did your school teach you how to carefully evaluate political candidates and ideas? Did it teach you how to read a credit card contract? Did it teach you how to read through a real property purchase agreement? Did you learn how to say "no" to your child? Did you learn how to effectively solve your professional and personal problems

Part II: Introduction

Why doesn't—why can't—the public school system in the United States teach our children these things they genuinely need to know?

The public school system in the United States fails for two reasons: first, it tries to teach things people don't need to know and don't want to know. Second, the assembly-line system makes any kind of general education impossible.

The schools are set up for failure.

Set Up for Failure

Part II:
Reasons for Failure

Section A:
The Curriculum

PRELUDE

*Education is what survives
when what has been learnt has been forgotten.
B.F. Skinner*

    The accident happened when the high schools evolved from the formal Academies in the late 1800s, and the Committee of Ten decreed that terminal students and college preparatory students should have the same basic course of study. From that point on, all young people who shuffled through the halls of learning in the United States endured the same required courses.
    Do you remember those halls?
    With paper schedule clutched in your hand, you stumbled through the halls—be they indoors or outdoors, as at the high schools in the Southwest—from door to door until you found the

Part II – A: Prelude

assigned room for first period, English Literature. You eked your way to the back of the room where you slumped down into a rigid seat-desk. You glanced suspiciously at the poster of some old guy in a dingy brown dress: did that say Chaucer? Who cared.　God,　I　hope　I　can　pass.

Or, you had already walked your entire schedule the Friday before school started, so you knew exactly where to find your classes. Once at the class room door, you eyed the entire room, then aimed yourself toward a second row seat, slightly to the left so you could have an unobstructed view of the board. English Literature: At last, you would be able to find out whether Shakespeare was really Shakespeare or whether some obscure playwright had actually penned the famous words, as you had suspected all along, (or at least since ninth grade). Lord, I　hope　I　can　get　an　"A+".

The second student relishes learning the academics, which compose 90% of high school curriculum; the first student resists learning them. The second student succeeds wildly in the academics; the first student barely gets by and maybe not until the second try. The second student goes on to college, armed and loaded with a brain full of academic minutia, aching for the opportunity to put it to use and show it off. The first student quits school after getting hopelessly far behind in credits. His brain aches for something that makes sense to him.

Between the first and the second student fit most of the rest of us, willing but not eager, responsible but not particularly responsive.

Regardless of attitude, every young person goes through twelve years of education, and most of those people are in public schools. It's the law.

Yet, who makes the decisions about what these people should learn?

One hundred and fifty years ago, the teachers at the Academies made the decisions. Those teachers were well-educated.

Set Up for Failure

At the turn of the twentieth century, the Committee of Ten and others like them made the decrees, responding to current leanings of educational and social philosophers of the day. These people, too, were highly educated—college professors and the like.

Throughout the twentieth century, public school content became more and more elaborate and requirements expanded. College professors and political leaders teamed up with representatives of pressure groups and text book publishers to formalize and centralize the curriculum decision-making process; this would ensure equitable education experiences across the state, or so they hoped.

College professors, teachers, political leaders,—these are the people who determine what every public school student must study and, hopefully, learn.

All of these people have college degrees adorning their office walls. All of these people represent only a small proportion of the population. In 1998, college graduates composed only 15% of the United States population. Considering that a good portion of those graduates go into occupations not related to teaching, politics, or business, well less than 15% of the population tells the other 85% what they should know and be able to do. (Statistics from Education Watch 1998, page 6)

Does the heavy equipment operator contribute to the decision-making? Is the bank teller asked what he should know? Does anyone ask the hair-dresser? Has the stay-at-home mom given her input? Is the professional athlete part of the process? When does the grocery clerk, the policeman, or the flight attendant get to have their say?

No one has asked roughly 85% of the population what they should know and be able to do. As far as education policy-making is concerned, about 85% of the population has been disenfranchised. Omnipotent and all-knowing, the college-educated masters determine what is best for everyone.

Part II – A: Prelude

How would they know?
Does the future factory manager need to know the same math as the future computer engineer? Does the future veterinary assistant need to have the same writing expertise as does the future historian? Does the future flower shop owner need to know the same anatomy as does the future doctor? No. No, no, and no.
Does the future custodian need to be able to analyze the same political arguments as does the future Methodist minister? Does the future loan broker need to be able to understand the same electric bill as does the future librarian? Does the future inventor need to be able to decipher the same medical plan as does the future ornithologist? Yes. Yes, yes, and yes.
No, anti-elitism has not reared its ignorant head here. This is not an attack on the educated elite, those mindful people armed with a lust for learning and discovering ideas and possibilities, who delve into the past and mentally reach for the future. They are and ought to be the intellectual leaders of a culture. That's their deal, and they do it well.
But, it's not everyone's deal. In fact, the intellectual pursuits of knowing past literary masters, analyzing the Egyptians' cultural contributions, testing hypotheses, deciding where to put "only" in a sentence, and explaining why the Untied States went to war with England in 1812 are not the deal for 85% of the population.
Nor is this an attack on the 85% of the population who, in all honesty, couldn't care less about probably 85% of the public school subject matter—not as student, nor as adults.
It is, rather a plea for reason.

Set Up for Failure

Part II:
Reasons for Failure

Section A:
The Curriculum

Chapter 2
Students don't need it+
Students don't want it =
Students won't learn it.

Where is the life we have lost in living?
Where is the wisdom we have lost in knowledge?
Where is the knowledge we have lost in information?

T.S. Elliot

Signs of a good school

    In 1999, Houghton Mifflin published *The Schools our Children Deserve* by Alfie Kohn. Named by *Time Magazine* as "perhaps the country's most outspoken critic of education's fixation on grades [and] test scores," Kohn, a former teacher

Part II – A: Chapter 2

turned author and lecturer has written several books about the problems with the nation's education system.

Alfie Kohn's is not a household name. Most likely, few educators know him. That's not surprising, however; few educators knew Howard Gardner until his research on multiple intelligences was more than ten years old. But what Alfie Kohn has to say about what ought to happen in classrooms remains indisputable. Without even knowing him, knowledgeable teachers and administrators will view his descriptions of a productive, pro-learning classroom as solid, tight, and thoughtful. I will refer to his descriptions, not because Kohn reigns as the latest education guru, but because the descriptions are succinct, clear, and well-reasoned.

In his book, *The schools Our Children Deserve,* Kohn lists eleven categories of signs of a good school. If you had wandered into my classroom during my last several years of teaching, you would have seen good signs listed in seven of those categories. In three categories, you would have seen what Kohn calls "Possible reasons to worry". One category referred to the entire school on which I had little impact.

My classroom rated high in these categories: furniture; on the walls; sounds; location of teacher; teacher's voice; stuff; and tasks. It gave reasons to worry in the categories of students' faces, students' reaction to visitor; and class discussion.

Category 1: furniture. Kohn says that chairs should be arranged around tables to facilitate interaction. The room should have multiple "activity centers", usually areas where students can find or prepare information on a specific topic. You also should see open areas where students could gather. In Kohn's mind, a classroom with neat rows of desks facing the teacher should cause big red flags to wave.

Our classroom perfectly matched Kohn's good signs. The room had a computer center for word-processing and Web searches; a library center for hard-copy research; an art center where students helped themselves to art supplies to create art for

Set Up for Failure

art's sake or to support another project; and a small group center where I worked with students individually or in clusters. Students grouped their desks in sets of two to four, facing each other. They used these desks as a base of operations, for whole class instruction, and for individual work. Open space did not exist: twenty-two students with furniture and centers took all the available space.

Category 2: On the walls. According to Kohn, the classroom walls should be covered with student work which should show evidence of collaboration among students. Any direction-giving signs or lists of subjects or schedules should bear witness of the students' creative hands—he abhors those commercially-created signs and posters that advise all about all.

He worries if he sees rooms with nothing on the walls, or only the "best" student work displayed, or lists of rules (with consequences) created by the adults in charge.

Partly for selfish reasons, I never created the décor in our room. So, students plastered their projects and papers and art work all over the walls. It wasn't elegant, but the walls did belong to them. We posted rules, but the students generated the rules and designed the posters to illustrate the rules. If *National Geographic* maps constitute "commercially-produced" material, then I sinned, for we posted relevant (and sometimes not-so-relevant) maps whenever they came out.

Category 3: sounds. The good classroom should be a hum of activity with students exchanging ideas, presumably about the work they are attacking together or individually. Kohn would worry if he heard silence, or if the teacher's voice rose loudly above students' voices or the students' silence.

"Hum" is a key word in his suggestion, and one teacher's "hum" may be another teacher's "cacophony". The hum in our room rose and fell during any given work period from the hum of a gentle ceiling fan to the "hum" of a wind tunnel. As long as the conversations and discussions bore evidence of the topic or

Part II – A: Chapter 2

topics at hand, the hum usually roller-coastered without my interference.

Category 4: Location of teacher. Kohn's good teacher would be difficult to find in the classroom, since he most likely would be working with individual students or small clusters of students. A teacher who always stands front and center would give Kohn reason to be concerned.

Front-and-center teacher position had its place in my classroom, but only for a small portion of the instruction time—long enough for me to hand out general information about the school or to review the schedule for the day. With those tasks out of the way, I proceeded to the students' cluster center or individual students' desks. Being relatively small in stature, I frequently disappeared among the forest of teen-aged boys. Visitors would stand at the door, scanning the room for a good thirty seconds. "Oh," they would say when they found me. "I thought you were one of the students." A likely story.

Category 5: Teacher's voice. Kohn worries about teacher voices that condescend or control, or make one sick with "saccharine sweetness". Rather, the teacher's voice should be respectful, genuine, and warm. Like a parent's voice, right.

Warm, encouraging, pleading, cautioning, joking, cajoling—anything but saccharine sweet—, my voice chiding or cheered, but never condescended. Few people under few circumstances deserve condescension, and certainly not teenagers who have very few clues about what they're doing. (They only think they know what they're doing.)

Category 6: Stuff. If the classroom overflows with good books, art supplies, animals and plants, and science apparatus, then, according to Kohn, learning could flourish.

In our classroom, we had some of that stuff. The room was loaded with art supplies, from tempura paints to charcoal pencils to markers to watercolor to pastels to recycled items. I brought some of the stuff from home and purchased the rest with open purchase orders for the class. I balked on the animals—

Set Up for Failure

teenagers seem to be overly fearful or overly focused on animals. At any rate, I thought it best to spare the animals from the flighty and fickle young people. Several good books—well, I thought they were good—and aging computers (which constituted the science experiments) filled out the complement of Kohn-approved stuff. We kept the textbooks behind the cupboard doors when we weren't using them, and the occasional worksheets were filed in a small plastic box in the corner. Kohn would approve.

Category 7: Tasks. Students deserve to have a classroom where different activities often take place simultaneously, and where the activities are frequently completed by pairs or groups of students. Kohn worries when he sees all students usually doing the same thing, or when students work alone unless they're listening to the teacher.

In our classroom, three to five different activities might be going on at the same time, with most students working with partners or small groups and a few students working by themselves. They might be interviewing the custodians about their occupation, or searching—art paper and pencil in hand—the campus for examples of various shapes. They could be working on vocabulary on the computer or working through their math problems with the tutor. Only once each day did they all do the same thing at the same time: at the beginning of the day, we watched the news together and took notes before we discussed what we observed.

Signs of reasons to worry

So much for the classroom and activities. Kohn would approve. However, while the classroom measured up to Kohn's descriptions, the students did not.

Category 8: Students' faces. Do the students look eager and engaged—good signs—, or blank and bored—possible reasons to worry?

Part II – A: Chapter 2

My students, sad to say, wore blank and bored expressions much of the time, unless, that is, they were discussing a notorious sports figure or a "tight" music video or a "stupid dude" who got into a fight or their awesome new shirts. They approached many of the activities with a "Let's get it over with" demeanor. Some of the students calculatingly opted to ignore particular activities or assignments with an "I can afford to not do that one" attitude. The students' body language spoke loudly and clearly of disinterest, and the occasional "This is boring" or "This is stupid" proclamation projected over the gentle din of student busy-ness.

Category 9": Students' reaction to visitor. Kohn would like to walk into a classroom and encounter students who welcomed him, eager to explain or demonstrate what they were doing. Perhaps he envisioned students pulling him over to their desk to ask him to help them. Perhaps he wasn't walking into my classroom.

The visitor to our room would usually be cause for distraction from the assigned activity. This, in Kohn's mind, gives reason to worry. I know it worried me. At the beginning of the school year, the students and I practiced how to handle visitors to the room. We discussed what would be appropriate behavior, and then we practiced it. For a few weeks, they did as practiced. But gradually, they resorted to long-established habits of turning away from their work to interact with the new-comer. Back we went to the practice—repeatedly.

Category 10: Class Discussion. We regularly held "discussion sessions" about timely topics. "Are sports figures heroes? Why or why not?" "Why should kids go to school?" "What's the best way to keep a friend?" "What's more important: being a good friend or being a good son or daughter?" "What subjects should students have to study?" "What is courage?" "How would your life be affected if the U.S. got into a war?" "Who should provide activities for kids after school?"

Set Up for Failure

I structured these discussion sessions to pose a set of lower-level questions first. With the factual basis established, I began to ask analysis questions: compare this to. . . , how is that different from. . . , what caused that. . . , why did he do that. . . . And the synthesis questions: what if she had done this instead. . . , what other solutions could he have tried. . . , if you combined these two. . . , what do you mean by. . . . By the time I was asking the more thought-provoking questions, most students had already contributed to the discussion and felt comfortable about expressing their ideas.

The students loved these discussions. They eagerly pulled chairs around the two big tables we pushed together. Participation was voluntary, and they received credit for contributing, for asking questions as well as giving responses. Occasionally, they stayed at the discussion even into the lunch hour.

In these sessions, the students' behavior matched most of Kohn's "good signs": students talked to each other as well as to me, and they thoughtfully explored complex issues. Kohn would like to hear students pose questions of each other and the teacher. Unfortunately, my students seldom demonstrated a curiosity in other people's ideas.

Discussions of mandated content, however, looked and sounded quite different. Questions like "What would be the best diet for you over Christmas vacation?"; "How does she use the grocery bag as a metaphor in the story?"; "What are the conflicts in this story?"; "What's the best way to organize these sentences into a paragraph?"; "How does his use of dialect create the character?"; "Where would you start searching for that information?" elicited responses like "I dunno," or "Who cares," or "This is stupid".

The most often asked student-question was, "Why do we have to do this?"

The most honest teacher response would have been, "I don't know."

Part II – A: Chapter 2

The standard educator response explains that students need to look beyond themselves; to look to literature as a way of learning about themselves; to be able to analyze good sentence structure so they can write better; to understand our past so they will better understand the present; to exercise their brains so they will think better. And I believe these explanations have truth. But not for all students at all times.

What I believe, however, has little bearing on what the students believe. And students—in what proportion, I can't say—believe that most of what they are taught in public school is useless information. That is what they told me over and over, from my first teaching year to my last.

Why do the students disengage?

Herein lies the puzzle: our classroom matched all of Kohn's descriptions of "good signs", indications that learning would go on in that environment. It should follow, then, that my students should match his descriptions of active, involved, eager learners. They did not. Why not?

As a university field supervisor for teacher candidates, I observed many classrooms over a three-year period, spending probably fifteen hours a week watching teachers work with students, from kindergarten through twelfth grade. I noted that students' transformation from enthusiastic learner to bored inmate correlated directly with the number of years in school. The younger the students, the more they exhibited a love of learning.

Kindergartners, first and second graders, and many third graders busy themselves eagerly into the activities, ask questions, share books and crayons, cut out pictures, and scrunch up to the easel for shared writing. Student desks cluster in groups of four or more, rooms hold four or five different "centers", and student work covers the walls and hangs from the ceilings (in spite of the fire marshals). The teacher meets with students at their clusters

Set Up for Failure

or works with them at the centers. I can't remember ever seeing a good primary-grade teacher sitting behind the desk.

To the very young students, everything they learn is like a brand new freeway to a weary commuter: wide open, fresh, exciting, fun. Each new idea is huge and crucial to making life better.

Every state has a set of content standards, and almost without exception, every specific standard for the primary grade students has merit and value to the learner. You can ask "Why should they know that?" of each standard and it will hold up to scrutiny. For example, according to the English/Language Arts content standards for California public schools, kindergartners should "know about letters, words, and sounds. They apply this knowledge to read simple sentences." Who would argue with that?

Classrooms change for the upper elementary students. In many rooms, desks face toward the source of direct instruction (be it the teacher or the television), centers disappear, and the teacher appears front and center handing out worksheets and information like he was dispensing laxatives. Students and teachers eschew the story-time-on-the-rug of the earlier grades, and they opt instead for more individual activities like computer-assisted instruction or tutorial instruction with an aide.

States' curricular standards become more detailed for the upper elementary students; while most seem logical, some raise questions. "Create a multiple-paragraph composition," the State of California tells fourth graders. The purpose seems clear. "Describe the structural differences of various imaginative forms of literature, including fantasies, fables, myths, legends, and fairy tales," it also commands of the same age group. Why, one asks, must all students describe the different structures of creative literature? Students begin to ask the same question.

While the upper elementary students still greet visitors with friendliness, their eagerness has waned. They move with less enthusiasm from activity to activity, they often prop their

Part II – A: Chapter 2

heads on one hand, elbow resting on the desk, and they become more and more careless with books and supplies.

By the time students reach the pre-high school status of seventh and eighth grades, they—with painfully few exceptions—sit in neat rows facing the source of knowledge. They carry three to five five-pound books, stuffed tightly into the backpacks, so they all look like wind-bowed trees, struggling to make it to one of their five or six different classes where they sit for 45 to 55 minutes while the knowledge maven attempts to inspire them to care and learn about the remote and the ridiculous.

The most common sitting position of seventh and eighth grade students appears to be the semi-reclining position. The students shuffle into the room as close to the tardy bell as possible, plop their backpacks onto the floor, and slide into the rigid seat-desk—I'm not certain, but I have reason to believe those desks date from the medieval torture chambers—, and slump into apathy. They take out pen and paper only when prompted; many will pronounce, "I don't have a pen," as if that forms a legal proclamation relieving them of any liability for work for that day.

Curriculum standards: the wolf in sheep's clothing

A quick study of the curricular standards provides a clue as to the student's abject disinterest in the subject at hand. "Analyze idioms, analogies, metaphors, and similes to infer the literal and figurative meanings of phrases," commands one California Department of Education English/Language Arts standard for eighth graders. "Understand the most important points in the history of English language and use common word origins to determine the historical influences on English word meanings," says the next. "Determine and articulate the relationship between the purposes and characteristics of different forms of poetry (e.g., ballad, lyric, couplet, epic, elegy, ode, sonnet," demands another. Blah, blah, blah, blah, blah.

Set Up for Failure

Good Lord! The next time you go to the airport, ask a pilot, "Would you mind determining and articulating the relationship between the purposes and characteristics of a ballad, a lyric, and a couplet?" Hell, ask him what a couplet is! In fact, go to your child's school, and ask the assistant principal to do any of the above. Or the principal. Or half of the teachers. Or any of the school district administrators.

Why, I ask, and why, the students ask, do students need to know this stuff?

By the time a student reaches seventh grade, at twelve years of age, he or she has reached the Formal Operations stage, identified by the 1950s and 1960s imminent child psychologist Jean Piaget as a time when the youngster can begin to formulate abstract conclusions and barely begin to understand cause-and-effect relationships. The California State Department of Education's mathematics standards for twelve-year-olds defy this theory about abstract reasoning: the standards are riddled with mandates to use abstract thinking. Students will "Convert fractions to decimals and percents and use these representations in estimations, computations, and applications;" "Understand negative whole-number exponents;' "Simplify numerical expressions by applying properties of rational numbers;" "Know and understand the Pythagorean theorem and its converse and use it to find the length of the missing side of a right triangle and the lengthen of other line segments and . . . empirically verify the Pythagorean theorem by direct measurement."

Will knowing these skills help the young people decide about a career, where to live, how to score in a job interview, or how to buy a car; choose a political candidate, a job, or a mate; know when someone lies to them, how to be a good neighbor, or where to find the best interest rate?

How many of those math skills will the students remember as they mature? How many do you still remember? How many do you need to be successful in your daily life?

Part II – A: Chapter 2

Should subject-matter experts know these skills? Of course. And just what percentage of California's high school graduates plan to be professional mathematicians or linguists? Why, then, must all students become proficient in the English language and mathematics to the extent that they could write and defend a Master's Degree thesis on each subject?

In my classroom, one student took five different prescription pills each day; one student's father was in jail and his mother was on house arrest; one student spent all of Thanksgiving weekend in jail; one student spent several years living under a bridge with her father before her aunt adopted her; one student's father died the year before; half of the students took medication for ADHD; three students had probation officers. They should care about "inferring literal and figurative meanings of phrases as revealed by an analysis of idioms, analogies, metaphors, and similes?" Who is kidding whom?

The students in seventh and eighth grade classes assume the "I don't give a damn about this stuff" position because they DON'T give a damn. How can they, when the information they are expected to know and understand is light years removed from real life, or from anything that WILL be their real lives?

"Compare and contrast motivations and reactions of literary characters from different historical eras confronting similar situations or conflicts", the California English/Language Arts content standards demand. "Analyze the relevance of the setting (e.g., place, time, customs) to the mood, tone, and the meaning of the text." These standards refer to fourteen-year-olds, for crying out loud. The college students I taught couldn't meet these demands.

"Connect the student's own responses to the writer's techniques and to specific textual references", the document goes on. "Present information purposefully and succinctly and meet the needs of the intended audience." The school district administrators can't do that! Have you ever read their memos?

Set Up for Failure

The eleventh and twelfth graders are expected to meet even higher standards, I think, than anything most of their teachers can achieve.

The English/Language Arts standards, for example, ask the juniors and seniors to "Analyze the use of imagery, language, universal themes, and unique aspects of the text;" to "Demonstrate an understanding of the author's use of stylistic devices and an appreciation of the effects created;" to "Identify and assess the impact of perceived ambiguities, nuances, and complexities within the text." Have you asked a recent high school graduate to define "ambiguity" and "nuance"? Perhaps if those concepts were taught in the context of the love life, they might understand; they might even care.

In delivering oral communication—that is, speaking to one another—, California's juniors and seniors should "Use rhetorical questions, parallel structure, concrete images, figurative language, characterization, irony, and dialogue to achieve clarity, force, and aesthetic effect." Furthermore, they should distinguish between inductive and deductive reasoning, syllogisms and analogies, and should "Use logical, ethical, and emotional appeals that enhance a specific tone and purpose." You're a high school graduate: can you do these things? Does it matter?

The content standards, indirectly measured by the various standardized tests, raise the expectation bar so high that a majority of students don't even try to meet them. Almost from the beginning, students fail to comprehend the concepts being presented simply because what they are asked to learn is beyond their developmental capabilities, not to mention their give-a-damn factor.

Not all of California's English/Language Arts content standards for juniors and seniors cause one to screw up one's face. Students should "Recognize strategies used by the media to inform, persuade, entertain, and transmit culture (e.g., advertisements; perpetuation of stereotypes; use of visual

Part II – A: Chapter 2

representations, special effects, language). They should "analyze the impact of the media on the democratic process (e.g., exerting influence on elections, creating images of leaders, shaping attitudes) at the local, state, and national levels." Yes, indeed they should. These standards are among the few that relate to real-life decisions students will need to make as they become participants in the democratic society. Finally: we read standards that actually reflect a real-life purpose, and when taught, generate a tremendous amount of interest from the students.

The California Department of Education's English/Language Arts and Mathematics content standards documents have served as examples of the standards movement gone berserk in the United States. Reading them (and attempting to comprehend them) gives tremendous insight about the reasons for student apathy toward the mandated core curriculum. In a painful revelation, they teach us why kids hate their core subjects.

The public school system, in its zeal to placate ignorant politicos—few political leaders have any clue about how people learn or what they should learn—have crammed school curriculum with minutia, trivia, and otherwise useless concepts, but, boy, does that stuff look good on paper. "Make the standards tougher and tougher," the politicos cry in haughty indignation, "and the students will rise to the occasion." Only if they choose the occasion to arise to.

Young people who see high school as a necessary step toward their ultimate goal of a college degree will be motivated. Kids whose parents value greatly the worth of knowledge will try harder. Students who burn with curiosity and a passion for learning might take the tough standards as a challenge. Those students, however, comprise only a small proportion of the public school population, the 10 percent to 15 percent that actually graduate from college.

Set Up for Failure

The rest of the students will never use the skills and knowledge that content standards say they must have, and consequently, they see no reason for them.

Standards are essential. They express the shared values of the people, they translate the values into the expectations for the students, and they focus the work of the teachers. They are the meal at which the students should gather and be made strong to survive. The public school systems, instead of serving a balanced and nutritious meal in reasonable portions, have ordered the students to stuff themselves with a ten course banquet, and then it wonders why the forced
guests choke and puke, depart from the table before the dinner is over, or leave half of the food on the plate.

Should students WANT to master the demands of the public school's content standards? I don't know. That's a different issue. The truth remains that most of what they are presented in public schools is useless to them. They know it, they resent, they defy it, and they don't learn it.

That is why my students didn't match Kohn's descriptions while my classroom did. As with a "Dear John" letter, the delivery system worked but the content sucked.

Without perceiving a need, students can't/don't/won't understand.

To appease his loving (and very sexy) wife, Mark fussed himself up, forced his chubby neck into a white tie on top of tuxedo shirt, vest, and cummerbund, and escorted her to the opera. Generally speaking, Mark's music-of-choice had more of a twang and a slide. Still, the prospect of a particularly satisfying late night encounter motivated him to endure piercing high notes and words he couldn't understand even if he did know the language.

His attention span, however, was another matter. Shortly after the overture ended, Mark's head took a dive for his chest, and his brain checked out of the concert hall. Motivated to

Part II – A: Chapter 2

attend, he was; motivated to comprehend, he was not. His biological needs had taken him as far as he could go.

Sarah, throat swollen and sore for the third day in a row, puckered out her lower lip, rolled her eyes in the most pathetic manner, sighed from the bottom of her toes, and opened her little mouth to accept the bitter, slimy concoction her Gramma shoved toward her. Through the lips, onto the tongue, and down the throat—the nasty stuff was in.

Not even for all the Teddy bears in the world would Sarah drink that medicine of her own choice, unless, as was the case now, she understood that it would help her get better. In other words, she was highly motivated to do something she highly hated, so she did it.

Fourteen-year-old Tim slumped lower into his desk-seat in his first period Language Arts class, shoved his worksheet away from him, and slapped his pencil down on the desk hard enough so it squirted onto the floor. The teacher, leaning against the overhead projector with pen in hand, stopped in the middle of his sentence and looked toward Tim.

"Is there a problem?" Mr. Peters inquired gently.

Tim said nothing, just adjusted his seat and reached to the floor to retrieve the pencil.

Mr. Peters waited a short moment, then continued with his "discussion" of the poem. He had made a crude drawing of stairs and labeled each stair tread with one of the lines from the poem. He had asked several students to describe how a splinter felt on the foot, what a broken-down staircase might look, smell, and feel like, and what a crystal glass looked like.

Of the thirty-six kids in the class that day, two raised their hands to answer any of Mr. Peters' questions, and no one ever asked a question, until Floria raised her hand right after Mr. Peters asked "What would you tell someone who was about to make a mistake?"

"Ya know, Mr. Peters," Floria began, "I don't know enough to tell someone what to do. An' even if I did, I'd just tell

Set Up for Failure

'em like it is. I don't see why this person doesn't just say what's on her mind instead of talkin' about crystal stuff. Why doesn't she just say it?"

Mr. Peters started to answer when Ramon blurted out, "Yeah, this stuff is just too boring. Can't we just talk about what we think instead of reading this junk? I mean, shit . . . . "

Mr. Peters stood up from the stool, turned off the projector, pulled down his glasses with great deliberation, and carefully placed the pen on the transparency.

"Here it comes," sneered Halloway, folding his arms and stretching his legs into the aisle. "The lecture on 'Why we oughta care'." Several others snickered.

"Well," Mr. Peters said quietly, "you should care. If you. . . ."

"Wait, let me say it," pleaded Kelly, sitting bolt upright in her chair. Mr. Peters smiled a patient and friendly smile, and said, "OK, Kelly, take it away," making a sweeping gesture and a bow.

"OK, here we go. You oughta care because you gotta know this stuff to pass the test; and you gotta pass the test to pass this class; and you gotta pass this class in order to go to ninth grade; and you gotta get to ninth grade if you hope to graduate; and you gotta graduate in order to get a good job. So, without this discussion, you won't get a job." She looked up for approval. "Did I get it right?"

"Yeah," Mr. Peters admitted, relaxed, looking in amusement at the young girl with tattoos on her ears, arms, and fingers. "Yeah, that's pretty much it. That's pretty much it." He shook his head, a little sadly, and looked out at the patient kids. "That's pretty sad, isn't it?"

Tim, like most of the others, seldom put up a fuss; the pencil incident was unusual for him. For the most part, he cooperated, came to class with pencil and paper each day, and filled in the worksheets with a little collaboration among friends. He did most of the assignments, but he seldom understood them.

Part II – A: Chapter 2

He couldn't tell a sentence fragment from a phrase, or a preposition from a conjunction. He couldn't explain the author's point of view or the purpose of a ballad. He could define a new vocabulary word for you, but he couldn't tell you what it means.

Still, he got by with checks and "OK"s and "C"s on most of his assignments. He never read Mr. Peters' comments on his essays (three paragraphs, at best); he just looked for the grade and wadded up the paper and threw it away. Like Kelly and Ramon, he saw no purpose to all the talking and reading and writing about stories and poems; he couldn't understand why he had to figure out which sentence sounded best; he couldn't figure out why he had to pick out the best title for a selection. None of this made sense to his fourteen-year-old mind.

He could remember learning only one thing for that whole year: how to read an advertisement. Now, that had been fun. The kids had worked in groups, scanning through newspaper and magazine ads to look for and read the "small print". Then they had to figure out which of the "buys" had the best value (they had to use some math for that). Finally, they had to create their own ad for a product of their choice (within reason) and add all the fine print they wanted.

Tim had struggled with reading the ads, for the fine print syntax challenges even adults. But he helped a couple of kids and a couple of kids helped him, and they learned to look for key words and break the sentences down into manageable pieces.

"Yeah, this is cool," he remembered thinking. "This makes some sense. Now I know what to look for when I get ready to buy a CD player."

When the task and concept had some meaning for Tim, he worked hard and he learned it. When it meant nothing, he didn't try and he didn't learn it. End of analysis.

In any situation—Mark's, Sarah's, or Tim's--, the person's motivation determines comprehension and behavior. If the person is not motivated, whether by need or by desire, the

Set Up for Failure

person will seldom understand the concept or do the task. End of explanation.

In the upper grades, where so much of the curriculum means nothing to the students, students give up trying to comprehend it. The tasks and concepts become exasperatingly difficult for them.

When the young child in lower elementary grades first begins to learn numbers and letters, nothing has much meaning—it's pretty much all gibberish. However, these kids are driven by curiosity and by a will to please. They will try to learn something simply because someone asks them to. They will feel an interest simply because the ideas are new and fresh to them. They will try to learn, even when the concepts and tasks pose great difficulties for them.

At the early stage of kindergarten and first grades, almost all children are motivated to try to learn.

Then the learning path suddenly forks: the motivated children go to one side and the unmotivated to the other. The motivated children either have had success in their learning, their need to please remains strong, or curiosity still burns within them. At any rate, they keep trying.

The unmotivated kids have met with failure, so they have stopped trying. For a variety of reasons, their cognitive skills didn't match the demands of the concepts and skills being presented. Perhaps the child had not yet developed to the requisite cognitive level; perhaps he had a physical impairment; perhaps she missed some crucial chunks of knowledge and she couldn't put together the network of concepts, so she fell behind.

In the early phases of learning something new, failure wet-blankets the experience. Imagine you have arrived at the dock, poured yourself into a borrowed wet-suit, and stood ready and eager to learn how to water ski. With a little help, you clamber into the boat, and listen as the captain shouts a few cursory tips to you as the boat swooshes to the middle of the river.

Part II – A: Chapter 2

Your friends dump you overboard into the bitterly icy water. You think your goose bumps will poke through the wet-suit. They toss the tow rope to you. "OK," they shout to you. "Now hang on. Don't try to stand up. Just let . . . ." And their voices fade into the background of the outboard motor. You shake so much from cold that you're not certain you could stand even on land.

This is not a pretty sight. Once, twice, seven times the friends on the boat toss you the rope, seven times they holler "Just try harder." Seven times you feel yourself jerked face first onto the river's surface. Seven times you almost drown. So you quit. You give up, and go back to where you began. In the boat and to the dock.

We should not be surprised when young students give up on trying to learn after they have failed repeatedly. We, as adults, will do the same thing. We'll stop trying to make a soufflé after the third flop, or trying to change the car's oil after turning the driveway into an oil slick, or trying to write a book after the tenth rejection letter. Why do we think students will do otherwise?

As children work their way through the elementary years, the motivated and unmotivated pathways grow farther and farther apart, and the latter trail picks up more and more travelers. Besides the ones who have no success, the trail now carries older kids who lose their curiosity for things that don't come easily or things they don't like, especially as they become more inclined to have their definitive likes and dislikes. They take a shortcut over to the wide and well-worn path of the unmotivated

Without curiosity and without essential skills, they have no inclination to try things they don't understand. At the least, however, many children still carry a will to please the adults in charge. By the time children reach middle school, their caustic culture and wrong-headed peer-pressure dictates that they lose even that.

Set Up for Failure

I watched in pain as my fourteen-year-old students sat, three in the group, heads leaning on their hands, struggling with adding unlike fractions. I help them, the aide helps them, a capable student helps them. They push their papers around, start to kick the kid on the other side of the table, flip the book open and closed—anything to avoid trying to understand.

"I don't get it," whined one student.

"I don't either," agreed another. "This is stupid. It doesn't make sense."

Indeed, the notion of changing two different fractions into fractions with the same denominator while they maintain their individual values, then adding only the numerators of the fractions, will challenge a person who still adds using fingers and toes as most of my students did.

Where there's a will, there's a way. Conversely, where no will exists, no way will someone learn, regardless of how much we think they should learn.

What happens when the schools teach something that matters?

Grove Public Charter High School in Redlands, California, maintains a curriculum that prepares students for college. Using a method that encourages students to explore individual interests, it demands independent thought and self-motivation. The requirements encourage students to spend time on the land and with nature. Consequently, their school on its nine acre campus provides space for students to grow produce, and it houses several farm animals including chickens and goats and pigs.

Late one October, the pregnant sow began to give birth to 18 piglets, an unusually large number to a first-time mother pig. Piglet Number 18 was still-born, and its delivery caused an infection, commencing a series of problematic events for the sow's health. The sow, Velma, began to turn a disinterested attitude to her mostly healthy piglets. Her normally pink skin

Part II – A: Chapter 2

turned black and blue on one side as she developed mastitis, an infection of the mammary glands.

Within twenty-four hours, death threatened to take her. She wouldn't eat or drink, and she wouldn't nurse her hungry piglets. One student, with a cardiologist mother and anesthesiologist father, stayed the night. She enlisted the aid of another student whose parents worked with small animals as a vet's assistant. They gave Velma antibiotics and hydrated her with fluids through a tube directly into her stomach.

Unable to locate a large-animal vet to work with the sow, the band of animal health warriors took to the internet to search for information about using an I.V. They had no luck, so they continued with the treatments they had begun.

In the mean while, the piglets received hand feeding from the principal and another student who took them home to care for them.

With the combination of antibiotics, hydrating fluids, and constant vigilance by the students and adults, Velma perked up. By the third day, she ate a little pumpkin and apples. Soon her litter returned to her, and she took over the motherly chores.

Students and adults had worked together to solve a serious problem, serious, at least, to the pigs. The students learned about research, medicine, biology, animal husbandry, persistence, kindness, and trust. They had to trouble-shoot the problem and experiment with possible solutions. In this one three-day situation, inadvertently set up by the curriculum at the school, students had learned more about life than they could have in a semester of prescribed classes.

"Even though the situation had the potential to go bad, we all learned a lot," the principal said. "To see kids and grown-ups working side by side on something that matters to them, that's what it's really all about." They learned because they were involved in something that really mattered to them.

What our public schools ask our students to learn—that stuff doesn't matter. And they don't learn it.

Set Up for Failure

Part II – B: Chapter 3

Part II:
Reasons for Failure

Section B:
The system

Prelude

Consistency is the last refuge of the unimaginative.

Oscar Wilde

Through the immense power of long-term memory, call up a picture of the schools in the United States one or two generations ago.

At the elementary schools, you will see one teacher for every 25 to 30 students, confined to one room with those kids for six and a half to seven hours per day. All the kids in a given classroom will be the same approximate age. The teacher will run the kids through the same basic lessons every day: a little math, some language arts, some reading, social studies occasionally, science if the teacher happens to know anything. Sometime in each day, kids and teacher are blessed with one to two twenty-minute recess sessions. The kids can scream, yell,

Set Up for Failure

run, hit, kick, trip, and get into fights to work off some of their frustrations and anxieties after having been locked in a classroom for extended periods of time. The teachers often feel like doing the same things.

Take a look at the junior high school of two generations ago. You find 1,000 to 2,000 kids—again, roughly the same age as each other—going from one class to another throughout a six to seven hour day. During that time, they will receive instruction in six different subjects, one isolated from the other, as prescribed by the wise and sage elders of the school board of education.

All students receive the same information, in the same manner. As you watch the kids scurrying from class to class during the five minute passing period, you hear them hollering terrible expletives at each other and see them knocking the books out of the other kid's hands, and you stand out of their way as they run to make class almost on time after they have rushed a quick cigarette behind the gymnasium (remember, this is two generations ago). The girls squeal hysterically to find out that one of the boys "likes" them, while the boys walk with their books strategically placed to conceal their raging hormones in action.

At the local high school, the scene looks surprisingly like that at the junior high school, only the kids are bigger, and the girls and boys are locked in bone-crunching hand-holds, at least. The fights are meaner, and the misbehavior in class more rude and defiant. All the students are taking the same basic core classes that the local and state boards of education deemed essential to a successful life, and, as in the junior high school, receive the information in the same basic style.

These scenes were acted out during the Roaring Twenties, the Depression, through a global war, as the "happy days" turned, during the entire civil rights/free speech/and anti-war movements, with and without baby-boomers, in the big cities and small towns, big schools and small schools. With very

Part II – B: Chapter 3

minor adjustments, schools throughout the United States have functioned in identical ways for generations.

The assembly-line system of public education began at the turn of the other century. In her 1997 book <u>The Right to Learn</u>, Linda Darling-Hammond wrote, "The application of scientific management to U.S. schools [in the early twentieth century] followed the rush of excitement about the efficiencies of Henry Ford's assembly-line methods. Schools were expected to be the most efficient means to produce a product whose uniformity and quality could be programmed by carefully specified procedures." (Darling-Hammond, p. 39) According to Darling-Hammond, those procedures included adopting "grades and textbook series for sequencing instruction and examinations for evaluating curriculum mastery and placements." (Darling-Hammond, p. 39)

In the beginning of the 1900s, when the births of factories seemed to outnumber the births of babies, procedural streamlining ruled like a newly-declared king. Make things more efficient, cried the factory managers, focused on the bottom line. The more efficiency and the less waste of time and energy expended, the less the cost and the greater the profit.

Cost efficiency experts, in an effort to educate the greater and greater numbers of young people coming to the urban areas at that time, designed ways to cut costs in education. Begin, they said, by replacing small schools with large schools. Darling-Hammond cites a 1926 source as writing that, "Chicago superintendent William McAndrew noted that building a school of 4,000 pupils could save $11.80 per pupil over the construction costs for a school of 2,500." (Darling-Hammond, p. 41) Build one cafeteria to serve the 4,000 instead of two at two separate schools. Build one expensive gymnasium to serve the big crowd instead of two expensive gymnasiums. And so on.

Carrying the assembly-line concept to the extreme, William Wirt developed the "Platoon School" in 1908. "Hoping to save on wasted plant space and

Set Up for Failure

solve overcrowding, Wirt devised the system in which students circulate through the school from one classroom to another, with different teachers teaching them different subjects for short periods of time." (Darling-Hammond, p. 41) According to Wirt, this efficient system would lower costs of operating the school and the costs of each teacher per pupil. It would, in its perfection, eliminate waste. This system, as you might recognize, remains in use today.

If the "good ol' days" were working—that is, were turning out what constituted an educated society--, we should hail them and keep them. They weren't doing that then, and they aren't doing that now. Schools like they "used to be when I was a kid" are not working. Clinging to this system marks a significant reason for the failure of public schools today

While the game is the same, the players have changed—significantly. Today's young people are not the same as one, two, or any generations ago. They are different.

More than fifty percent of them live in broken, extended, or single-parent families; many live where there is no parent at all. Young people in suburbia come home after school to empty houses, to which neither parent/guardian will come home until after rush hour. In many communities, well over forty percent of the high school aged young people have jobs where they work for at least twenty (and often forty) hours per week. It is not uncommon for a high school kid's schedule to go like this:

7:30 a.m.: begin school, until 2:30 or 3:00 p.m.

3:30 p.m.: begin eight hour shift at work;

midnight: close store (by himself), go home (where everyone else is asleep), study homework for twenty minutes before falling asleep in papers, at 1:00 a.m.;

6:30 a.m.: get up, head for school, after parents have already gone to work.

For those high school kids that don't work, it is not uncommon for them to plop themselves down in front of the television and the almighty VCR for the next three hours after

Part II – B: Chapter 3

school to watch the soap operas they taped while they were at school, or to stare, stupid-faced, into a computer screen.

Because of television and very explicit movies and cable programs, young people know more about sex than did most young adults of one or two generations ago. Two generations ago, children heard about a girl who had to go to "visit her aunt" for six months or so: no one <u>ever</u> came to school pregnant, and no one ever kept her hapless offspring.

Young people have access through computers to information and skills and labor- and brain-saving aids that we never contemplated except in sci-fi books. Calculators make fingers and toes obsolete.

Easy access to credit cards, cars, the seeming failure of their parents' generation to be happy, new and old incurable diseases, instant access to anything their heart desires, even an "instant" war, and the obvious failure of their parent's generation to solve the injustices of America, have bred a different young person. These young people are wary, skeptical, afraid, pragmatic. They want events in their lives that are meaningful, but, hey! If they can't have that—and, who can?—they'll take what they can get. They want things immediately because immediate gratification feels good. Because of their life-long addiction to the television and movies and music-videos, they cannot tolerate anything that is not flashy, fast, tantalizing, full of action, sexy, and otherwise pointless.

We are not talking about Ricky Nelson, Beaver, Dobie Gillis, not even Fonzie, nor Michael Doonesbury. We are talking about the young people of the early twenty-first century. He and she are different from anything like our nation has ever raised before.

Why, then, does the United States continue to offer the same old education stuff to a completely different student body? Would you continue to feed puppy food to your adult dog? Would Disneyland keep the same profile it had in 1956? Any product manufacturer who ignored the demographics of the

Set Up for Failure

consumers and continued to make things the way he "always had" would soon be out of business. By all rights, most schools in the United States <u>should</u> be out business. The traditional organizational system of public schools in the United States makes education impossible.

Some sage said, "Custom is everywhere a hindrance to the progress of mankind." The traditions of the nine-month school year, placing 25 to 35 students in any given class, assigning letters to indicate a student's accomplishments, and prescribing instructional programs according to age, (and all the related practices), are binding education with inch-thing chains attached to house-sized concrete blocks and throwing the whole mess in the ocean. Progress in enabling young people in our society to become informed, critical, and curious citizens living satisfying and meaningful lives will <u>NEVER, NEVER</u> happen as long as the public of the United States clings to the customs of schools "the way they used to be when I was a kid."

Part II – B: Chapter 3

Part II:
Reasons for Failure

Section B:
The System

Chapter 3:
The assembly line system assumes everyone is identical

A people, it appears, may be progressive for a certain length of time, and then stop. When does it stop? When it ceases to possess individuality . . . . Whatever crushes individuality is despotism, by whatever name it may be called.

John Stuart Mill

The Ideal Assembly-line System

    Assembly-line production systems rely on consistent quality from one ingredient to another in order to produce a

Set Up for Failure

dependable product. If the items, let's say, tomatoes, vary in quality, the final canned products will differ. The whole, peeled tomatoes in one can might be mushy while in another can, they might be dry. Customers would never know what to expect, and most likely would shun that brand name.

Therefore, at the start of the assembly line, before the preparation and packaging begin, "sorters" sort the recently-picked tomatoes to be packaged. These sharp-eyed inspectors inspect each tomato that gets dumped into the system, comparing the hopeful red fruit to an "ideal", centerfold-quality tomato.

Those tomatoes that compare favorably continue their production journey; those that don't pass muster get dumped. Perhaps they get funneled into another production line where tomatoes of inferior quality are used for juice or paste. Perhaps they get rejected completely. At any rate, they never receive the chance to contaminate the final product with their less-than-desirable quality.

As the tomatoes bounce from one stop to another on their assembly line to the can, "assemblers"—people well-trained to handle the food gently with gloved hands—shuttle them in one direction or another. Each tomato receives the same treatment as every other tomato, all the way to the end of the journey, which is the Tomato Commencement Occasion. Then the can lid sucks onto a seal with the edge of the can, the cans are neatly and swiftly snuggled into shipping boxes, and sent out into the real world.

No matter which can of whole peeled tomatoes the consumer picks out, the quality will be identical to the high standards set by the packaging company, the store, and the buyer. Another story of a successful assembly line production ends perfectly when the garlic-oregano-basil-laced tomato sauce bubbles luxuriously just before it's served with freshly-made pasta.

Part II – B: Chapter 3

In the Administrator's Dream

With an eye toward efficiency and a heart to produce a typical American graduate, the educators of the early twentieth-century United States modeled the public school system after the assembly line of the highly successful factory system. Like the tomato on the conveyor belt, each student receives the same treatment and is mixed with the same ingredients at the same pace as every other student.

In the eyes of educators, administrators, parents, and citizens in general, each finished student who shuttles through the assembly line of public education should be identical to the ideal "centerfold quality" student and meet the high standards set by that student's society. At commencement time, the student will be "packaged" with a guarantee (high school diploma) certifying that the student has met all the minimum standards. The student then will be shipped out into the real world for use, as it were, and society should be able to enjoy the contributions made by each and every graduate. In their dreams!

This never happens. Unlike the consistent, predictable quality of the packaged tomatoes, the quality of the "packaged" students defies predictability.

The patently simple reason shouts out. While the production systems appear similar, they differ on one monumentally important aspect: the public education assembly line omits the "sorter" at the beginning of the line.

For the school-factory to be totally efficient and successful, the "assemblers"—administrators, counselors, and teachers—would have to be able to control the entry-level quality of the students they would be assembling. They must be able to compare candidates to the "ideal" student, and reject those that don't fit. The rejected students could be shuttled off to other functions, or "left in the field", i.e., at home, to rot.

With this initial sorting process in place, the accepted students should be nearly identical to the ideal student and the production process should hum smoothly along.

Set Up for Failure

Imagine the plant, uh, school, filled with students identical to each other. Everyone would understand every concept at the same time. No one—not students, nor teachers, nor administrators—would become anxious or frustrated. Discipline problems would cease to exist. (Whatever would the assistant principal do?)

One textbook would work for every student. Class size could be increased beyond the school district administration's wildest dreams: with the elimination of any need for individualized instruction, fewer teachers would be needed. Talk about efficiency!

At the end of the line, every student would receive a totally valid stamp of approval, and the assembly line production system would have succeeded. Of course, the society would be wondering what to do with the ninety-percent of the young people who had been sorted out at the beginning of the assembly line.

What Really Happens

Expecting students to learn and prosper in an assembly-line education system is like expecting bread to rise in the refrigerator, or water to mix with oil, or cars to never break down, or a football star to like opera. It happens, but rarely.

The production-line fallacy starts with assigning students to a course of instruction according to their ages.

Here's the problem. As a person learns, dendrites—little hook-like things—form on the brain cells where the learning is taking place, and hook onto other brain cells, gradually forming a massive web. (Cognitive scientists, please forgive the grossly simplistic explanation.) Each person's dendrite-formation rate occurs at its own pace, prescribed by that person's genetic structure and environmental stimulation; it may vary from another like-aged person's development rate.

If you have raised more than one child, you know it is not necessary for researchers or scientists or educators or anyone to

Part II – B: Chapter 3

tell you that each child learns differently, speaks or walks at different times, and reacts differently to the same stimuli than other given children, even within the same family.

Why, then, do we still prescribe instruction according to age rather than according to developmental level?

The only possible justification for such an unsound and illogical practice is "convenience"; to handle all the learners, it becomes convenient to give the same instruction with the same materials to masses of students at the same time. Dealing with individual differences becomes grossly inconvenient when we have to face 30 to 40 students at a time for a short period. In fact, developing a specially-designed educational program for each individual, according to that individual's developmental level, is an absolute impossibility for teachers, given the numbers of students they must "teach".

State and federal governments, however, have recognized the value of such individualized teaching practices, and have mandated that students who qualify for special education programs (learning handicapped, English-as-a-Second-Language, educably mentally retarded, severely emotionally disturbed) must have an Individual Educational Program (IEP) planned out for him or her by specially trained teachers, a counselor and/or psychologist, an administrator, and the parent/guardian. (The success of the actual delivery of those programs, however, must be examined with a jaundiced eye.)

Well, that addresses the students who are at risk for "falling through the cracks". What about the rest of the young people who might provide meaningful leadership and direction to civilization in the future? Are we to assume then, that they do, indeed, develop and learn at the same rate as everyone else? If the young person is age eight years and three months, he is ready to learn multiplication of single digits. If she is age nine years and six months, she can now begin to learn about photosynthesis. He cannot possibly understand the concept of state government until he has reached age ten. At age fourteen, she *will* learn to write a two-page argumentative essay. No one will be expected to understand micro-economics until he or she has reached age seventeen.

Who is kidding whom?

The concept of the un-graded classroom was argued before by no lesser authorities than John Goodlad and Robert Anderson in their 1959 book, <u>The Ungraded Elementary School</u>. In such a classroom, the teacher works with youngsters of different physical ages but similar developmental ages. Decades later, the ungraded classroom remains nothing more than a proposal except in the cases of a few visionary school districts.

In the one-room schools of a century ago, the more advanced kids—regardless of age—helped less advanced kids. Youngsters could start their learning at the point where they had left off, unrestricted by mandated curriculum and not dictated by age limits. Oh, sure, (you say), and they probably only had a few kids in the classroom at any time. Teachers had the time and energy to work individually with kids. So true. Does that tell you anything about what we need to be doing, if, that is, we really want the public schools to be worth their cost?

One-size-does-NOT-fit-all in public education. Students vary in every conceivable way. If we expect students to succeed in a system that operates based on a need for homogeneity, we have our heads buried in a deep and dark place.

Part II – B: Chapter 4

Part II:
Reasons for failure

Section B:
The System

Chapter 4

Teaching strategies ignore what we know about how people learn

The dead might as well try to speak to the living as the old to the young.

Willa Cather

When your partner refuses to admit that (what became) the vacation-in-hell really was a bad idea, you chalk it up to stubbornness. When your best friend, having pains in his chest and arms, refuses to go to the doctor, you chalk it up to stupidity. When your boss refuses to give you the new assignment, even when it's obvious you're the best person for the job, you chalk it

Set Up for Failure

up to politics. To what can we "chalk it up" when the school system refuses, in the face of the clear and obvious, to make adaptations and adjustments?

Until fairly recently, teachers have operated by the seat-of-the-pants when attempting to help kids learn. No one had a clear understanding of how and why people learned. We taught students to memorize information because we had always done that. We prescribed certain subjects for them to learn because those were the subjects we had been taught.

Until fairly recently, little empirical evidence existed to prove that memorization, drill and practice, phonics—and stuff we were taught in school—really did help all or any kids learn.

No one had a concrete explanation of what made a successful teacher. The few existing instances of excellent teaching just happened. "The teacher has a gift," would be the accepted explanation of what made one teacher inspire students and another depress them. No one had systematically analyzed what the "gifted" teacher did in the classroom that other teachers did not do.

Even as late as 1969, when I earned my teaching credential, college and university courses offered very little (if any) explanation as to how people learn, and how we should teach in order to help them learn. I had only one course—"Child Growth and Development"—that touched on the subject. In fact, even my ten-course Master's Degree program in Curriculum and Instruction at a respected university presented only one course on how people learn, and that was in 1982.

Can you imagine someone getting a certificate to work on cars without learning how the car works? Or worse, a person getting a license to operate on hearts without learning everything about how the heart and body and all related elements work? Still, people receive licenses and credentials to help kids learn without knowing <u>how</u> they learn.

Perhaps this oversight could be justified in the past by explaining that teacher candidates were taught all there was to

Part II – B: Chapter 4

know at the time. True, very little information existed about the learning and teaching process. Furthermore, the relative "success" of previous generations to educate students offered some basis for continuing the teaching practices in use.

Since those dinosaur days, the information picture has changed significantly. In the late 1960s, researchers at major universities began to ask the question, "What makes an effective teacher?" The studies that followed inspired the "effective teaching" movement, aided by the work of Madeline Hunter at the University of California, Los Angeles. This movement identified and labeled exactly those things that excellent teachers did in their classrooms that made them successful. The research revealed significant common behaviors which, if practiced consistently by the vast majority of teachers, could generate more and more student successes.

The research also inspired a flurry of studies about teaching practices. In turn, these studies have revealed a plethora of data about what works in the classroom and what doesn't, and why it does or does not work.

If we could know how the human brain functions, about what happens as data is taken into and processed in the space between the ears, we could become even better at helping kids learn. What if teachers could know what happens in the brain that tells it to keep this piece of information and throw that piece out, or arrange these letters backwards and upside-down, or take in any information at all?

Until the past three decades, we had few answers to these questions. Now, answers abound. Not all of the answers are indisputable, and not all are finished. But they have opened the doors—the floodgates, even—to understanding how to match teaching practices with students' brain functions to make learning happen.

Since the Association for Supervision and Curriculum Development (ASCD) published a list of 32 books by cognitive scientists and science writers about cognitive development, we

Set Up for Failure

have learned volumes more about basic brain mechanisms, brain research developments, brain neuron behaviors, split-brain research, memory, endorphin research, mental illness, and body/brain rhythms and cycles. What we know today about the working of the human brain most likely is just a small pond compared to the ocean of information that we can know. But it is a veritable Great Lake compared to what we knew in 1970.

We also have learned about how the physical environment for learning affects success in schools. We know how color influences people, and how people react to various sounds. Some people find more comfort sitting in a straight chair at a table, while others would rather lie on the floor with feet propped up against the wall. Some types of learners are so sensitive to heat and cold that they simply cannot concentrate on a task if the temperature is uncomfortable. We know these things about people and their learning environment, and with this knowledge, teachers have the capability of breaking down age-old barriers to learning.

Still, They Don't Change

In spite of all the brilliant and enlightening information that teachers can know today about how people learn, about what makes for effective teaching, and about how the environment can help or hinder learning that makes successful things happen—in spite of all this, teachers teach just like they did when we knew almost nothing. They cannot claim they are doing the best they can based on what is known today; in reality, they do practically nothing based on what is known today. It's as if the teachers have deliberately buried their collective heads in the nearest sand trap to keep from hearing or seeing or otherwise sensing new ideas, provocative thoughts, and challenging concepts.

Imagine President Bush, at a briefing during the War on Terrorism, announcing to the media that he is planning to distribute bows and arrows and spears to the ground troops for weapons because those were effective weapons in the past. I believe the President wanted to win a war, with as few casualties as possible, and with the greatest speed. Absolutely without a doubt, he, therefore, would use the very best and advanced weaponry and information available to mankind, based on the most current research and development, and sparing little expense. In short, if something would help him win the war, he would use it.

Don't schools and teachers want to "win the education war?" Don't they really want to help kids learn as much as they can in order to be well-equipped to live a productive and rewarding life? Don't they want to do this with as few casualties as possible, and with the greatest speed?

Why do schools—management and teachers—reject and/or ignore the stunning revelations about human learning and human relationships, and go on about their teaching business as if the information they had twenty years ago was finite and they knew all there was to know? Why does the public of the United States let this happen? When it comes to making education work, ignorance is no excuse, and when it is deliberate ignorance, it is shameful.

Let me show you what I mean.

What We Know About How People Learn. . . .

Each person learns things in a somewhat different manner than the next person. A person may learn best if he has things explained to him, or if he talks about it out-loud. That is the auditory learner, roughly 25 to 33 percent of all learners. Another person learns most easily if she can see the subject written down or drawn. That is the visual learn, also about 25 to 33 percent of all learners. Others, from 33 to 50 percent of the learners, learn things most quickly if they can act them out, do it themselves, pace while they read, gesture with their hands. Those are the kinesthetic-tactile learners. (Even the name suggests a lot of movement.) We label these different ways of learning as Learning Styles or Modalities.

Set Up for Failure

All of us can learn in any style, to a limited extent. However, we each have a preferred strength for learning one way or another.

Do you find it easier to put together Christmas toys by reading the directions aloud and painstakingly following each step (the auditory learner), or by throwing all the parts in a big pile and just sort of putting things together until they feel right (the kinesthetic-tactile learner [K-T])?

Are you more likely to remember faces (the visual learner) or names of people you meet (the auditory learner)?

Do you prefer to read dialogue (the auditory), descriptions of action (the K-T), or descriptions of scenics (the visual)?

Do you have a neat and very expensive date book to help you keep track of your life (visual), or can you remember your schedule by repeating it aloud to yourself (auditory)?

Is your desk neat and clean (visual), or a massive junk-pile of papers, folders, clippings, receipts, used tickets, and fast-food wrappers (K-T)?

If you were to take an objective view of your spouse or significant-other, you might agree that she isn't really a slob, she's just a kinesthetic-tactile learner who is not the least bit impressed by a neat, tidy, orderly house and kitchen.

Each of us will learn most quickly and with greater retention when presented information in the mode that matches our learning style preference or strength. This knowledge is not new; it has been researched over and over again since the late 1970s. Since then, many researchers have added their findings to the pile. As a result, we have an extremely complex picture of what the human mind and spirit are all about.

We know that each person has two sides to the brain, and that (in most people), one side predominates over the other. Each side—hemisphere—features different characteristics of thinking and responding. The person who is dominated by the left hemisphere of his brain will tend to be more sequential and

Part II – B: Chapter 4

think in a linear fashion. This person shines at organizing events that require a step-by-step process. Algebra would be easy for her, she will excel at filing, following or giving sequential directions, or keeping records of the local fundraising event. This person thinks first in terms of details, then she organizes the details into a finished product.

The person dominated by the right side of his brain thinks in terms of the big picture. He understands things spatially, in shapes. He does much better at geometry than at algebra. The artists are likely dominated by their right brain, as are the architects and the farmers.

The right-brainer has the visions, while the left-brainer worries about the details. The first envisions the brilliant ideas while the second figures out how those ideas become realities.

This concept is called hemisphericity, and it, too, has been around for many years. It has been around long enough, in fact, for various theorists to de-bunk it, saying that people really aren't one way or the other. True, people are multi-dimensional, but the right-brain/left-brain concept adds one more facet to understanding how people's brains work.

Cognitive science took another leap at education with the early 1980s work of Howard Gardner at Harvard University. As he studied idiot savants and people with severe brain injuries, he observed that people could be completely limited in most fields yet unimpaired in one field. Mozart, for example, functioned poorly as a business person yet scored off the charts with his music. He might point out super-star athletes who perform feats no one could dream of, yet be incapable of handling their daily lives.

This research led Gardner to theorize that a person could be positively astounding in one component of her life yet totally dysfunctional in all others. Many years ago, theorists identified exact locales in the brain which function as headquarters for specific skills, such as language/words or numbers. Could the brain have more specialty headquarters?

Set Up for Failure

In the 1980s, Gardner surmised that each person has intelligence in at least seven specific domains (he has identified more since then): mathematical/logical, interpersonal, intrapersonal, musical, visual/spatial, linguistic, and bodily/kinesthetic, and each intelligence can be found in a particular portion of the brain. Each person may be highly developed in one or more of these intelligences.

Because of the implications for how people learn, Gardner's theory of Multiple Intelligences had the potential to profoundly influence how we teach. He suggested that these findings could open doors for students in the public schools. Whereas only those students who could read, write, and compute well had been considered "smart", he suggested that any student could be intelligent in any one of the categories, and that each of the categories carried the same significance. He believed that a student with high bodily-kinesthetic intelligence—say, a stellar tennis player—might not comprehend the scientific principle of photosynthesis if merely hearing or reading about it, but he might understand it if he physically manipulated blocks and lights and colors. A young piano protégé might have difficulty comprehending multiplication until the teacher helps her memorize a tune to a poem about the times tables. A boy with strong interpersonal intelligence (an insight and interest in people) might better understand the notion of sentence structure if he can be in charge of helping other students learn it.

Gardner's theory took hold of public education ever-so-slowly; not until fifteen years after he first published <u>Frames of Mind</u> did his work receive regular attention in teacher education classes.

Since the research on learning styles and the multiple intelligences, educators and cognitive scientists, philosophers and psychologists have pooled their intellectual resources to learn more about the human brain. David Kiersey and Marilyn Bates in <u>Please Understand Me</u> write that several types of personalities

Part II – B: Chapter 4

exist, each with its own strengths, and each best-suited to a particular occupation and role in life.

Rita and Kenneth Dunn, more than twenty years ago, defined as many as 18 elements that affect how an individual learns. According to Dunn and Dunn, each person receives influence from environmental, emotional, sociological, and physical elements, and each person processes influences slightly differently from the next person. One student may need a lot of light, no sound, a cool temperature, and a very structured arrangement of desks in the room in order to learn easily and retain the information. The very next student may learn most easily in a warm and semi-dark room with soft music playing while she sits cross-legged on the floor. The Dunns researched their theories extensively and accumulated massive amounts of proof.

So, what does all this hocus-pocus about how people learn have to do with teachers? The idea that each student learns differently from the next does not rattle the windows, but the knowledge about the specific ways we learn, should.

And, it means this for teachers: if we truly want to help kids learn, we must present the information in the styles and modes and intelligences in which kids will learn best. We must accommodate those different learning styles, and at the same time, show kids how to stretch their own styles to adapt to other types of presentations. Generally, that's all this means.

Specifically, it means 1) a teacher must present a lesson using auditory, visual, and kinesthetic-tactile stimuli. For example, she reads a description of World War I trench-warfare after she has distributed a written copy of the description to each student. Then, she has students move the desks around until they form a series of spaces that resemble trenches, and the students "hide" in these. Then, with the "soldiers" in the "trenches", she shows films and slides, and plays a sound-track of exploding bombs and mines, and she turns off the lights in the room. Each trench has a handful of soldiers, each with a dog-tag, a name and

Set Up for Failure

a history and a family. Each handful of soldiers has a commander who has the job of making decisions, giving orders, meting out discipline, and boosting morale. At some point, the troops in one trench must try to take those in another. When it is all said and done, students understand some of the difficulties of enduring and over-coming trench warfare, and they understand some of the soldiers' terror, and they understand one reason why the bloody and devastating World War I cost so many lives.

This lesson appeals to all learning styles. The "auditories" have heard an explanation, and they have heard the bombs and the commander's orders and the cries of dying soldiers. The "visuals" have seen the written explanation, and they have seen the bombs exploding and the dirty, impenetrable trenches and the terror on their buddy's face and the frustration on the commander's face. The "K-Ts", who neither heard nor read the explanation, have experienced trench warfare, they have felt the closeness of the trenches, the discomfort of the tight quarters, they felt the explosions of the bombs, they sweated when they had to over-take another trench or when their own trench was under attack. Each, in his own way, knows something about what trench warfare was like for the millions of young men in the War to End All Wars.

This very powerful lesson could be learned by all students in that room, not just those who could listen to a lecture, or those who could watch a film.

2. Each lesson needs to be prepared to reach both sides of students' brains. Is it possible to give a lecture about the Constitution (usually a sequentially organized subject) so those flaky right-brainers (who think in spaces and shapes and often seem as if they're out-in-space) can understand it and care about it? Yes!

On one side of the board or screen, the teacher writes the lecture notes in a linear pattern. (If the teacher expects the visual learners to understand a lecture, he must write notes.) On the other side of the board, the teacher draws pictures of what each

Part II – B: Chapter 4

part of the Constitution means. Stick figures work fine; the kids won't care. And, best of all, the right-brained students will "get the picture." For K-Ts, the teacher uses verbs that show action, uses large hand gestures during the talk, uses analogies to activities in the kids' own lives, and passes around a parchment-like copy of the Constitution for the kids to feel. Voilá! Everyone wins.

3. The teacher must know the students' personality types and offer tasks and opportunities to each accordingly. He asks the extravert to lead the class discussion, and the introvert to keep written records. Each student learns from the discussion through a task complementary to his or her personality. Must a teacher be a clinical psychologist in order to determine personality types? No, indeed. Many efficient and simple surveys and inventories exist that can be given by a teacher to students, and yield reasonably accurate results. With knowledge of those results, the teacher can help each of her students learn more quickly and efficiently.

4. The teacher must be aware of the types of environments in which his students learn best, and suppress his own preference for environment. This doesn't happen easily. Suppose the teacher is truly right-brained, not a sequential bone in his body. His desk has ceased to exist; only a six-foot high "stack" of papers and trash remains. Student desks are arranged helter-skelter. Text books are not arranged on their shelves, they are "put over there." For many students in the room—the right-brained auditories and many K-Ts--, the room is next to Heaven. For others—the left-brained visuals and other K-Ts--, the room makes them nervous and anxious. They have trouble concentrating on the academic tasks, not because they can't think well, but because their environment seriously distracts them.

Of course, they <u>can</u> learn under these circumstances. That's obvious. Students have been getting along in spite of their environments for decades. Yet, if the object is to help students

Set Up for Failure

learn, why not give them every possible opportunity? Why not enable them with every possible advantage?

Accommodating different environmental needs doesn't cost money or take time. Allow students to study on the floor in a dark corner, or drag a desk outside of the room into the bright sunshine, or park her desk neatly in front of the teacher's desk, or arrange several desks in a small group so the kids can be close together, or. . . or whatever will help a young person learn quickly and efficiently.

Simply stated, student differences must be acknowledged, and accommodated. There are square students and round students and hexagonal students and upside down students and inside out students and we cannot make them all fit neatly into the pentagonal hole that the powers-that-be have decided is best. The few pentagonal students will fit fine and be model students. Some other students will fit if forced, but their edges will be damaged. Most of the students will be so chinked-up and battered by the unforgiving, rigid lock-step system that they will be permanently damaged: they will hate school by the time they are in third grade, and they will begin to hate themselves as they have failure after failure. Some will give up trying to fit, or resent being forced to fit, and just drop-out. You know people like this.

Schools and Teachers Remain Inflexible . . . .

Acknowledging and accommodating student differences requires great flexibility from schools. That flexibility does not exist. Here is a description of what actually happens in the vast majority of classrooms. (If your child's school differs from this description, consider yourself and your child lucky; but, get yourself to another school and take a look at the "usual" classroom, just so you can get the total picture.)

If you follow one student for one whole school day, you would find (in elementary and secondary schools) that:

- 80% of class time is taken up with teacher-talk;

Part II – B: Chapter 4

- 75% of the questions asked by the teacher ask for lower-level thinking, like pure recall;
- Desks in most classrooms will be arranged in neat rows;
- Lecture, presented with few visual aids, still rules as the most common teaching technique in secondary schools;
- All students in the classroom are expected to be on the same page of the text on the same day, regardless of mastery of subject-matter;
- While reading levels may range from third-grade to eleventh-grade, there will be one text book at one reading level, and there will be no alternative instructional technique.

And you would find yourself desperately bored, looking for any possible distraction. In one school where I worked, a few teachers bit the bullet and "shadowed" students for a day. Well, for part of a day. Halfway through the shadowing, the teachers invariably bugged-out. They grew weary from sitting in the tiny, rigid seat-desks; they became uncomfortable from rooms that were too hot or too cold; they couldn't follow the teacher's presentation; and they drooped with boredom from observing the same ol', same ol' in class after class.

Teachers have many excuses for the same ol', same ol' in classrooms across the nation. Curricula adopted by the state and district do no allow teachers the flexibility they must have to respond to differing learning styles. The task of responding appropriately to 30 different students (elementary schools) or 165 different students (secondary schools) every day truly overwhelms the teacher. They receive minimal training in pre-service or inservice to present several different types of lessons at once. And some teachers and administrators still believe that it is not necessary to accommodate students' differences, which, they say, have no significance after all.

Set Up for Failure

Ignorance about how people learned once worked as an excuse to teach the same way we learned when we were in school; it doesn't work today. Plenty of information exists, and, as research continues, we will know more. In the mean while, a gap—a Pacific Ocean—exists between what we know and what we do about what we know.

What We Know About the Effects of the Learning Environment . . .

Imagine being in a room with bright red walls and ceiling. Under normal circumstances, would you take a nap in that room? Imagine prisons with bright red walls. What would prisoners be like? People have long believed that the color red inflames people's passions. Colors, as it turns out, do have a dramatic effect on people's emotions and abilities to concentrate.

One study, conducted by Alexander Schauss, at the American Institute of Biosocial Research in Tacoma, Washington, cast great light on the subject of color and learning. He found that the color of soft- to medium-pink calms people. Hospitals use this color on the walls in their patient areas. Workshop presenters wear pink-colored clothes when they present in order to sooth the fears and suspicions of their audiences. Schauss also found that pink color decreases the appetite. (Maybe we all should paint our kitchens this color.)

He found that light blue relaxes people, orange stimulates people, and solid green walls depress people. Yellow, he discovered, increases the heart rate and respiration. Furthermore, yellow stimulates the left hemisphere of the brain.

Further research was conducted in Canada. In one study, the sides and front inside the classrooms were painted a yellow color. These were the areas that students could see easily. The back of the room, which the teacher faced whenever he was presenting a direct lesson, was painted a light blue. Using a control-group for comparison, this research found that, at the end of a school year under these conditions, the group with the yellow/blue walls scored 12 points higher on IQ tests than did the control group. Also, the teachers in the test group reported feeling less stressed and more relaxed than they had felt at the end of other school years.

Even assuming that the study needs more research to verify it, one must admit that this information provokes thought. The study was not one that was part of an obscure doctoral thesis. In fact, I found this information in my local newspaper. Can't we safely assume that the information was released to more than just my newspaper? In other words, it has been available to educational and legislative institutions all over the nation. What have we done about it?

Remember the classrooms you visited while "shadowing" a student for a school day? What color were the rooms? Drab-beige? Finger-printed off-white? Brick?

We have additional revelations about the effects of lighting on students' capabilities to learn. In Sarasoat, Florida, Dr. John Ott found that full-spectrum lighting (incandescent), when used on hyperactive children, calmed them down. These children rapidly overcame learning and reading problems. Also, students working under incandescent lighting on a regular basis have scored higher on IQ tests when compared to students who work regularly under fluorescent lighting.

Back to that school: What kind of lighting did you see? Most likely, you saw fluorescent lighting. OK, so it's cheaper to operate. So, what is it we want to happen: save money, or help kids learn as much and as well as they can? Here is that gap, again, between what we know to be true, and what we do about what we know.

What We Know About Personnel Relations and Management

The mentor system, in which one mature and experienced teacher guides a new and inexperienced teacher, operates in many states, initiated as a partial response to the 1983 report "A

Set Up for Failure

Nation at Risk". After discovering that being a model teacher did not necessarily translate into being an effective helper for teachers, school districts and states began to prepare mentor-candidates for the coaching skills they would need. In the best coaching training sessions, mentor-candidates learned they must build trust before any new teacher would accept their help. Once a trusting relationship grew between mentor and mentee, productive work on the new teacher's skills could begin. Since most teachers—experienced and inexperienced—view anyone offering advice with great suspicion*, trust-building is a painstakingly slow process.

*(This is a sad-but-true paranoia which occurs as a result of years of the public denigration of teachers and the pre-tenure treatment of teachers by administrators and school boards).

Administrators have long-since been charged with the task of guiding new or troubled teachers. Still, not one of the thirty-plus site-level administrators I worked for ever lived up to that task. They faced two problems: 1) the administrators lacked knowledge of teaching skills; 2) the administrators lacked knowledge of skills for coaching fellow-professionals. They approached the teachers under their charge as a despot-to-subject. Build trust? Never. Result? I know of no occasions (in my experience) where real and genuine improvement in teaching skills came about as a result of a conference with an administrator.

Today, we have no excuse for such administrative bungling in assisting teachers. Information abounds about how to effectively work with adults. We know now that any manager of an adult must gain that adult's trust and confidence before help will be accepted. A person in the position of being helped by a "boss" automatically feels threatened; he feels the boss is casting aspersions on the quality of his work; he feels put-down by the boss (and, possibly, by other employees); he might feel disliked; he might even feel his job is in danger. Quite honestly, all this may be true. One thing is certain: the person's performance will not improve as a result of help from the boss unless that person trusts and believes in the sincerity of the boss.

Have you ever been counseled by a psychologist or minister or friend? You know that these people can help you, but only if you want them to help you. The same is true for teachers being counseled by administrators. And no amount of "ordering" the teacher to improve will force that teacher to improve. Genuine changes in teaching skills will come about only if the teacher wants them to.

How is trust built? Very simply, the helper (administrator or mentor) listens to the teacher. She listens for the teacher's agenda—what is important to the teacher. After all, the teacher won't deal with anything until her needs, as she views them, are being addressed. The helper sympathizes with the teacher, acknowledging the importance of the situation, as the teacher sees it. This is not easy for the helper. Sometimes the teacher's peeves seem incomprehensibly miniscule. But they are real and unpleasant to the teacher, and must be recognized. The teacher will construe—and rightly so—this acknowledgment of her problems as acknowledgment of herself. The result becomes trust in the helper. This may happen in one session, one month, or never. Much depends on the amount of "teacher" that remains after burn-out, or on the pliability of the new teacher, or on the suitability of that person to the teaching profession in the first place.

Once trust exists, the helper must work to enable the teacher to become self-evaluative, to judge his or her own work and progress. The task must be one of enabling the teacher to control his or her own growth of teaching skills. It is a long, slow, yet eminently satisfying process, for both teacher and helper.

The intensity of the time involved looms as a major roadblock for this kind of help taking place. Administrators, especially the second- and third-level administrators at sites, do not have anywhere near the time they need to do even the "student discipline" part of their jobs, let alone the part where they actually help teachers.

Time, however, cannot be blamed for administrators not offering this kind of effective help. Mostly, administrators have no training to "coach" teachers. They receive training to evaluate or judge teachers. But evaluation serves no purpose, because teachers cannot be fired based on one (or even several) negative evaluations. (The firing process is terribly complicated and more time-consuming than a genuine helping process.) Evaluation certainly does not improve teaching.

How to help teachers improve is not a mystery. Researchers, psychologists, counselors, ministers—they know how to do it, and have published extensively about it. Again, we have a gap between what is known, and what is done about what is known.

There's more. Information about personnel management abounds. For years, managers complained about employees not being motivated. Eventually, business managers have discovered that their companies become more productive, hence more profitable, as their employees become more empowered.

What breeds motivation? Control. Simple, but real control of one's own destiny motivates one to perform better.

In American automobile factories, managers found that, when the employees had a "say" in how an engine is put together, or in what kind of material would be best for comfortable seat cushions, or about the best colors, those workers had a "stake" in how the product was received by the public. Suddenly, the onus for whether or not a car received rave reviews fell at least partially on the worker. Suddenly, high-quality work became very important, not to just the manager and president and stock-holders, but to the people who actually did the work. This kind of motivation for doing a better job comes about when the employees have control over their job.

The same rings true for teachers. As they have more control over the school in which they work, and as they have a

Part II – B: Chapter 4

voice in the teaching techniques, the books, and the supplementary materials that they use, they become more motivated to see the school and its students become more successful, because, you see, the success or failure of that school now reflects on them, not merely on the administrators or school board.

Researchers and reformers strongly suggest that management systems in schools must become more teacher-oriented. Some have suggested even that district-level administration be cut to bare bones, and teachers at sites become empowered with the tasks of running the school. Some have suggested that each school have rotating principals: several competent teachers who will be released from their teaching duties for a semester or a year to act as principal of the school. Others have suggested that each school be run by a committee of teachers.

Empowerment of teachers means accountability. As teachers have the responsibility and the privilege of managing their school, they also get the credit or blame.

Can teachers do administrative work? Don't be silly. Any teacher who is capable of managing 30 to 36 reluctant young people in one 250 square-foot area for seven hours in a row, ordering supplies, diagnosing students' strengths and weaknesses, accurately assessing personality styles, directing students' activities, planning appropriate learning experiences for each child, entertaining the kids with timely pleasantries, meting out dignifying discipline, cleaning up disasters, cleverly decorating the room, detecting and acting on health problems, and maintaining smooth relationships with parents and colleagues, can certainly do the same tasks on a larger scale.

So, that is what we know about the effectiveness of teacher autonomy. Now, what do we do about it?

In a few places, teachers have received power. However, in most school districts throughout the United States, management exists the same as it did ten, twenty, forty, or sixty

Set Up for Failure

years ago. It was and is what I call "convertible" management: Top-Down. There are "us" and there are "them." This is "our side" and that is "their side."

District superintendents tell assistant superintendents what to do, assistant superintendents tell directors what to do, directors tell coordinators what to do, and so on. Any of these administrators may tell the principal what to do, who tells the assistant principal what to do, who tells the teacher what to do, who tells the students what to do.

As each of my 26 years in the public schools went by, I found myself saying, "This is just like it was when I started teaching. Things have not changed." Most likely, this Convertible Management style in place in most school districts around the country will not change in another twenty years. In spite of the tremendous amount of empirical evidence we have about the profound effects of teacher-empowerment, nothing will change. Unless the public demands changes, nothing will change, and the system will get more and more bogged down until it sinks into oblivion.

We know even more about personnel management. We know that any professional—the doctor, lawyer, engineer, teacher—needs regular inservicing in order to stay fresh and enthused about his or her work. This process resembles taking the car to the service department on a regular schedule so that all the parts are kept in smooth working order and defective parts are replaced, except that the professional's inservicing needs to add new, more advanced parts to the existing repertoire.

These inservices, in order to be effective, must be perceived by the recipient as being useful (not just something the administration thinks the teachers "ought" to have), and they must be intense—at least one day to one week in length. Half-day workshops are virtually useless—a serious waste of taxpayers' money and teachers' time. Furthermore, inserviced teachers must receive intensive follow-up coaching. We know that, when learning a new technique, a teacher must practice the

Part II – B: Chapter 4

skill, with coaching, fifteen to twenty times before he or she feels comfortable using it with unpredictable and unprogrammed students. Although this means considerable expense to pay for substitutes and coaches or for summer/off-track workshops, nothing less will do if we expect genuine improvement and development of teachers' skills.

As you might guess, school district and site administrators never give that strong a commitment. "Students can't afford to miss that much time in class," they argue. And, besides, the district can't afford it. Worse, parents become extremely hostile about teacher inservice days, days when teachers go to work but students stay home. On any given inservice day, the district office can count on several complaint calls from parents. Do those parents think the teachers are having a party at school? Parents say they want the teachers to be more skilled at their art, yet they are unwilling that teachers should have the time and money necessary to become more skilled.

Sadly, in truth, the one-day in-services really serve only as morale boosters, rather than as vehicles to improve teaching. Remember, genuine improvement in teacher skills—something parents, community, and district office should demand—happens with even more time and money than they are now spending. Will parents allow that to happen, or do they want something for nothing?

We know lots, but we do nothing. This gap between what we know and what we do about what we know challenges comprehension. The situation makes me think of food and clothing donations being stacked up in store-houses never being doled out while needy people in third-world countries starve by the thousands. How can civilized people let this happen?

We have the storehouses and bumper crops of knowledge and information that can make schools in the United States give

Set Up for Failure

their students the power of knowledge and the love of learning. Why won't we do something with that knowledge? It's not a secret. It's available to any educator, legislator, parent, and community member.

Today, it is an unforgivable case of deliberate ignorance. Tomorrow, it will be the same thing, and it will be too late.

Part II – B: Chapter 5

Part II:
Reasons for failure

Section B:
The System

Chapter 5:

The system's schedule ignores what we know about how people learn.

The schools will be structured just like they were when I went to school:
Seven hours each day, five days a week,
every class every day, nine months a year.

It seems that, when free public education in the United States was first being fashioned, the schools in most of the country lost most of their students during the months of the year when the kids needed to help on the family farm. Those were the

Set Up for Failure

months when crops were planted, tended, and harvested—the late spring, summer, and early autumn. Survival—that is, putting food on the table—being somewhat more important than the three "R"s, school systems eventually structured themselves around the needs of the farming community. In the early 1800s, that constituted more than 80% of the population. Thus, the nine-month, September-to-June schedule evolved.

Why do we have that schedule today? How many kids do you know that need to be planting, tending, and harvesting crops for three or four months out of the year? What possible reason do we have for the continuous nine-month school year in the United States where the bulk of the population lives in urban or suburban areas? No legitimate reason exists.

Consider these arguments.

The first refers to how we keep data in our mental memory banks. According to accepted retention theory, in order for a person to retain or remember what is being learned, the person must practice the skill or concept in mass at the beginning, then practice it every so often forever. This intermittent practice may focus on the skill or concept itself, or may incorporate it into some larger skill or concept. Without the intermittent practice, the skill or concept will be dropped from the memory banks, and to some degree, will have to be learned over again. This rings especially true for those skills or concepts for which the learner has little or no motivation to learn, i.e., much of what the schools teach.

A middle-aged person's experience at "learning" the computer provides a good, small example of this retention theory in action. She was barely literate in the language and use of this labor- and brain-saving device. When faced with the necessity of sorting and putting data into columns, her first step was to put off the task as long as possible. Procrastination finally went as far as it could go, and she had to call her friendly computer geek to help. He manipulated the computer (with which he had no experience) at lightning speed. In no time, all the data lined up

Part II – B: Chapter 5

in neat, logical columns. He then showed her how to do the same thing, and watched while she successfully arranged information. Then he left. She has not used the "sort" function since, and as of this writing, has not one clue as to how to "sort" data on her computer.

The practice was not massed at the beginning of learning and, more importantly, did not follow a schedule of intermittent practice of the skill. The skill was lost, and will have to be completely re-taught and re-learned.

This is precisely what happens to newly learned skills and concepts during the three months that the student's brain goes fallow while he or she wastes away on summer vacation.

When September comes around, teachers, especially in the elementary grades, must, to some degree, re-teach skills or concepts that were "learned" in the previous year and subsequently deleted from the memory during the summer. Valuable time evaporates. In the worst cases, teachers simply don't bother to re-teach: they just go on with their planned lessons because they have so much material to "cover". Students get left behind because they don't have crucial chunks of information and skills firmly in place, and without those chunks, new learning can't happen.

Providing a three month hiatus from learning looms as a grossly unsound teaching practice. It makes no sense whatsoever. What does make sense is to continue the teaching-learning process in a reasonably continuous stream without major interruptions damming up the whole process. Some form of a year-round schedule, (designed for use in some districts simply as a means of handling overcrowded facilities), sets students up for more success by chunking the time in school into palatable time periods followed by short breaks.

Still, teachers resist the schedule. Mention to teachers the possibility of switching from traditional to year-round schedule, and watch their eyes glaze over and their brows break into a sweat.

Set Up for Failure

Why do they resist giving up their three-month vacation? It's because, you say, teachers and students desperately need relief from mental overload after nine long months. So true. Hence, the second argument against the traditional school year maintains that the instruction becomes one long, boring concrete channel, unbroken by the occasional tree-lined parks and bikeways; the result—learning becomes grossly inefficient.

Observe the anatomy of a school year. The first nine weeks or so of any school year seem fairly productive. Students, teachers, and administrators are refreshed and somewhat agreeable about being at school. (Parents celebrate for several days in a special September prayer, giving thanks that no serious damage was done to the house, the neighborhood, or the family's reputation during the summer.)

Just when the sameness of the daily schedule of school begins to grind mercilessly on the toughest nerves, the holiday season intervenes and provides the much-needed distraction. The general peace and tranquility of the school are saved, but not much gets learned during those two months of concerts and holiday programs and parties.

The school year slides all down hill from there.

With January comes the end of the term. Teachers and students suddenly panic as they realize just how much stuff needs to be "covered" in a few weeks. The pressure to get through the stuff becomes intense. Students who were left behind from September are completely lost by now, and resort to acting out or bailing out.

After the intensity of the end of the term comes . . . no break. That's right, students and teachers, without an opportunity to heave a big sigh or to recharge their mental batteries and gear up for another semester, are thrust back into the thick of things. The next several weeks grind on the best of constitutions. The weather is bleak, teachers are hostile and impatient, students become lethargic, and, again, very little learning goes on.

Part II – B: Chapter 5

The situation only gets worse until June. The spring break provides a margin of relief: perhaps the wild flings of teenagers during their spring vacations are almost understandable now. (Not acceptable, just understandable.)

Then, the weather warms, and if ever students (and teachers) wanted to be somewhere other than the classroom, this is the time. Keeping the kid's attention on iambic pentameter, or the Marshall Plan, or rules for field hockey, or conjugating "shut", or the pulmonary system becomes a frustrating exercise in futility. Brains are taxed to their max. The teachers get angry with the kids and complain that they don't care; the kids get resentful because they really <u>don't</u> care. Only with the application of various extrinsic motivators, such as the threat of a failing grade and the threat of restriction—does any learning take place at all for many students.

By the time the end of the school year mercifully materializes, teachers hate the kids, kids hate the teachers and the whole school, and the administrators hate everyone. (Parents are beginning to pray and fast in preparation for the next three months.)

Students have been mentally and physically over-loaded since the middle of January. Logically, this brain over-load for the kids shouldn't happen. We know that we use very little of the whole potential of our brains. Surely, kids should be able to focus and absorb and seek volumes more information and ideas than they do in schools. But they don't.

The interminable sameness of the school routine, droning on and on for nine long and longer months, without brief intermissions to let thoughts settle, is like trying to force eight lanes of freeway traffic into three: some ideas get through, some get off at the nearest exit, and some crash and burn and get completely mixed up with the others.

One of the major motivators for students—for anyone, for that matter—is novelty. Advertising agencies know this very well. That which is different from the norm is that which sells.

Set Up for Failure

The clever, the unique, the off-the-wall, the change-of-pace—these things catch attention. That which is the same as everyone else's, or is the same as it's always been, gets tuned-out and turned off. School routines are the same thing, over and over and over and over again for nine months. Students and teachers tune out and turn off.

The traditional school year poses two problems that interfere with learning: 1) the three-month vacation from instruction allows skills and concepts—not well-learned in the first place—to fall out of the memory banks; 2) the uninterrupted nine-months of instruction is so long and monotonous that students' brains grow numb and teachers' energies drain out. The traditional school year is like driving straight through, without break, from coast to coast; somewhere after the first 300 miles, the driver and passengers become unresponsive to anything they see or hear. They may get to the end of the trip, but they gained nothing along the way.

Alternatively, a schedule of continuous instruction with brief respites would allow learning of concepts and skills to be retained without the mind-numbing factor of the monotonous school routine.

Whose interests rule the schedule decision-making? Do we schedule instruction to fit the needs of parents? Do we plan the year based on the interests of the tourist industry? Are the schedules arranged to fit the football schedules? Or do we hang on to the traditional year because it's what we've always done?

Extensive, valid research, backed by common sense, tells us we learn best when we receive information in small chunks, in terms of amounts and time, each chunk tied to the previous chunk. We also know that brief breaks between chunks help keep instruction fresh and learning efficient.

Still, educators and the public cling to that traditional school year schedule like a scared child clings to its teddy bear: it is somewhat comforting, but it offers no real help.

Part II – B: Chapter 5

The problem with the traditional schedule of classes at secondary schools

The traditional school year constitutes only part of the schedule problem. In secondary schools, the traditional schedule of classes also violates common sense. Volumes of learning theory research prove that this routineness only contributes to the malaise of the learning coma.

Consider this argument against traditional scheduling. Research proves (as if we needed research to tell us) that the brain will absorb only as long as the rear-end will endure. In other words, we can stay attentive only as long as we remain physically comfortable. For presentations which hold little interest for us, that means about ten to twelve minutes. After that time, our minds begin to engage in thoughts that interest us more, like speculating about why the person two rows over has a sock clinging to his pant leg, or what your last night would have been like if you had called her by the correct name, or what the teacher would look like naked.

How many minutes must middle school and high school students endure in each class? The various laws prescribe anywhere from forty-five to sixty-minute classes. This length of class time violates intelligent thought. What happens if students and teacher become thoroughly engrossed in enlightening discussion and the bell rings? Do their brains suddenly, involuntarily switch into a neutral position while they leave that room and find their next class, at which time their brains switch onto the next channel? Nonsense.

Will the student stay attentive and interested and polite just because seven minutes remain in the period designated for that subject? Ridiculous. Absolutely and utterly ridiculous!!! Do you have yourself so arranged that you will switch from thought to thought on the signal of a bell? Are we all Pavlov's dogs? Why does this thoughtless, mindless organization and planning of the school year and daily school schedule continue? Can anyone explain that?

Part II:
Reasons for Failure

Section B:
The System

Chapter 6:

Class size: More is only more, not better

Have you ever seen any research that proves that teachers can be most successful and effective in their teaching if they have 25 to 35 students at a time in the class? Where is the logic to expecting one adult to relate adequately to and communicate well with 25 different psyches at one time? Have you thought about how different each child in any given class is from the other children?

Throughout one seven-hour day in an elementary class of 25 students, a teacher has approximately sixteen minutes to spend with each individual student. Granted, that's twice the average amount of time a father spends talking to his teen-age son during an entire week. However, this is all the time a teacher has to instill a motivation for, then an understanding of as many

Part II – B: Chapter 6

as six different subjects, giving each subject approximately three minutes each.

During a fifty-minute secondary class with 35 students, a teacher has one and a half minutes to spend on each individual young person. What kind of teaching and/or learning can be done in one and a half minutes?

In an elementary class of 25 students, on any given day:
- Nine students argued with their parents before leaving for school;
- Eight students did not have a decent breakfast;
- Five students did not see their parents at all before they left for school;
- One student had a pet die during the night;
- Nine students didn't sleep well;
- Seven students watched their parents/guardians and/or siblings fight;
- Four students had a fight with each other the day before.

(Yes, it adds up to more than 25 students, but some students have multiple problems.)

Of those 25 students,
- six are primarily auditory learners, six are primarily visual learners, and thirteen are primarily kinesthetic-tactile learners;
- three are dyslexic;
- four are learning-handicapped;
- ten have Attention Deficit Hyperactivity Disorder;
- three are English-as-a-Second Language students;
- three are gifted;
- one is hearing-impaired;
- one suffers from epileptic seizures;
- two have asthma;
- One wets her pants;
- three are seeing the school psychologist;

Set Up for Failure

- and four have private psycho-therapists.

In an eleventh-grade class of 35 students,
- ten had fights with their parents/guardians before school;
- eighteen did not have breakfast at all;
- fifteen worked for four or more hours the day before;
- seven had fights with their significant others the day before;
- five had fights with their significant others just before class;
- ten watched a fight between two students just before class;
- five were sick the night before
- thirty did not do their homework;
- five spent the night with their significant others, (or wished they had).

In the same class,
- Twelve are auditory learners;
- Twelve are visual learners;
- Eleven are kinesthetic-tactile learners;
- Three read at third-grade level, eight at sixth-grade level, thirteen at eighth-grade level, six at tenth-grade level, three at eleventh-grade level, and two at twelfth-grade level;
- two are hearing-impaired;
- three are visually-impaired;
- one is a victim of multiple-sclerosis;
- three have asthma;
- one has seizures;
- five are in the special-education program;
- two are ESL (one of which cannot speak English at all);

Part II – B: Chapter 6

- three are gifted;
- three have attempted suicide;
- four are seeing the school psychologist;
- and six have private psycho-therapists.

(And ten percent of the girls are pregnant, or wish they were.)

(The above numbers are based purely on anecdotal evidence and the professional observations of the author.)

When attempting to deal with this kind of diversity in these kinds of numbers, it absolutely amazes me that any teacher can have one success in every five kids—"bat 200"—on any given day. It's like sending a blind-folded player up to the plate with a Swiss-cheese bat to swing at one tiny ball-bearing.

Obviously, schools fill classes with 25 to 35 students because of economics. Probably, the number would be twice that if teachers could or would bear it. In order to reduce classes to no more than 15 students each, school districts would need to spend from 20 to 30 percent more money for added teachers, classrooms, and materials. What an enormous expense that would be! Can you imagine an education budget that was bigger than the defense budget?

What guarantees would we have that such an investment would bring results? It's true: cutting class size in half would not reduce the diversity of skill levels and concept comprehension in any one class. It would, however, give the teacher more time for each student. In an elementary class, this can translate into two fifteen-minute reading groups, twice a day, instead of four or five ten-minute groups once a day. And, it's far more reasonable to expect a teacher to monitor seven or eight students working independently during reading groups than to manage twenty "independent" students.

Furthermore, the teacher would have twice as much time to spend on evaluating student work and providing essential feedback. Sadly, teachers often forego the feedback part of instruction for lack of time. The result? The student has no idea

Set Up for Failure

what he or she did wrong (or right!) so that the mistake can be corrected or the progress can be repeated. This benefit alone would pay for the investment in smaller classes.

To break with the class-size tradition of 25 to 35 students per class will take either a considerable investment of money, or some very creative and clever options. The state of California has already made this break in grades one through three and grade nine English classes, choosing the investment option, although in financial crunch-time (which seems to be most of the time), schools receive a waiver for this mandate.

The very same teachers we have today, if allowed to work with half the students they now face, would be wildly successful. However, with the reality of overwhelming numbers of students in their classes, they continue to be set up for failure.

Part II – B: Chapter 7

Part II:
Reasons for Failure

Section B:
The System

Chapter 7:

Letter Grades De-Grade Learning

Have you ever wondered why the letter "E" is omitted on the traditional grading scale? I suppose the argument goes that people would confuse it to mean "Excellent" or "Exceptional." However, it could mean "Especially Bad" or "Extremely Poor" or "Essentially dumb" or "Egregious". Some teachers might use it to mean "Exasperating."

This ridiculous letter-grading system itself probably will not bring public education crashing down. However, it does illustrate the pointlessness of much of what has become traditional in schools.

What, exactly, does "C" mean? Does it mean the student performed adequately, so-so, or much the same as most students perform? Many students perform the best they can, and still receive a "C". They did better than "adequate" or "average" in proportion to their capabilities, yet, when compared to the

Set Up for Failure

general population, they were merely "OK". Other students put out no effort at all and, by virtue of being quick with words, being able to schmooze, or just being cute, still get a "C". Does that letter tell anyone how lazy that child is, or how potentially capable? In fact, it in no way indicates the amount of effort students may or may not have put into their work, and it has even less to say about what the student knows.

What does "F" mean? It means, some say, that the student failed the subject. What does that mean? From that letter grade, can anyone tell if the student was absent most of the time, depressed and unable to function, disinterested, missing vital pieces of information, or just plain stupid?

Letter grades cannot possibly mean one student is better or worse than another. Better or worse at what? Taking tests? Writing essays? Talking off the top of the head? Cheating? Working hard? Copying? By themselves, and at best, a letter grade can mean only that Mom or Dad or Grandparent will or will not be giving the kid some money at report-card time.

The system gives no clues as to what a student can and cannot do academically. It does not say in what areas the student is deficient or what he or she *has* managed to understand that can be used as a basis for building new learning.

If at the beginning of the term, the teacher looked at the previous term's report card and saw an "A" for social studies, would that teacher know that the student understood the geography of the United States? Well, that would depend on many things: did the previous teacher even teach the prescribed curriculum? Would the grade by itself tell that the student knew how to read map legends? Identify land forms on a map? Describe the economy of the southern states? Nope, none of the above.

A letter grade cannot tell whether the student can comprehend what he reads, do basic computation, write a complete sentence, explain the concept of democracy, compare

Part II – B: Chapter 7

and contrast results of a scientific experiment, solve problems, provide leadership in the classroom, or make a value judgment.

Evaluating student work constitutes an essential part of teaching. Reporting that evaluation should provide useful information to future teachers, employers, parents, and the students themselves. Such information could then be used as a basis for new instruction or for the re-teaching of unlearned concepts. The letter grading system does none of this.

If every teacher evaluated student work according to the identical criteria, and if every teacher taught exactly the same things in the exact same amount of time, perhaps the current grading system would have some meaning. As it is, assigning letter grades is an arbitrary action. One teacher's "A" is another teacher's "C".

Some teachers pride themselves on being "tough", and consequently, bestow only one "A" per term. At the high school where I taught, science teachers took great pleasure in being the department whose students earned the lowest grades. If science students averaged better than a straight "C", their instructors felt like they had failed as teachers. They failed to realize that the low grades were more indicative of the teachers' performances than the performances of their students.

Some teachers use an "A" to indicate 91 percent accuracy on an objective exam, others use it to indicate 95 percent accuracy. Some teachers give an "A" if the third grader can write his name on a paper, while others insist on a multiple-paragraph essay. The more student-oriented teachers award "A"s and "B"s to encourage the children to keep trying, regardless of how much they actually learned. The more subject-oriented teachers won't give an inch on the basis of a student's effort.

What does the United States public want from an educational grading system? If it wants a simplistic, meaningless indicator of nothing, then it should be happy. If however, it wants a system that provides useful information about each

Set Up for Failure

student's accomplishments, then it will have to give the letter grade system an "F" and throw it in the trash.

Letter grading interferes with learning in yet another way: the almighty grade becomes the Holy Grail; learning the concept becomes a by-product.

At the first class session, students—even the disinterested ones—want to know what "it takes" to get a C, or B, or A. They want to have it in writing, and their parents want to see the written truth. Weekly, some students ask to see their grades.

"What's my grade?" they ask at the most inopportune times, like when the teacher is starting the VCR to show a clip from the previous night's PBS news broadcast, or when he's halfway through the discussion on "The Nacirema". In the students' minds, of course the teacher should 1) be able to instantly recall that student's grade (out of 165 students), or b) stop immediately to search the grading program on the computer.

English teachers, especially, try to carefully read each submitted paper—potentially 165 of them, but realistically only 80—, providing written commentary so the student can know what she did well or poorly. Armed with this knowledge, presumably, the student will either continue using the technique or adjust it. This feedback could have the most powerful impact on learning.

Thoughtful teachers write the essay's letter grade at the very end, hoping that the student will not discover it until she has looked through the entire paper and read all the lucid and erudite comments. After all, the teacher spends up to fifteen minutes reading, evaluating, and commenting on each paper; hopefully, the student will peruse the comments and consider them carefully.

Ha! The student spends less than fifteen seconds shuffling through the graded and returned essay, searching for the grade. Discovery made, the student either stuffs the paper into his backpack or tosses it into the trash can.

Part II – B: Chapter 7

An empty concept, void of meaning, the letter grade system mirrors much of what goes on in public education, and it contributes to the set-up for failure.

Part II: Reasons for Failure

Section B: The System

Chapter 8:

Misplaced priorities say learning isn't important

Ask most Americans about the purpose of free public education, and most will tell you it is to teach young people to read, write, and do arithmetic. Some might take a more comprehensive view, and say that the purpose of schools should be to prepare young people to be conscientious, thoughtful adults in a democratic society. Few would argue, however, that the main function of the schools is to teach young people basic academic skills. Few people would argue that, but, by all appearances, the actual activities of few schools would support that.

Part II – B: Chapter 8

Schools have misplaced priorities:

What you would see if you personally visited most public schools, would be anything but an academic focus. You would see the main social worker for the community (as it provides health services, speech therapy, and physical therapy), a food service for kids whose families cannot afford to feed them in the morning, psychological testing and services for troubled youths, and the main source of social life for the kids. In secondary schools, you would see a "farm club" for college athletics, a "farm club" for kids going into trades and businesses, and an entertainment center for the community.

Of course, you also would see building after building of classrooms where young people receive the academic wisdom of the elders of their society. You have to stay on campus for only one day, however, to get the real picture and understand that, what goes on in those classrooms takes a seat farther and farther back in the bus to any number of non-academic functions. The priorities of the people in charge of the schools become obvious, and are mirrored by the students.

Parents:

I am confounded by the perennial complaints of parents of kids in schools. Teachers and administrators will never hear from 98 percent of the parents of their students unless and until a problem arises, either for the particular kid or for the school in general. They say they believe school is important, yet they very seldom put that belief into action. The priorities of too many parents are far removed from their child's academic progress. When they, themselves, don't demonstrate a valuing of education , how can they expect their kids to think learning is important?

Teachers:

Teachers, too, have misplaced priorities too often. When their number one priority should be providing the best service to their students that they possibly can, (under admittedly adverse circumstances), they play politics with the administration, they vie with other teachers for the room closest to the parking lot, they argue about another teacher's activities, and they serve their social needs by hanging out with the "Lounge Lizards" during their conference hour.   While these characteristics may not be the norm for most teachers, it is normal for too many teachers who view teaching as just a job. It's a job like any other job, where you clock in and clock out, do what you're told to do and nothing more, and collect your paycheck once a month.

Wrong priority for this line of work! Teaching young people ranks as too significant and too special a task to ever be thought of as "just a job". Too many teachers carry this misplaced priority on their shirt-sleeves for all to see.

It's no wonder today's kids don't value their free public education: no one else does, either. They're not deaf, mute, and blind, you know. The society's misplaced priorities become the kids' priorities.

Non-Academic Focus

As goes the football team, so goes the high school for the whole year. This misplaced priority, while largely focused on the high school, probably influences all the schools in the district. The school year opens one or two weeks after Monday Night Football airs for a new season. College football teams already have played a skirmish or two. And, before the first week is over, the high school team vaults onto the brightly (and expensively) lighted field, players' arms and fists punching the air as they leap over invisible obstacles. Loud, objectionable guttural sounds emit from their throats, threatening excruciatingly painful damage to enemy team members. They bravely run the gauntlet of buxom, giggling, wiggling cheerleaders, and hurl themselves through a large hoop covered with a paper painted with a hapless caricature of the enemy. After the last yellow flag has flown, the ambulance has driven off

Part II – B: Chapter 8

with the season's first fallen warrior, the coaches have sent in their last desperate plays, and opposing team captains grudgingly shake hands, one team—and its entire high school student body—will be labeled "loser".

"Losers" have very little to talk about on Monday morning. Except, of course, their studies. How dull. They have nothing to sustain them for the week. Except, of course, the skills and concepts they are supposedly learning in class. Nothing much there.

"Winners", on the other hand, zing with energy. They re-play every key play in the game. They dream-up new adjectives for the various key players in the game. They talk about the moves of one man, the speed of another man, and the strength of still another. They, too, have studies to attend to. Very strange, however: classes don't seem so boring as usual.

Within the next few weeks, the "loser" or "winner" status of a school is sealed for the entire school year. That status depends entirely on the success of their warriors on the field of football. The doldrums that accompany "loser" status will hang on a school and its student body every day of every week of each semester. Other schools see them as "losers", the school board sees them as "losers", and they see themselves as "losers". As the American public knows too well from its experience with Vietnam, that "loser" status kills the morale.

Some "loser" schools come to life for a short while in the middle of the school year when their basketball team begins to play. Even with a fine showing from these new warriors, the school eventually resumes its "loser" morale. The "loser" cement was poured and set early on, and nothing the school does seems to break it up. The school can have a championship debate team, receive several literary awards, dominate a state-wide art competition, and end the year with five SAT scholarship winners, and still be viewed as second-rate when compared to the other school in the district whose football team won the league championship.

Set Up for Failure

Who takes the blame for this misplaced priority? The public. The public buys the newspaper which prints the stories about the football heroes. The media prints what the public wants to read. Face it: the only people who would eagerly read the play-by-play of a speech contest are the parents of the speakers.

The school districts produce the entertainment the public will pay to see. Football games generate more revenue than all the other athletic events put together. Besides, would you pay to see American History students taking their Advanced Placement exam? The American public gets exactly what it wants; therefore the American public must accept responsibility for this misplaced priority.

This misplaced priority on football and other athletic events infects the high school in other ways. Schools spend inordinate amounts of money on transporting teams to and from events. Figure that an average sized high school—2,000 students—has anywhere from ten to fifteen different sports each year, fielding teams for men and women. That might mean up to 30 different athletic teams that must be bused to an average of ten events each. That means a minimum of 300 shipments for 5 to 100 miles each at a cost of $2.00 per mile, plus stand-by time for drivers. Does $60,000 sound like a lot of money for bussing kids around so they (and their coaches) can play games? For an interesting activity, you might check with your school district's accounting department to find out what they spent on buses for high school athletics for the year.

This bussing problem causes another problem. Football and basketball usually are the only sports scheduled for play in the evening. All other sports are scheduled for the afternoons, except for tournament play which often takes the entire school day. The team members must leave early enough to travel and arrive in time to warm up for the game or match. This means they must leave before their last class of the day ends. They call

Part II – B: Chapter 8

this "early release". The schedules for some teams necessitate their players having "early release" twice a week.

Do you have any idea what this "early release" does to the kid's study efforts for those missed classes? On more occasions than I can count, I watched students' grades sink from "A" for one quarter to "D" for the next, just because the kids had "early release".

The grade slippage does not bother me as much as the message that we deliver to kids by "early release". Loudly and clearly, the students hear the schools saying, "Academics are not important enough for us to schedule athletic events so they do not interfere with your reason for being here." If the schools don't seem to think academics are important, why should the kids think they are important?

Athletic competition at high schools is as much a part of the system as is the tardy bell. As with most of the system, it needs to be changed. It costs incredible amounts of money and it distracts from the main purpose of the public school. It fosters only bad feelings for opposing high schools. It breeds stinkingly low morale at all but the few schools that are lucky enough to be "winners" in the fall. And, of course, it is a hell of a lot of fun . . . for coaches, parents, board members, administrators, and community members.

Athletic prowess and good sportsmanship can be taught—in fact, should be taught—at schools that focus on building the educated society. They can be taught within the curriculum that first honors the intellect. They seldom get taught through athletic competition among high schools.

If public schools had nothing but money, they could enjoy the luxury of providing the athletic development opportunities for the young men and women so inclined, and the entertainment for the community. Without the endless money supply, schools have no business being in the athletic business which pulls money away from expenditures which could benefit the entire school, not just the athletes.

Set Up for Failure

The stature and priority that athletic competition has achieved need to be seriously and drastically reconsidered.

It's just a job.

How many classrooms have you walked into where the teacher was sitting behind his desk, skimming through a magazine or other unrelated fare? The kids may have been watching a movie, or doing book-work, or themselves lounging at their desks, attending to unrelated business. They may have even wandered out of the class, unnoticed. Do you remember "Mr. Ditto" in the movie "Teacher"? Here is an example of a mentality that says, "If I give them enough dittos to do or papers to write or problems to complete, I can relax and read my book or chat with my colleague." In the first school where I taught, many teachers put their students to work on assignments, then retired to the lounge for a smoke. As unbelievable and unforgivable as this sounds, it happened then and would happen today if smoking were permitted on campus.

The only way a teacher can convey the significance of the skill or concept he tries to teach is to be constantly teaching it. That means walking the rows of desks, bending over students' shoulders, kneeling beside a desk to question the student. Teaching is not a sit-down job. It is not routine. It is not "just a job".

The complete act of teaching also means being involved in school-wide decisions. Herein lies the catch-22 for teachers. Too few schools allow for any genuine teacher involvement, let alone teacher autonomy. For teachers to serve on after-hours school-wide committees often becomes a pure waste of time, as the committees lack any authority to make decisions or policy. Why bother? the teacher asks. I have things to do at home that are far more important to me. Partly for that reason, when the last bell of the day rings, many teachers beat the kids to the door. They clock in and they clock out and they don't give the school any more than they are contractually required to give.

Part II – B: Chapter 8

This "just a job" attitude resonates with the kids. Eighty percent of the message that people receive from other people comes from non-verbals: gestures, facial expressions, body-language. The teacher doesn't have to say a thing for the kids to know how he or she feels about the job. From those teachers who come to school just to get a paycheck, the kids get the message that education does not particularly matter.

The parental excuses and abuses
Probably the biggest culprit in the de-prioritizing of education is the parent. No matter what kind of a school system exists, no matter what the priorities of teachers or schools or administrators or school board members, if the parent believes and teaches that education is the most important thing the child can be doing, then the child will believe it. Those of you who conscientiously read to your kids, help them write stories and thank-you letters and poems, and use every conceivable opportunity to help them practice things they are learning, will say "Amen!" about now. Those of you who don't will say, "There it is! The parent-bashing from the teacher!" Parent-bashing or not, it speaks the truth.

Parents convey their negative messages whether they intend to or not. And students read their messages, loudly and clearly. Here are some examples:

From the parent who keeps the 13 year-old daughter home from school so she can baby-sit with the infant while the mother goes shopping, the daughter gets the message that Mom's needs weigh more than hers, and that school does not teach anything important.

From the parent who writes a note excusing the child's over-sleeping by saying it was for a doctor's appointment, the child gets the message that it's not important to be on time for anything, and that you do not have to be responsible for yourself.

From the parent who never asks about the kid's schoolwork, the kid gets the message that what is being taught in

Set Up for Failure

school is not important, and that the parent is not interested, anyway.

From the parent who never goes to parent-teacher conferences, the son gets the message that his education is not important enough for the parent to trouble himself, and that the teacher does not know anything the parent does not already know.

From the parent who never goes to meetings about curriculum or policy, the child hears that no one can do anything about bureaucracies, so there's no point in getting involved.

From the parent who buys every conceivable electronic gadget for the son, the son gets the message that there are a lot more interesting things out there besides education, and that it's OK to get whatever you want (but not necessarily what you deserve).

From the parent who lets the teen-ager work more than twenty hours each week, the daughter gets the message that school won't get you anywhere.

From the parent who storms into the office when the kid gets suspended and demands that the teacher be fired, or, at least, the kid be transferred to another teacher, the kid gets the message that whatever he does is OK with Mom and Dad, and authority figures don't deserve your respect.

From the parent who calls the school board member when the kid gets a difficult assignment, the kid gets the message that you should not have to do hard work, and that you don't have to learn to fend for yourself, because Mom or Dad will pull strings to get you out of anything uncomfortable.

From the parent who lets the kid quit the team, play, or club in mid-stream, the kid learns that it's not important to live up to commitments.

And from the parent who begs for school to start in the fall so he won't have to see the kid all day, the kid knows that school is only good as a babysitter, and the parent doesn't really like him.

Part II – B: Chapter 8

The bare-bones message from all of these parental excuses and abuses says that education is not important. When the parents think this way, the kids think this way. While the school system may be a disaster, education and learning remain vital. They must not be shelved at 3:00 p.m. every weekday. They must be sought-after and promoted by the parent every time he or she spends time with the child. They must be valued, for the child's sake and the society's sake.

Misplaced priorities—by the schools themselves, by the teachers, and by the parents—bear part of the responsibility for the failure of the public school system. As long as they remain as they are, the schools will continue to be set up for failure.

Part II:
Reasons for Failure

Section B:
The System

Chapter 9:

Lopsided Budgets for Education's Corporate Structure Spell F-A-I-L-U-R-E.

Would you put your hard-earned money in a system that ranked as both "bureaucratic and blind?" Certainly not.

In the heat of this information age, would you look for leadership from an organization that was "trapped in the centralized, industrial-age model?" Not if you had any sense.

Journalist Ronald Brownstein, in a 1998 edition of his "Washington Outlook" column, flung those epithets at the venerable, impenetrable, unmovable American system of public education, no less. He cited school finance expert Sheree T. Speakman as saying that only about 32 percent to 43 percent of a school district's total budget goes into teachers and curricula—those things that directly affect how and what students will learn.

Part II – B: Chapter 9

Where do the other 58 percent to 68 percent go? It disappears "into overhead and management." It pays for monitoring the myriad of educational programs developed since 1950, programs established to fix the even greater myriad of problems of public education. In reality, the administrative bureaucracy in public schools, with its disproportionate chunk of the school budget, robs the classroom—hence, the students—of the resources that truly could fix the problems.

Linda Darling-Hammond, Professor of Teaching and Teacher Education at Stanford University and passionate proponent and activist for education reform, studied the staffing and budgeting practices of two school districts, one in the Southern California city of Riverside, and the other in Zurich, Switzerland. The districts were similar in numbers of students and total dollars spent per pupil. At the time of the study in 1990, Riverside had 29,100 students and Zurich had 28,800 students; Riverside had 1,223 teachers and Zurich had 2,330 teachers. Even with almost twice as many teachers as in Riverside, Zurich's school district paid its teachers nearly fifty-percent more than the Riverside district paid theirs.

Knowing that these two districts spent the same budgets, one might think to ask, "Where does all the money go in Riverside?" Darling-Hammond's study also found that Riverside had 142 certificateded administrators and Zurich had zero; Riverside had 836 classified administrative and office personnel and Zurich had 113. Put simply, Zurich's school district handled the same amount of students and almost twice as many teachers with a total of 113 administrative staff, including certificated and classified personnel, while Riverside used a total of 1,005 administrative personnel. Who, you may ask this time, aghast at the low numbers of administrators for Zurich's schools, does all the administrative work? It's simple: they don't generate all that work in the first place.

"Their schools do not hire specialists to supervise, write curriculum, and run special programs. Instead teachers develop curriculum [Isn't that what they are supposed to do?], and manage school affairs. They also serve as guidance counselors for their students, . . ." and because they are well-trained to meet students' learning needs, they do not send their students to pull-out educational specialists: they are the educational specialists. (Darling-Hammond, 1997) Darling-Hammond says that the school district in Zurich, like other foreign school districts she studied—in Belgium, Japan, Italy, Australia, Finland, France, and Denmark—invested their resources in ". . . supporting the efforts of better-paid, better-prepared teachers who are given the time and responsibility for managing most of the work in schools." The lower-paid, less well-prepared teachers in the United States receive their direction from an enormous corporate-ladder style cadre of administrators, supervisors, specialists, coordinators, and facilitators. This lead weight of administrator-rich organization sucks up the money while Zurich spends its money on its teachers.

How did this expensive administrative bureaucracy come to be? Before the 1950s, most school districts had one superintendent and one assistant, and most schools had one principal and two assistants. Then came the baby boomer tsunami which resulted in huge schools and huge classes. With more students per class and more students of diversity, the rigid, lock-step instructional strategies of lecture and worksheet failed more and more students.

As students began to sink into anonymity and "slip through the cracks" and more and more problems swamped the lower decks of public schools (namely, the classrooms), legislators and school boards found band-aid solutions in mandated programs. Darling-Hammond succinctly says, "Rather than humanizing the educational experience to prevent some of these problems, the bureaucratic solution is to create new offices, job titles, and programs that seek to compensate for the effects of an ill-designed system. . . . When the problems are not solved, still more offices are created to meet the increased 'need' for services . . . . Thus bureaucracy feeds on the fruits of its own labor, and resources for schools and classrooms are drained away." The formula looks like this: inadequate schools systems + ill-prepared teachers + core-family breakdowns (not discussed in this section, but still a major factor) = student failures = creation of special services = less money for classrooms and teachers = more student failures = creation of more special services . . . .

Enter the corporate ladder into public education.

What is this public school corporate ladder?

When the British rock group Pink Floyd composed their classic album tracing one man's journey into insanity, one significant lyric involving the schools hit it big in the United States. The factory or corporate model the song described struck a chord with many Americans, and for good reason. Any reasonably intelligent person is struck by the public schools' uncanny resemblance to a factory. Even a child can see it. Even a child resents it. When the alarming chorus rang out, "We don't need no education!" it wailed not against learning, but rather the way in which the process was delivered.

The corporate ladder structure of the public schools in the United States is no accident. The "ladder" rose in the early 1920s with the hope of duplicating, in the world of education, the astounding success of the American factory system. Predictably, it progressively dehumanized not only its product, i.e., students, but in significant ways, the professionals who were charged with the responsibility of shaping the next generation.

As if it were a plant cranking out widgets, the public school system, like a major corporation, has a ladder-design management structure. It has entry level positions, various levels of middle management positions, and a full complement of executive positions, including a chief executive officer with an attending coterie of underlings. As in a corporation, the entry level positions offer the lowest pay, the least status, the fewest

Set Up for Failure

perquisites, and no real policy-making power. As ambitious people move up the education career ladder, they gain in all these categories.

As in a major corporation, the person at the entry level position—the teacher—is closest to the product. This person knows the ins and outs of the product, knows most about the performance of the product, knows what damages the product, and has a fair idea about what might improve the product. As with their brothers and sisters on a factory assembly line, teachers know what would make the process easier, faster, and more effective. They know what makes workers come in late or arrive early; they know why some quit early or stay late. They even care about whether the product lasts a lifetime or breaks on the first use. Of course, workers/teachers at this level have virtually no say about how things are done at any stage.

In a major corporation, the highest management positions are the farthest removed from the product. Typically upper-management personnel haven't seen the inside of the factory since the second promotion, haven't talked to a worker since the last strike, and can't clearly remember what the beginning stages of the product look like. Still, they make all the major decisions about expenditures for the manufacturing process, including how much will be allocated for production, public relations and advertising, and their own salaries.

In the schools, these management creatures come in all shapes, sizes, and genders. At the top, there are superintendents, assistant superintendents of this and that (numbers may vary from district to district), directors of stuff and nonsense, coordinators of something or other, program specialists in thingamabobs, consultants for the implementation of whatsits, and others which appear and disappear like Alice's Cheshire cat leaving only a smile.

As is true with the corporate counterparts, the person at the bottom of the school system ladder—the teacher—has the greatest responsibility for the quality of the product that the

Part II – B: Chapter 9

"plant" produces. Here the analogy ends: unlike the products of a factory, each product of the schools considers himself or herself to be of immense significance. And they are—not only to themselves, but to their society.

The ladder-climb in the school system usually follows this pattern. A young person, having in mind a career in education, gets an appropriate university degree and a teaching credential. He seeks and finds a teaching position. Usually this individual must spend three years in charge of a classroom (note the absence of the word "teach") before being considered for a "promotion". At some time during this period, the future administrator makes a depressing discovery. He has made a career choice mistake. The issue may be financial, status-related, stress-related, or he simply may be inept in the classroom. Teaching, or pretending to teach, is not for him.

He begins to take courses at night and in summer school aimed at becoming an administrator or a guidance counselor. Rumor has it that at some point in this process, he is subjected to a surgical procedure which removes a significant portion of his brain matter and sterilizes him. In simple terms, he is figuratively lobotomized and castrated. This is to curb any tendencies toward intelligent thought or independent action.

Presumably, his internship in the classroom has taught him "the ropes" of the school system. He ostensibly knows how to manufacture (educate) the product (student).

Frequently, those who choose the path of the guidance counselor as the first rung of the ladder find that they have made another error. They find they have become a glorified clerk. They dislike the glorified part as much as they do the clerk part. Although they have this really keen office and a phone, they find their only function is to complete paperwork. They distribute surveys, administer group tests on careers, they put up college posters and give out brochures. A mildly competent secretary could do their job (and frequently does). Many of their counselees (code word for "student") remain strangers to them.

Set Up for Failure

The only students they see are the good, the bad, and the ugly. They have no happiness in their work, they don't make enough money, or they can't seem to do a very good job at this either. Back to night school. Next stop: administration.

Some eager chipmunks skip the guidance office altogether and make a leap directly from the classroom to administration. After the apprenticeship in the classroom, the mouse who would be a rat applies for, or is recruited by the management team for a bottom-level administrative position. If the said rodent has done a good job, and has done her course work, she steps up another rung. "Good" does not mean to imply any expertise in actual teaching. Good means "a team player", a volunteer for committees, one who takes on extra duties no matter how meaningless (with pay, of course). She may or may not be an effective teacher. You see, in today's educational establishment, teaching becomes irrelevant to advancement. However, before she leaves the classroom, she is required to memorize a litany describing how much she loves the kids and the classroom, and how she simply felt she could do more good at another level. She was, as she modestly will tell you, a very good teacher.

Case study on recruiting Young Up-wardly Mobile Administrators:

The youngish high school teacher had taught for ten years or so, and he was extremely popular with his students. Coincidentally, he was a reasonably effective teacher. He was also popular with the teachers: he took part in union leadership and served as the voice of reason. Oddly enough, the administration liked him, too. He helped coach and referee at the various ball games, at which point he rubbed elbows with the office administration. He was a genuinely good guy.

And he gave no indication that he wanted to be anything other than a teacher, until the principal began to hint that he

Part II – B: Chapter 9

could probably get an administrative job if he even started to work on his credential.

So he did, until an assistant superintendent said, "If you'll come over to our side, I'll make sure you move right over the guidance counselor job and the dean's job and get an assistant principal's job, and you won't even have to interview."

With that offer, he pulled his potential career ladder off the wall.

If one is not recruited, as with this popular teacher, he must struggle to move up. After several humiliating rejections, he gets rewarded for his persistence, and receives a bottom-level management position. In most school districts, this is an assistant principalship. This means he does all the jobs the head principal doesn't want to do. He disciplines students (because teachers won't or can't). He takes charge of equipment, or supplies, or furniture, or disaster preparedness, or all of the above. Lately, many assistant principals have foisted off many of their disciplinary duties onto the guidance counselors. This accomplishes two things: first, it gets part of the onerous duty off the shoulders of the assistant principal; second, it gives some training in "discipline" to the counselor who may someday join the ranks of the elite.

The assistant principal walks the halls, often with a walkie-talkie (they have such neat toys), looks for fights, dress-code violations, drug deals, or other rude behavior. All assistant principals, whether they wear slacks or skirts, high heels or Rockports, walk and stand like cops. After a typical day of breaking up several fights, assigning numerous after-school detentions, issuing suspensions from school, fielding phone calls from angry parents, writing multiple memos, chairing committee meetings (which half the teachers involved in forgot about [because they didn't read the memos] and the other half didn't listen to), skipping lunch, and not leaving for home until 6:30 (unless they have a ball game to patrol), a light comes on in the

Set Up for Failure

assistant principal brain: this is not what he was trained to do.

Because the assistant principal seldom deals with anyone besides the orneriest students, the most recalcitrant teachers, and the angriest parents, emotional calluses form. Attitudes about the very nature of humanity may be altered especially concerning students, teachers, and parents. This attitude altering is invariably negative. The job of an assistant principal will be involved with fielding complaints about everything connected to the school and writing reports about them. Tenure as an assistant principal qualifies as a baptism by fire.

Of course, the position comes with some rewards. The assistant principal gets a salary increase, a nifty office, a secretary, and the opportunity to plan inservices for teachers. This is a biggie. Usually it involves ordering refreshments, ordering furniture to be moved about, acquiring a presenter, and composing the agenda. The role flirts with stardom.

The position has one more benefit: the evaluation of teachers. This process is supposed to ensure that the quality of instruction remains high (if it ever was). The linchpin of this process is the classroom observation. The assistant principal goes to a classroom and watches the teacher teach. Each teacher receives an evaluation every third year, depending on the contracts. This gives the assistant principal time to write all those memos and reports. The average assistant principal will observe and judge the qualities and techniques of teachers who are not only better teachers than he, but are often teaching a subject about which the administrator has little or no knowledge. No problem. He has a clipboard. On the clipboard is a checklist filled with little boxes. The assistant principal loves these little boxes. It serves as the perfect engine for his purposes. It looks objective while it is entirely subjective. One has become a god.

A teacher may be chided for insufficient classroom control, or for writing too many referrals for discipline. He may be criticized for the way he dresses, for the way he talks, for

Part II – B: Chapter 9

over-reliance on the text, for not using it enough, for using too many videos or for not utilizing available technology, or for having a less-than-exciting bulletin board (put together at the teacher's own expense, of course). The list goes on. In different evaluations, a teacher may be castigated for something by one assistant principal and three years later, be praised for it by another (or sometimes even the same one, if her memory fails).

Case Study #1 on Assistant Principal's Qualification to Evaluate Teachers:

The young man "taught" for three years in the social studies and fine arts departments of the high school. He put in a few extra hours as coach now and then. All the while he worked on his Master's Degree and administrative credential. Then he began his move. He applied for—and was hired for on the first try—the dean's position at his school. Next he applied for—and was hired for on the first try—an assistant principal's position at another school. Then he applied for—and was hired for on the first try—a principal's position in another school district. Then he earned his doctorate in education. From the very first administrative position, he, with only three years of lame teaching experience, was in charge of evaluating teachers who had taught successfully for ten, fifteen, twenty, and thirty years.

Case Study #2 on Assistant Principal's Qualification to Evaluate Teachers:

The teacher had taught secondary Special Education classes for twenty-three years in three states and one foreign country. He had developed curriculum for district-wide and state-wide committees; he had presented inservices and workshops throughout the area; he had authored and co-authored numerous project proposals and reports. All that alone did not qualify him as an effective teacher: his successful students, however, did.

Set Up for Failure

His evaluator for the year had taught secondary social studies classes for four years, and for the past fifteen years, had floated around the area in various assistant principalships. He came to the teacher's room with check-list in hand, watched the goings-on, and took a few notes. One bi-lingual student was explaining the directions to a limited-English-proficient student. The other students were working in pairs on various activities, specifically geared for those students. At the post-conference, the assistant principal reviewed the check-list with the teacher and offered fine compliments, then said, "The room seemed to be a little noisy. I felt like the students were talking too much."

"Well," reasoned the teacher after he had calmed down, "one negative comment in twenty-three years is not all that bad, especially coming from someone who doesn't know Special Education or teaching."

The next career ladder step

An assistant principalship is nobody's career goal. It serves merely as an internship for a head principal's position. Normally, after a few years of working twelve hour days, skipping lunches, and constructing a baby ulcer, the Young Upwardly Mobile Administrator (YUMA) moves up the ladder into what is in reality the most vital administrative role, a school principalship.

The creative, dynamic, dedicated, courageous building principal provides the inspiration for her teachers. The good principal points the direction for the entire staff and the school campus. The good principal becomes that advocate for the needs of the school, its students, its teachers, its entire population, pleading the causes to the central office. The central office management team is joined only insofar as it is necessary to get the needs of the school met. The well-being and improvement of the school stand as the absolute priorities. The good principal imprints the campus with her own dynamism. The staff at a

Part II – B: Chapter 9

school with a good principal would lay down their lives for her. Their school shines as a jewel among pebbles.

The typical YUMA principal, however, joins in with the central office team as often as possible for whatever excuse can be created in order to curry favor and get that next promotion. This may mean serving on several district committees (during school time, of course), or working with county or state committees (ooohh! What this does to a resume!), or helping to prepare district reports, or taking time away from the campus to work in various central office departments. The YUMA has very little contact with the campus staff, although he may know by first name every secretary at the central office. The YUMA does not visit classrooms, has no idea what's being taught or how, and seldom attends school site council meetings. The students do not know what their YUMA looks like. The YUMA-run school is a dirt clod among pebbles.

Case Study on the Unknown Principal:

The modest-sized middle school had a principal and one assistant principal. The assistant principal, in his first administrative job, handled all the discipline and all the parent complaints, and did all the evaluations of teachers. During lunch and between classes, he was out on the campus if he wasn't in his office in a parent meeting; he greeted students, played a little basketball, and kept his eyes and ears open to the goings-on of the school. The principal was at the central office meetings, county office meetings, or conferences. A teacher at the school asked her students to draw a picture of something—anything— about their school. One child drew a picture of a school bus with the principal hiding behind it.

What does the YUMA do during those odd times when forced to actually spend time on campus? No one is quite sure. One enterprising rising star went on a two week quail hunting trip with some of the central office people. No one except his secretary even knew he was gone. Alas, they do call staff

Set Up for Failure

meetings. Now, this is a bully pulpit, indeed. This becomes a show where one person can be the star, the producer, and the director, and even play all the supporting roles, if desired. In many schools, these meetings may be called as often and may last as long as whim dictates. What delicious power! What an ego trip! One can almost see the visions of superintendency dancing just overhead as the YUMA commands the stage, the podium, and the microphone, directing the teachers in the audience to do this or that.

The YUMA's Next Step

The YUMA soon applies for a bottom-level central office position, a coordinator of something or other. If he has paid his team-joining dues, he receives his reward with a position on the second or third application. The task is—well, we're not sure what the task is. It is probably irrelevant. It does have an extended job description which lists writing various reports, meeting with various committees, studying various government reports, and assigning tasks to various site personnel as necessary. It does have at least one secretary and one clerk. And, it has a nice office with new furniture. It includes a boost in salary, full benefits, including a massive life insurance policy worth ten times that of a teacher's policy. Often, a district-owned car is included for "official" use.

Of course, one's time is not one's own. Workdays, which begin at a 6:30 breakfast meeting may extend until 11:00 p.m. for a school board meeting. But entry into the inner sanctum has been achieved. The YUMA is limited now only by luck and her ability to suck up.

And the climb goes on

From here, the climb up the ladder becomes more like an escalator ride, but only for as long as the YUMA continues to be a "team player". He cannot bad-mouth (speak honestly about) any district policy or administrator. He must do whatever he is

Part II – B: Chapter 9

asked (ordered) to do by upper management. He absolutely must not discuss any district-office improprieties or irregularities (whistle-blow). That means sure death. Since most central office administrators do not have job-protecting tenure, they must rely on their ability to be the perfect toady, the ultimate crony, the best good-ol'-boy (gal) on the block. They may even be allowed some minor moral peccadilloes as long as they are discreet.

From Coordinator, the YUMA moves to director. This means another hefty increase in salary and two secretaries and two clerks and a bigger office. From director, he moves to assistant superintendent. This means an astronomical increase in salary and benefits, everyone else's secretaries, and an office with a waiting room.

One would naturally assume that, from here, the next step would be the superintendent's office. Since a district has only one superintendent, this career move happens more slowly. The assistant superintendents decide that the only way to move up (and move up their salaries) is to design new titles, leaving their old ones to be taken over by up-and-coming YUMAs, creating yet another rung on the corporate ladder.

Case Study on Expanding the Ladder:

The superintendent had dutifully worked his way up the ladder, serving his time as a junior high school science teacher, assistant principal, and principal before moving up to the central office where he moved quickly from coordinator to director to assistant superintendent of personnel. When an ugly strike prompted the school board to send the old superintendent packing, the home-grown boy moved in. The school board like him: he was affable and nice-looking, and he smiled readily. For heaven's sake, he himself had been a student in that district. In the process of moving up the ladder, however, he never bothered to look beyond to the possibility of moving to another district, and he never took time to earn a doctorate degree of any kind.

Set Up for Failure

Clearly, from his point of view and from the school board's point of view, he was not moving out of that central office.

Therefore, the assistant superintendents, in order to improve their respective status, gave themselves more elevated titles: Deputy Superintendent, Associate Superintendent, Vice Superintendent. They also received more elevated salaries. The central office grew to a conglomerate consisting of one superintendent, three associate/deputy/vice superintendents, six or seven assistant superintendents, ten or more directors, and who-knows-how-many coordinators, assistant coordinators, and facilitators.

This is a typical management structure for a mid-sized school system. The bigger the district, the more elaborate the structure. And the longer the career-ladder. In a mega-system like that of Los Angeles, the district is broken into sub-districts (called "clusters"), each with its own central office. The chief superintendent has an extraordinary salary, and an expense-account, and a chauffeur-driven limousine. When was the last time he spent a day in a second-grade classroom to teach a lesson on addition and subtraction? How long has it been since he experimented with a variation of the cooperative-learning teaching method? When was the last time he had to comfort a ten-year-old whose parents were getting a divorce? What was the last lesson plan he had to write? By the way, what does he do?

What do any of them do?

According to a colleague who is now a principal at a middle school, the district-office team generates memos—sometimes identical memos from each different department—directing the site administrators to do this or that. At least twice a year, they go on recruiting trips to round up the finest quality (and cheapest new) teachers they can find in quaint places like Boston, Massachusetts, Ann Arbor, Michigan, or Santa Fe, New Mexico. Often, they go to conventions and conferences where

Part II – B: Chapter 9

they learn things like how to play hardball in negotiations with the teachers' union.

Supposedly, they help improve instruction in the classrooms. They provide assistance to teachers by way of keeping them informed of new district policies (which they write), about government requirements, or maybe about requirements for the teacher's own continuing education. None of these realizes any improvement in instruction. In fact, for central office administrators to help improve instruction is an impossibility, especially since they almost never go into a classroom.

Case Study on Central Office Administrators' Infrequent Visits to the Classroom:

One assistant superintendent had been on the job for a year and a half before any teacher saw her on a school campus; she said that was because she was in the process of "organizing her office". For what??? A military inspection? Her title was Assistant Superintendent of <u>Curriculum</u>; you know, the stuff that teachers teach and the ways they teach it. She attended conferences on conducting meetings, drawing flowcharts, and writing reports. What does this have to do with finding creative ways to teach topic sentences to third-graders?

The major impact on the teacher's job of having this enormous central office staff is an increase in the number of committee meetings a teacher is encouraged to attend. They are asked to attend committee meetings on implementing the new state science framework, on recommending a lay-out for a new school, on selecting employees to be recognized and rewarded by the school board, for improving relations among schools in the district, for coordinating athletic events and plant usage, and for preparing for state reviews. None of this committee work

Set Up for Failure

includes empowerment: the teachers have absolutely no decision-making authority. They recommend—provide input, as the district calls it—and the district decides. One can seldom find a correlation between the recommendation and the decision.

Without a doubt, central office administrators work long hours and they work hard. The problem is that their long, hard work does not result in any real improvement in how kids are taught, and in what kids learn.

Their long, hard work does result in a complex bus schedule, and safely-maintained (we hope) buses. Buildings and grounds are maintained (event if it does take two and a half years to repair the door-closing device, and a letter-to-the-editor of the local newspaper to get the hole in the wall fixed and the mouse community eradicated). Supplies and materials are ordered (and delivered, and they will come within the current school year if the teacher calls the business office once a week to check up on the paperwork). New teacher-candidates are recruited, interviewed, and hired. New text books are selected, but not until several teachers have procured samples, reviewed at least six, and submitted the reviews to the principal who forwards them to the district office. Budgets are put together, but not until each principal has prepared his own school's budget and submitted it to the central office, which then compiles the principals' budgets, and subjugates those budgets to the central office budget.

These tasks have a logistical nature, and the central office makes them happen. Unfortunately for them, this is not the military where battles are won more often by logistics than by strategy. In education, good teaching (and subsequent learning) goes on with or without the logistical support. You can be sure that my colleague whose room was shared by students and mice didn't wait until the logistical support of the maintenance crew came before she began to teach. This is not to say that schools don't need a supply line for materiel and other resources. But, please, is it necessary to pay $22,000 per month to rent office

Part II – B: Chapter 9

space for a staff of hundreds to supply one school district with the materiel essential for smooth operation? (1992 figure)

This enormous school management system did not always exist. One superintendent, an assistant superintendent, and a principal with two vice principals per school ran the district. Then the schools changed. School boards and central office administration became factory-minded. They began to reorganize according to the industrial model of management. Perhaps school administrators secretly coveted the job-title and accompanying prestige and salary of the leaders of industry.

Probably, however, school district management grew because they believed more management was necessary to handle the plethora of government mandates coming down for education. Desegregation orders required management. Tougher graduation standards to beef-up post-Sputnik science programs required management. Equality in opportunities for men and women in athletics required management. Multitudes of baby boomers in schools required management. Orders to provide equal education for disabled people required tons of management. Educating the non-English speaking youngster required management. Providing social aid to children of poor families required management. And, so, management it was and is.

The problem lies not with trying to provide the services needed; the problem lies with the maze of self-perpetuating jobs created to meet those needs. Central office administrators hold meetings to plan their tasks, they write reports to explain their tasks, they make projections about their tasks, they hold meetings to plan policy about their tasks, they write reports to discuss the policy about their tasks, they hold meetings to coordinate their tasks with other departments' tasks, they write reports to evaluate the significance of their tasks, they write reports to justify their tasks. They issue memos to lower-level management about how the tasks will impact them. Lower-level management writes memos to the people in the field about the impact of the tasks on them. The people in the field write an appropriate response to the lower-level management memo, and proceed to do exactly what they have been doing all along. In the end, unless and until the purse-string cut-off is threatened, nothing much changes in the day-to-day operation of a teacher's classroom. And still the management structure flourishes.

The Education Career Ladder sets up the schools for failure

How does this lopsided budget and over-weight corporate management structure set up the schools for failure?

First, it denigrates the status of the teacher. The teacher, who, daily, touches the hearts and minds of the young people, for better or for worse, is viewed and rewarded as nothing more than a beginning step up the education career ladder. One of the latest educational reforms is to create greater career opportunities for promising young teachers. They take excellent teachers out of the classroom, where they excelled, and put them in a position that has no correlation to their expertise. Who, then, takes the place of that excellent teacher in the classroom? A struggling new teacher. Who benefits from this process? Certainly, not the student.

The job of the teacher is treated as if it gives no opportunities at all, when, in reality, it offers the most fantastic opportunities to influence society. If anything, the position of teacher should be viewed as an end in itself. It should be treated—in status, respect, and remuneration—as the ultimate career opportunity in education.

This belittling of the status of the teacher most assuredly discourages likely candidates from entering the field.

Secondly, it is illogical to require teaching experience for the move upward in education management. The essential tasks (and the key word is "essential") provided by central office staffs do not require teaching expertise. Foods services, buildings and grounds maintenance, accounting, and personnel management tasks can be performed quite admirably without a teaching

Part II – B: Chapter 9

credential. Yet, each of these services is managed by several certificated people.

The curriculum and instruction department is the only one that might be done better by someone who knows teaching. This certainly would be true if the curriculum and instruction department offered genuine services to teachers: instructional methods workshops; content-area workshops; coaching for teachers; help to keep communication channels open among schools. Painfully few schools provide such services from the curriculum and instruction department. What do they do? Testing: but, that's another issue.

Teaching expertise—knowing how to evaluate a students' historical-process essay, sensing and using the "teachable" moment, determining which type of presentation will help a particular student understand the concept, being able to dignify the student's error, planning a whole series of meaningful lessons—these magnificent, powerful, and exquisite skills (or is it artistry) are not necessary for successfully locating and recruiting new teachers, for planning and maintaining buildings, or for keeping track of state and federal government requirements. It is destructive to require the position of teacher to be the first stepping stone on the path to the corporate headquarters, aka central office.

Third, the report- and memo-writing staffs at central offices drain unbelievable amounts of money from the school district budgets. In districts where only 43 percent of the budget (as cited by finance expert Speakman) goes into teachers and curricula, at least three new teachers could be hired for every district administrator. If you deduct the expenses of clerical help and office space, at least one other teacher could be hired. That's four teachers whose impact is obvious and significant.

Fourth, the corporate leaders, who make the policy and budget decisions for what happens to kids, sit far removed from the subject of their decision-making. Physically and intellectually and emotionally, they are removed. You should

Set Up for Failure

ask any of your district's administrators how long it has been since they taught 36 kids in one crowded classroom. Remember that the central office—corporate headquarters—looms several years up the career ladder from the classroom. Former teachers tend to forget quickly the daily grind of taking roll on three different forms for each class, dealing with the faulty air conditioner, planning three or four different lessons around two pep assemblies, grading a six-inch-high stack of papers, disciplining seven tardy kids, answering three parent phone calls, working on the text-book selection committee, etc., etc., etc.. Former teachers who become administrators soon become embroiled in their own disasters and survival needs. After two years as an assistant principal, three years as a principal, and one year as a curriculum coordinator in the district office, she forgets what it was like to face the thirteenth kid in a day who "forgot my book."

As a result of this distance, the YUMAs clambering up the corporate ladder have little idea about the realities of teaching.

Furthermore, they don't care. They don't care about the daily details such as the twenty-seven broken chairs in the lecture hall, the fifty gym lockers that don't work, the bell that blasts so loudly you think you were hit in the ear with a hand grenade, the third-year teacher who comes late and leaves early every day, the twenty-fifth-year teacher who does nothing but show films, or the library's half empty shelves. They don't care because these are very small parts of a very big system, and they are too far away from the forest to see the individual rotten trees. So, if one tree rots off and falls, it's no big deal, because the forest still stands, more or less.

What's worse, the individual teacher with the nit-picky detail problem cannot get to the department that handles the problem without going through the . . . you guessed it, the chain of command. Do you, the fourth-grade teacher, have a problem with the quality of paper for your kids? Write a memo to your

Part II – B: Chapter 9

Grade-Leader, who writes a memo to the assistant principal, who contacts the principal, who then brings up the problem at the next (one month later) principal's meeting. If a central office coordinator happens to be at that meeting, then the problem might be carried to the central office. Fat chance.

Woe unto the teacher who by-passes the various links on the command chain to go right to the person who can solve the problem. That faux pas will guarantee you nasty letters in your file for being insubordinate, or a nasty evaluation, or an involuntary transfer to another school. No matter how much your students will benefit from getting the air conditioner fixed in their afternoon classroom, or from having books with dark enough print to read, or from not having to endure 180 different films from Mr. Media in one year, you must work your tedious, frustrating way through the chain of command to get the problem examined. If you have any energy left, you can teach.

Fifth, the corporate ladder climbers will be the last ones to agree to make significant, creative changes in the school systems. In order to prevent the inevitable failure of the schools, the public itself must "exorcise" the system of the corporate ladder. It must put the vast majority of that wasted money back into the classrooms. It must put the wasted expertise of former teachers/now administrators back into the classrooms. Clearly, school district office administrators will not go down quietly. They will do whatever they can to block serious changes in the system. You can hear them crying now. Ask any central office administrator what he or she thinks of this book, and . . . mark . . . my . . . words.

Major corporations in Japan realized long ago that the corporate ladder management system was faulty, at best. They realized that it bred a self-serving ego trip for self-serving ego-maniacs who soon lost all regard for the product or the process or the

Set Up for Failure

purpose of the corporation.

Many major corporations in the United States have seen the light, also. They have abandoned middle-management, and placed greater and greater decision-making powers—along with the commensurate accountability—on the people who make the product. They have found that this worker-autonomy stirs up a long-sleeping pride in the worker, who now sees some purpose for trying to do a better job.

Successfully restructured schools, those where the top priority of student learning results in genuine progress, have abandoned the corporate ladder structure and made the site teachers the accountable decision-makers.

However, schools notoriously react slowly to trends of thought. The industrial era was long underway before schools adopted the industrial management program. How long will it take for the schools to figure out that the education career ladder has led to a hole in the roof and set up schools for failure?

Long time friend and colleague and veteran teacher Jim Bowers contributed to this chapter.

Part II:
Reasons for Failure

Section B:
The System

Chapter 10:

The Media Interferes

She could have been a total knock-out, a Godiva of eye-candy. The teen-aged girl, with harshly dyed brown hair, stark black lines encircling each eye, and a purple tattoo of a scorpion etched into her left cheek, sat in her small, foreign car, waiting at the stop light. She wore a vacant expression as she jutted out her chin and unconsciously rocked back and forth to the pulsations of the booming car radio, and lightly tapped her fingers on the steering wheel.

"No ho's gonna beat mah . . ." the radio blared. "Ah'll whip her ass with a ty-ah ahrn and choke her skinny neck with a chain." Except that she mouthed the words to the piece, the observer would think that the young girl at the wheel didn't seem to notice the hideous lyrics.

Two buxom women slithered toward each other, dragging their tee-shirt-clad double "X" breasts through the mud before they squatted face to face and licked each other's tongues. They

Set Up for Failure

turned to the camera, and sang (as it were), "I'm gonna find love, somehow, somewhere, someday, in the wet, warm . . ." The five teen-agers—two girls and three boys—watching the music video stared vacantly at the TV screen as they shoved chips and soda into their mouths. It was 3:15 in the afternoon.

Three ten-year-old boys peered intently into the computer screen as the middle boy furiously worked his fingers over the keyboard and aimed to "kill" every human-like figure on the screen. "Yeah! Tight!! Oh, man, you blew his fuckin' head off!!" they shout as the video game warrior came closer to his final destination. "Quick, see if you can download the codes so we can win," one suggests to the others.

Two well-grown young men—only 14 at the time—strutted into the classroom, bobbing their heads, chins jutted out. "I think I wanna be President of the Eeeyuuuunited States," the short one pronounced, looking from side to side, eyes half closed. "An' ah'm gonna get an intern an' stoke some goooooood ceeeeegars!!!" The fifteen eighth-graders who came to class on time that day howled in gleeful laughter.

Well, the teacher rationalized to herself, at least they're paying attention to the news.

And, so, the teacher struggles. She must be quicker than a car commercial, slicker than a music video, funnier than "Mad TV", and more shocking than Jerry Springer. If he doesn't change scripts, props, or stage positions at least every ten seconds, he will lose his audience, assuming he had them in the first place. And this is seventh grade.

Few teachers in the public schools can successfully compete against the media for young people's attention. Few teachers embody the energy and force of personality to command belief that what they are doing is what the kids should be doing. Teenagers, naturally, prefer to hear and see messages about easy, sleazy sex than about using gerunds to make a literary transition. How can the teacher possibly be worthy of more attention than a music video with its split-second bites of flashy imagery?

Part II – B: Chapter 10

How can any rational, thinking adult on this earth today believe that what's on television and at the movies and on computer screens doesn't matter to the kids that suck up the sensual over-stimulation like a paper towel sucks up spilled milk?

Study after study discovers that teenagers who regularly watch television during early adolescence will likely be violent in later years. According to a study by Jeffrey G. Johnson of Columbia University and the New York State Psychiatric Institute, the rate of violence increases dramatically if the person watches TV for more than three hours a day. Johnson's study, which involved more than 700 people for 17 years, revealed a five-fold increase in aggressive behavior from less than one hour of television to three or more hours. Of the fourteen-year-old boys who watched less than an hour of television daily, 5.7 percent involved themselves in violent acts—assaults, fights, and robberies—by ages 16 to 22. The percentage jumped to a whopping 32.5 percent of the young boys who watched up to three hours of TV, and 45.2 percent for those watching more than three hours of television. And what are your children doing right now?

Network television smells like roses compared to the viewing fare on cable and satellite stations, which allow (nay, encourage) profanity and nudity and spectacular, graphic violence—all those richly exciting things that young people crave.

Music videos could easily function as the "birds and the bees" instruction for young people. Based on the musical and visual content of these ultra-popular features, one could surmise that the only thing Americans do all day is seduce each other in scanty, beyond-suggestive clothing, then hop into bed, or wherever.

Sadly, the impact of culturally depraved television hits much earlier than the young person's adolescence. *The Associated Press* writer Robert Greene reported on an Omaha,

Set Up for Failure

Nebraska teacher being hit, kicked, spat on, and bit by her first-graders, no less. According to Greene, a teacher in Aberdeen, Washington reported that her kindergartners "fly off the handle at the drop of the hat, throw chairs and throw tables because they didn't get their way." A second-grader in a class in Lagrange, Indiana, advised his friend to "just shoot him". Do the youngsters learn this aggressive behavior from the teacher? I think not.

Within a three year period, the small Southern California community of Rialto endured three brutal murders. The victims, elderly women alone in their homes, were beaten to death by teenagers who lived in the town. According to one news report, one assailant knocked the 89 year-old victim to the ground and " kicked and stomped her and dropped a portable air purifier on her head until she had 13 broken ribs, a broken sternum, a fractured skull and bruises the length of her body" before she died the next day. An 85 year-old victim was beaten to death by a 16 year-old neighbor before he set fire to her house. A 15 year-old girl is accused of using a lug wrench, monkey wrench, wood-splitting wedge and hatchet to kill the neighborhood "cat lady", and that according to the girl's own words.

These children learned extreme violence somewhere: could they have learned it reading books? Not likely, unless they read A Tale of Two Cities, which is even less likely. Could they have learned the violence by watching their parents? Probably not, since their parents would have been locked up had they perpetrated those crimes. Could they have learned it from church? From the teacher? From movies? From video games? From the Internet? From music videos? What's your bet?

In a 2001 story reported in New Jersey's Bergen County Record, researchers took magnetic resonance images (MRIs) of eight youngsters' brains as they watched either boxing scenes from the movie "Rocky IV", or blank scenes, or a film showing baby animals. The researchers found that the kids' brains processed the violence they saw in the Rocky movie the same

Part II – B: Chapter 10

way they process real violence, activating a part of the brain that is believed to store memories of traumatic events. A second study, this one of video game habits of more than 600 young teenagers, showed that those who play "a lot" of violent games—even players who weren't hostile by nature—are more prone to aggressive behavior than those who don't play the games at all.

In his 2001 book <u>Vulgarians at the Gate</u>, the late Steve Allen cited a 1999 report from The American Academy of Pediatrics as saying, "Children don't naturally kill. It is a learned skill and they learn it most pervasively, from violence as entertainment in television, the movies, and interactive video-games."

Allen also cited a litany of entertainment elements that directly contribute to the disintegration of our culture, including profane comedians; sex-obsessed sitcoms; music lyrics that glorify violence, sexual prowess, and a complete disregard for others; and shock-show hosts [and their producers and writers and camera men and lighting crew and anyone else involved with them including the stations that broadcast the stupid but phenomenally profitable shows] who operate with a total void of character.

In 2002, the Federal Trade Commission issued an Executive Summary on their investigation into unethical marketing of R-rated movies and M-rated video games to children as young as age nine. As a result of the report, movie studio chiefs admitted that they had deliberately targeted adult movie ads at adolescents and young teens. Film makers and video game manufacturers and marketing executives revealed that they had set up focus groups of minor-aged teens to evaluate violent and raunchy movies and games that should have been restricted to audiences over 17 yeas of age. Dick Rolfe, President/CEO of The Dove Foundation, reported that advertisers and film makers marketed 35 out of 44 randomly selected movies rated R for violence directly at children under age 17; ads for 83 out of 118 video games rated M for violence were targeted at the

Set Up for Failure

same age group; 54 percent of 395 movie theaters permitted minors unaccompanied by an adult to purchase tickets to R-rated movies; and 85 percent of retail stores that sell video games sold M (mature) games to minors.

These same young people who sit stupidly staring at the vulgar music videos, or hoot and holler at the hapless "guests" on the insipid talk shows, or calculatingly annihilate everything on the screen in the video game, or soak up the graphic blood baths depicted in the movies (and shout, "Oh, yeah, cool, tight!" when the soldier's severed head rolls under the feet of his comrades) come to school the next day, filled with lessons learned. They learned that killing someone quickly and painlessly (for the killer, that is) solves the problem. They learned that every female (or male, depending on the student) wants to have sex with them and that they should oblige. They learned that killing people is simple because no one has real feelings. They learned that it's fun and funny to make fun of other people. Presented to them in visually stimulating and pleasurable forms, the lessons make their deep impressions on the children, far deeper than any twelve-pound textbook, no matter how insanely busy and colorful the textbooks' graphic art may be.

Can children exist without television?

I knew a family who raised three children in a crowded suburban area of Southern California who never had a television in their home until the last child was fifteen years old and they received one as a gift. Every year the family, children included, had voted not to get a television; when this one came into their lives, they kept it covered with a blanket most of the time.

"You'll never be able to keep your kids at home," neighbors and friends had asserted to the parents, "because they'll be going over to their friends' houses to watch television."

It never happened. Instead, the home drew the neighborhood kids like an orange blossom draws honey bees.

Part II – B: Chapter 10

"We had more fun there," the kids would say, pointing out the myriad activities they could do like design and build a fort, invent dances, create costumes, make puppets, write plays for puppet shows, or conduct Olympic-style track and field or skating events.

This family's children went to a private Christian school until ninth grade when they transferred to the local public high school with all its ills and troubles. The kids never missed a beat, and thrived and excelled in the "cruel, real world" of public schools, becoming leaders of their classmates. As adults, they remain committed to helping make the world, locally and globally, a better place.

Few parents today have the insight or fortitude to ban the television and other multi-media devices from their homes. Instead, too many parents view these devices the same way they view the schools—as babysitters, something to keep their kids out of their hair and out from under their feet. These parents fail to realize that allowing the computer games or music videos or TV shock shows to entertain the kids is like asking the neighborhood convicted sex offender or armed robbery parolee to baby-sit their children. Would they do that, I wonder?

With or without an evil intent beyond lining their own pockets with platinum, the purveyors of the young people's media deliver a sordid and sickening product that deeply and darkly affects our young people's values, beliefs, and thinking. Like a thrice-convicted drunk driver behind the wheel again, their gross irresponsibility maims and kills the children's joyful and loving spirits. Today's media renders impotent the public schools' pitiful attempts to educate and sets them up for failure.

Set Up for Failure

Part III: Prelude

Part III:
Stop the Failure

Prelude

You can judge your age by the amount of pain you feel when you come in contact with a new idea.

John Nuveen

No one I know would ever say that education has no value. H.G. Wells said, "Human history becomes more and more a race between education and catastrophe." With education, people may be lead, but not driven; governed, but not enslaved, according to Lord Brougham. In our American society, where free, almost-universal public education first took root, education provides the opportunities to equalize the conditions of the haves

Set Up for Failure

and the have-nots. "The fate of nations depends on the education of the young," wrote Aristotle.

The fate of this nation hangs on the willingness of its people to change.

Consider the end of obsolete systems.

As I relax and comfortably snuggle down into my easy chair to watch a familiar show on the television, the TV picture begins to get fuzzy, blurry, and otherwise unclear. I employ the remote control—a clever device to enable the viewer to make changes without having to commit any energy—to switch to other channels: I want to know if this problem is in the television, or simply with that particular station. Sure enough. It's happening wherever I look.

Maybe I can handle this. I go to the television, and fiddle with some of the controls. The fiddling causes some changes, but nothing makes the over-all picture any better. In fact, the situation worsens.

Looks like a problem for the experts. But it'll have to wait, because I can't get to it until the day after tomorrow. Oh, well; I'll just watch it like this for a while. It's not too bad.

The expert arrives, and lovingly strokes the aging cabinet-encased television.

"Boy, she's a real beauty. I'll bet she was terrific in her day. Yeah, there's life in this baby yet. We'll get her working."

The expert maneuvers this gadget, works with that panel, tinkers with several different components. I don't oversee the project, because I'm trusting the expert to fix the "baby". The expert announces he has completed his task and the TV works again. He hands me the bill, somewhat inflated from the initial quote.

Part III: Prelude

"Well, ya never know what kind of trouble you're gonna find in these old systems," he assures me. Oh, well, the picture is clear again, and at least I don't have to buy a new TV. Yet.

The "fix" proves to be temporary. After that expert returns, and several more experts have consulted on the problem, the final prognosis appears clear: the baby is beyond repair. It will never again produce the kind of results it once did. And, actually, what it once did pales compared to what new systems will do. Therefore, getting a new TV, albeit very costly, will give me more than what I had before.

I make the decision. The "old" is out, the "new" is in, but only after thoughtful, critical analyses of several possibilities. The new television is delivered, located, and adjusted to fit its new situation. Sure enough, this new TV delivers far more than I had ever thought possible. Surround sound, split screen, DVD, and three-dimensional viewing on selected shows. Wow! I should have gotten rid of that old, out-dated box a long time ago!

Presumably, I and most people in the twenty-first century society of the United States would follow similar procedures and make similar decisions regarding most appliances, machines, and other systems that had failed or were failing to perform their intended function. Why, then, after decades of observing and decrying trouble after trouble with the public education system as it has existed since the early 1900s, do the people of the United States continue to cling bitterly, tenaciously, desperately, and defiantly to that old, battered, useless, failing, empty hulk of a public education system?

If the broken schools were broken TV sets, the people would have long since thrown them into the land fill.

In 1970, Charles E. Silberman published <u>Crisis in the Classroom</u>, and pleaded for change in the American system of education. He decried the failure of schools to facilitate a reduction of the differences of conditions between the minority groups and the American mainstream, and the "training" [my quotes] of kids into docile, mindless respondents, aided heftily

Set Up for Failure

by the pointless and thoughtless television programming. In 1983, the rousing indictment of education in the United States, <u>A Nation at Risk</u>, reported on the sad condition of schools. In 1990, the first report on education from the "education President" flatly stated that nothing had changed: our kids still could barely read, could to minimal mathematics, could write even worse than they could read, and could not think critically or analytically. A 2003 report by The National Commission on Writing announced that less than 50 percent of the freshman college class—the top 10 percent of high school graduates—could produce papers free of language errors or analyze arguments or synthesize information. At the start of the twenty-first century, only the bleakness of the situation has changed, becoming more and more hopeless.

In 1990, I wrote, "A report on education can (and probably will) be written in the year 2000, and it will say the same thing reports say today: American students are falling behind their European and Asian counterparts; school facilities are in deplorable conditions; violence at schools shocks society; teachers are not being innovative; parents are uninvolved; administrators cannot get control of their schools. People will shake their heads and their fingers, parents will blame the teachers, teachers will blame the parents, kids won't get it, and they <u>still</u> won't care." The reports have been written, and that is what they say.

The current system of public education cannot be fixed. At a time when financial, emotional, and intellectual resources are finite, we cannot go on doing things "the way it was when I was a kid." We must change the system. We must reinvent the wheel to carry the new and vastly different cargo of today's young people and tomorrow's future. We can't wait, and we can't make any more excuses.

Part III: Chapter 11

Part III: Stop the Failure

Chapter 11

Develop Effective Teachers

*In a truly rational society,
the best of us would be teachers,
and the rest would have to settle for something less.*
Lee Iacocca

Years ago, I heard that teachers made an average of 5,000 decisions each working day.

"You're kidding," exclaimed a businessman when I shared the information with him. "What's to decide? They have the standards, they have the textbooks, they have the workbooks; hell, the stuff could teach itself."

Is that all there is to teaching? In the minds of many people, teaching involves a simple schedule: the teacher arrives approximately 30 minutes before the students—say, 7:30 a.m.—so he or she can get out the materials for the students and still have time to go to the office, pick up mail, have a cup of coffee, and chit-chat with colleagues. They then spend four to six hours

Set Up for Failure

in direct contact with students, telling them what to do. After the students leave, the teacher spends another half hour preparing the next day's work for the kids. The teacher goes home around 3:00 or 3:30 p.m. and has the rest of the afternoon off. In addition, the teacher enjoys at least three months' vacation time and every possible holiday.

In the minds of many people, teaching is a cushy job: excellent benefits, decent pay, lots of time off. So, they have to put up with a few jerky kids; that's the price they have to pay.

Compared to this dim view of a teacher's work, reality will blind you. Look closely.

The real teacher's day

Mr. Welty arrived at his classroom door at 7:30 every morning. It never failed: three little third-graders were waiting for him when he arrived.

"How'd you get here so early," he would ask the kids each day.

"Mom dropped me off about a half hour ago on her way to work," one would answer.

"Everyone at home was gone, so I just walked over so I could have someone to talk to," said another.

Welty opened the door, and the kids squashed past him, tossed their backpacks on the floor near the door, and headed for the computers.

"No games," Welty hollered at them as he headed to his own desk.

"No, sir," they responded automatically.

Welty looked at the lesson plans he had carefully left on his desk the day before. He read the plans aloud, checking for problems:

8:00, opening activities, including flag salute, school announcements, birthday announcements, and school song.

8:15, SSR (Sustained Silent Reading) for 15 minutes;

Part III: Chapter 11

8:30, guest speaker – Mr. Zimmer from the bank will show them how to set up a savings account;

9:00, math (early for this day to segue from Mr. Zimmer's talk) on multiplication, the sevens;

9:50, recess for 20 minutes;

10:10, language arts lesson on standard #1.4 (antonyms and synonyms) for reading lesson;

10:40, language arts lesson on standard #3.2 (Comprehend basic plots of classic fairy tales, myths, folktales, legends, and fables from around the world) for literature;

11:30, lunch for 45 minutes;

12:15, settle-down game;

12:30, reading buddies with Mrs. Harrison's sixth-graders;

1:00, joint lesson with Mrs. Wright's class on photosynthesis;

1:50, art activity (students depict in a story board what happens to a plant with photosynthesis).

2:30, clean up;

2:40, "Loving Learning" share time;

2:50, dismissal.

He checked at all the stations to make sure all the materials were set up so students wouldn't have to wait between lessons. He discovered he had forgotten to make the antonym and synonym cards for the reading lesson, so he quickly went to the cupboard, found the 3 x 5 cards, and created several cards for the aide Mrs. Hopkins, a parent volunteer, to use with the kids.

During this time, he made one hundred and eight decisions: Where can I sit John after yesterday's shouting-fest with Miles? What will I have Clarence do if he comes in late again? Natasha isn't getting the idea of plot, neither is Kara or Elizabeth: Miss Hopkins can help them. I need to move Billy closer to me so he doesn't get distracted so easily. I need to write the directions on the board in at least three colors of ink. Wait, if I do that, they might get confused. No, I'll write in one

Set Up for Failure

color, but put a separate box around each direction; that way, they'll get it. I know if I don't let Brenda answer most of the questions, she'll pout for the whole day, so I think I'll let her help Mrs. Hopkins. No, maybe I'll have her help Mr. Zimmer set up his talk. I think it's time to call Ellie's mom again, because the kid is not settling down after recess. And I can't have Tanya sit at the same station with Margaret; they talk too much. Maybe I'll have Tanya work with a boy—maybe Jason. And so it goes.

By the time the class was completely prepared, he had only seven minutes before the other kids would come in.

"You guys, come with me to the office," he said to the boys on the computers. "I need you to help me carry some stuff."

They eagerly jumped up to go with Mr. Welty.

"Are you just going to leave those computers like that?"

They halted, ran back to the computers, and set them on stand-by, then rejoined him on the journey to the office.

"Mr. Welty," the secretary hollered at him, "don't forget that parent meeting during the morning recess. If you need, we'll try to get a cover for your class."

"Rats," Welty whispered, knowing that no substitute could follow his lesson plans, and knowing he had so little time to cover the lessons. "You guys, take this box and these two books to the class; I'll catch up with you. And, wait a sec, you know something? You're the best. Thanks for being so nice to me."

"You're welcome, Mr. Welty," they replied in unison, faces full of smiles.

He made a bee-line for the men's restroom and half-ran to class to beat the bell.

On his way, he made thirty-six more decisions. *I'll ask Ellie to greet Mr. Zimmer so she can feel important. Robert needs more one-on-one for math; I'll have to do that myself, maybe during recess. I'll pair-up the "savvy six" [a natural group of friends who worked particularly well together] and let*

Part III: Chapter 11

them work a little independently on the language arts literature lesson; that way they can go as fast as they need to. If Mrs. Priest comes late to that parent-meeting, I'll have to re-organize the antonym/synonym lesson because I won't be able to do the set I want to. And I don't think Mrs. Hopkins will know what I want. And so it goes.

Every piece of the lesson, no matter how carefully crafted, has the potential to come unraveled. Besides the individual issues each of the 28 kids might bring to class, outside events impacted what went on. On this day, several students had been involved in a big fight just before school. While none of his kids participated, they had friends involved, and many of them had watched it. When they came into class, they were breathing hard and were clearly agitated. They didn't sit down right away. The clock was ticking. The lesson plans began to disintegrate before the day started.

Welty looked around the room of squiggly eight-year-olds, twisting in their seats, listening to two boys describing the fight in vivid detail. The bell had rung, but the students had not settled.

In less than 30 seconds, Welty made forty-six more decisions. How can I use this event to set up the lesson on antonyms? How can I move them onto the flag salute? I can't yell at them to shut up—that's not an option. I'll write a message on the board, maybe the word "fight", then I'll point to other students—not to Barbie, she's too quiet—and ask them to throw out a word that means the same thing. I will move those two boys outside for a few minutes so they can calm down without getting any more feedback from the others. With the "fight" web on the board, I'll ask them to give me some good things and bad things about fighting, then ask for some alternative ways to solve problems. And so it goes.

By 8:30, the class had refocused. They had missed the sustained silent reading, but Welty had decided that to ask them to be quiet after the big fight would have caused a big fight

Set Up for Failure

between the students and him. He used that time to discuss the pros and cons of fighting, and while the students wrote a quick journal entry about their discussion, he had taken a few minutes to speak privately with the two boys he sent outside, and brought them back into class. By the time Mr. Zimmer, the guest speaker, arrived, the class seemed quiet and workable.

The day was only one hour old for Mr. Welty; he already was filling up his quota of decisions for the day.

An elementary school teacher prepares four to eight different lessons each day; a lesson might require 15 minutes to an hour to develop. If the teacher has not taught the lesson before, the teacher may create a script for himself or for the aide to follow. For each lesson, the teacher makes, buys, or borrows materials like audio or video tapes, computer programs, art supplies, or the antonym/synonym cards, or the teacher may happily find something surprisingly interesting from the textbook package. The teacher must match the lesson's objectives with the appropriate state curriculum standards. Each lesson generates student papers to evaluate, mark, and report in the grade book, a process that takes as long as or longer than the lesson itself. This usually gets done at home because the teacher has no time at work. The thoughtful teacher takes time to assess the success of the lesson and make suggestions for improving it for another time. Many teachers spend time after the work day to make brief reports in individual students' folders, describing a student's accomplishments or problems or conversations; these journals truly help the teacher plan effective strategies for each individual student, but they don't happen on a regular basis for most teachers.

Even with the minimum time spent on planning, preparing, and evaluating papers, the teacher has now put in at least two hours outside of class time; the 3:30 quit-time turns into 4:30, and suddenly, the teacher has put in a nine-hour day, and still has a stack of papers to evaluate.

Part III: Chapter 11

The secondary school teacher faces the same range of decision-making situations. That teacher prepares only two or three lessons for each day, but each lesson must be from 45 to 60 minutes long, time that can go painfully slow if the lesson doesn't click with the students. The secondary school teacher works with 150 to 165 students each day, considerably more than the elementary school teacher's load. That's 150 to 165 different psyches to try to carefully plan for, and to understand cognitively and emotionally.

Each secondary school lesson might require an hour to develop. The teacher's prep time allows only one hour, so the rest of the lesson-planning goes on before school, during lunch, and after school. Most classes generate some student work for grading, so the teacher could be faced with evaluating and reporting on up to 165 papers each day; if each paper took one minute to scan and record, the paper-grading activity has just added two and a half hours to the teacher's day. In reality, not nearly that many students submit finished work, and teachers learn any number of clever grading systems—peer grading (students evaluate each other's work together, a process that enables them to learn much more about the subject and the activity), quick quizzes, only one graded activity per week—to lighten the load. Still, sheer numbers force the teacher to side-step and short-change this critical teaching tool.

As the teacher plans the lesson, the teacher must consider the state curriculum standards, the course objectives, the textbook objectives, not to mention the teacher's own subject-matter expertise. The teacher bases the next lesson on where the students were at the end of the previous lesson and on where they need to go; he tries to fill in any learning gaps with side lessons for students that are behind. With reading levels ranging from 5th to 12th grade in any class, the learning gaps themselves require an entire curriculum. The teacher attempts to incorporate various learning modalities—visual, auditory, kinesthetic/tactile—into each lesson so all of the kids will have some opportunity to learn something.

If one class gets replaced for the day with an assembly or other school-wide activity, the teacher must figure out how to catch up the missed class with the other classes so her students don't miss important steps in the development of the concept. Many students miss the last class of the day so they can take part in team sports events. So those students won't get too far behind, the teacher then needs to plan special activities for them; those assignments never have real integrity because the student never gets the lesson behind them. Inevitably, students' grades decline during the terms when they have athletics.

Planning, preparing for, delivering, and evaluating an effective lesson for 30 different individuals at a time involves complex, far-reaching decisions that affect everything that follows, for better or for worse. The task demands multiple levels of thinking and organizing at any given time. It demands perceptive people skills. It demands content expertise. It demands a clear understanding of how learning happens and the techniques that enable learning to happen. It demands more than most teachers are trained to give. It demands, as business giant Lee Iacocca observed, the best of us.

More than any other child-adult relationship except for parenting, teaching impacts every child. As with parenting, teaching can be positive or negative for the child. It can instill a life-long passion for learning, or a burning distrust of authority, or a crippling fear of failure, or a joyous belief in oneself, or a cynical hatred of peers. Bad teaching can set up your child for on-going struggles throughout her school years; good teaching can turn on your child to everything around him.

Many teachers come poorly prepared

Most research asserts that teaching constitutes the single most important factor in whether or not your child learns. How can you accept anything less than the best for your child? How

Part III: Chapter 11

can anyone accept anything less than the best for the future of our culture? Yet we do.

We accept teachers who have no training. The 1998 State and National Data Book, Vol. II, published by Education Watch, reported that, in 1993-94, 16 percent of the teachers in the United States lacked a major in the subject they taught. That percentage rose to 21 percent for high poverty schools, and 20 percent or one-fifth of the staff for high minority schools. In 1996, only 44 percent—not even half—of the eighth grade math students were taught by math majors.

The 1996 report, "What Matters Most: Teaching for America's Future", showed that 72.6 percent of newly hired teachers in 1991 were, in fact, fully licensed; that means, however, almost 30 percent had either an emergency license or no license at all. Twenty-three percent of all secondary teachers did not even have a minor in their main teaching subject area.

Licensing itself does not guarantee quality teaching; the teacher preparation courses must be up to snuff, also. That same report showed that, of the 1,200 education schools in the United States, only 500 met common professional standards. That means that teachers coming from more than half of the teacher education schools have inadequate preparation.

Most schools require a baccalaureate degree plus some teacher education classes, but the subject matter courses are far removed from classes in pedagogy (the science of teaching), so the teacher sees no models of how to apply theory into practice.

In a standard program in the state of California, the teacher candidate spends a total of only twelve weeks actually working in a class with a master teacher and that teacher's students. In the internship program, the candidate gets assigned to a class of his or her own for the whole year, (at significantly lower pay than a certificated teacher), with no master teacher and no mentor assigned to assist the new teacher and the students.

By way of comparison, prospective teachers in Germany receive degrees in two subjects. They pass a series of essay and oral exams before they are allowed to enter pedagogical training. They then embark on a two year teaching preparation which includes teaching seminars, combined with classroom experience. Throughout those two years, college and school-based supervisors observe and grade no less than 25 lessons presented by the candidate to real, live students. Even after all this, the candidates need to pass yet another series of exams, including demonstration lessons, before they are considered ready to teach.

Teachers drop out, too

Teacher drop-out rate staggers the comprehension, especially considering the time, money, and effort required to earn a teaching credential. Some reports show that up to 50 percent of new teachers quit within the first five years, while others show that the same percentage leaves the profession within the first year. The 2001 report, "Action for All: The Public's Responsibility for Public Education", a survey by The Public Education Network and *Education Week*, showed that more than 20 percent of newly hired teachers leave the classroom after only two years.

The school district where I worked for twenty years frequently recruited fresh, cheap, young teachers from the east coast—conveniently pleasant places to visit on recruiting trips. Of the six or seven sweet elementary school teachers that started in one fall in the mid 1980s, half never returned from Christmas vacation at home; they simply quit in the middle of the year.

Why would these people leave such a "cushy job"?

1. They leave because they are not prepared.

If doctors received the same quality of preparation as teachers receive, and were expected to perform perfectly their first time in the examining room or operating room or emergency room, they would quit, too. If professional athletes didn't train and train and practice and practice, no one would come to see

Part III: Chapter 11

their pitiful games. If professional entertainers didn't spend a lifetime learning their craft and work for months in rehearsals, their performances would look like a middle school assembly. Public education is getting what it will pay for: inadequate, uninspired, under-prepared teachers.

While many public and private education schools have increased requirements and test-performance demands for their teaching candidates, they in no way prepare the candidates for the reality of facing 30 different, intellectually and culturally diverse individuals to guide through a curriculum that makes little connection to reality, while responding professionally to bureaucratic demands from district and state institutions and from parents who refuse to accept responsibility for their children's behavior. While many states fund mentoring services for beginning teachers, they do not acknowledge that the fledgling teacher—and that teacher's students—needs daily, on-site mentoring to help evaluate lessons, trouble-shoot problems, plan intervention strategies for needy students, locate materials and resources, and provide a soft and sympathetic shoulder when the time comes.

"Chance favors a prepared mind," says the old adage. If the policy-makers—whether local, state, or national—did nothing else but build the integrity of teacher preparation programs and on-going education, they would build an army of solid, highly skilled subject matter and pedagogical experts who light up their students with a lust for learning.

At the least, teacher preparation needs to include two years of internship at a "teaching" school, much like the doctor trains as an intern at a teaching hospital. At this school, which children and young people attend regularly, the intern is paired with two or more master teachers who coach the new teacher through all aspects of daily work. Like a professional baseball team that hires different coaches for different skills, the teaching school will assign different master teachers for different techniques—lesson designing, evaluating student work, using the

Set Up for Failure

many instructional strategies. With this constant coaching and shared responsibility for student success, the new teacher experiences two years' worth of possible problems, puzzles, routines, and joys before he or she ever steps into a classroom to assume the total burden of helping children learn.

2. They leave because they fall victim to new-teacher harassment from their colleagues.

Just before the new teacher arrives, the old staff gets together to give him the worst kids, the lousiest text books, and the crummiest classroom with leaky faucets, a broken screen, a remote-less television, and inoperable intercom. At the secondary school, the old staff conspires to give the new teacher the least desirable classes like the required ninth-grade social studies classes no one else wants to teach, while they divvy-up the plum elective classes which carry the lightest loads of the most advanced and motivated students. The least capable teacher ends up getting the neediest students in the worst situations. I know; I was there, on both ends.

To increase the effectiveness of teachers, schools must stop this practice. This is a no-brainer.

3. They leave because most of them come with a serious handicap.

They are excellent learners themselves, and without intensive training, they cannot comprehend that other people don't learn the way they do.

In order to get into college, teachers had to have graduated in the top 20 percent of their high school class. Clearly, they were successful learners for the predominant teaching style which was teacher-directed, text-driven instructional strategies presented primarily in the auditory and visual modes. When he was a student, the teacher responded happily to lectures and note-taking, essay-writing, filling in worksheets, and cramming for tests. The kids who monkeyed-around or got lost during class discussions or completed only half of the assignments—in short, the kids who didn't learn well with this teaching style—didn't tend to be among the top graduates.

When the new teachers enter their classrooms for the first time, they face children who don't learn the way they did. Unless they receive legitimate, extensive training and coaching in at least twenty distinct instructional strategies and the learning theories that support the strategies, they will resort to teaching the way they know—the way it was when they were in school. Twenty percent of their students will understand and thrive like they did, and eighty percent will not. It's deja-vu all over again.

4. They leave because they feel powerless.
Teachers have become the unwanted messengers of a trainload of edicts, mandates, directives, plans, programs, projects, laws, codes, titles, and guidelines, and they are getting shot down when they deliver the message. New programs begin with top management, maybe even with the politicians, with the expectation those programs will be implemented at the bottom. With a thirty-minute, Power-Point inservice at the end of a faculty meeting at the end of the workday, the new program meets its messengers who roll their eyes, slump further into their seats, and shuffle their stack of handouts. Within a month, the two-inch-thick document fills a slot on the shelf in the storage room—right next to the last three new programs in two years.

Top management, whether at district, county, or state levels, has not seen the inside of a classroom in five or six or ten ladder-rungs ago. They have long since forgotten the realities of teaching real children. For them to design and dictate any kind of program—remedial, academic, advisory, extracurricular, tutorial—without teachers involved from the start makes as much sense as the manager of a factory designing assembly-line tasks without the workers, or a tailor making you a suit without your measurements.

Set Up for Failure

Give teachers autonomy, and allow the individual schools to design the strategies that will help their students. Rely on the real experiences of teachers to plan what will work with the resources that school has. Let top management, if they must, provide general principles about what must happen, then let the teachers and the schools figure out how to make it happen.

Many restructured schools have only one administrator or maybe none at all; teachers and a small staff of clerks plan the curriculum, maintain the facility, handle the paperwork, and order supplies. A teacher could handle the pseudo-management position for a semester, then return to full class load while another teacher or team of teachers takes the position for another semester.

Research repeatedly has shown that when teachers bear the responsibility for both developing and delivering the curriculum, they teach better, their students learn better and perform better, and the school thrives.

5. They leave because they drown in a sea of overwhelming demands.

Whether facing 165 students in one day or 30 students for all day, the logistics of preparing lessons, delivering lessons, effectively evaluating student work, and communicating with parents and faculty floods over the teacher like storm water breaching the dam.

Lighten the load. Effectively restructured schools assign elementary teachers no more than 20 students, and secondary teachers no more than 45 students a day. Which would you rather face: 165 three-page essays on the reasons for the United States' participation in The Great War, or 45 five-page essays? Which could you grade more carefully? Which scenario would be more likely to help the students learn?

Expecting the teacher to provide adequate instruction to 165 kids at a time is like asking a single locomotive to pull a mile-long train up a hill. It can't happen: most of the train has to

Part III: Chapter 11

un-hitch before the little engine gets to the top; likewise, most of the students mentally un-hitch before they finish the course.

Scratch a teacher and you most likely will find a compassionate, dedicated worker who truly wants to do good work. Certainly, teachers do not choose this occupation for the money. Yes, the benefits generally provide a cushion of security, but they hardly compensate adequately for the unforgiving demands of an occupation that would be a profession if only the public wanted it that way.

"Without Mr. Barnes pushing me all the way, I never would have made it through school," says the high school senior.

"Mrs. Pletsky showed me how to persevere and stick it out when the going got tough," says the college freshman. "She showed me how to believe in myself."

"I never knew anyone who loved history so much," says the junior in high school. "She made that boring old stuff about boring old men come alive and dance all over the room. Because of Mrs. Ormistad, I'm going to study to be a history teacher."

"Mr. Walters wouldn't give up on anyone," says the new graduate. "He tried everything with me, and it finally worked. I owe a lot to him."

The teacher—that powerful yet powerless, brilliant yet baffled, incredibly human force that connects or disconnects with so many young people; that person in the classroom trenches of the education fight; that surly, loving, needy, giving man or woman who works with your child—the teacher, like no one else your child will know, holds the key to unlocking learning. Prepare that teacher, support that teacher, empower that teacher, and you can rightly expect that teacher to light the bonfires of education.

Part III: Stop the Failure

Chapter 12:

Create Meaningful, Relevant Standards, and Test for Achievement.

Minimize what the student needs to know, and maximize learning.

You're planning a two-week vacation to the capital of the United States for late June. You make a list of the clothes you will pack: five trench coats, in various colors; ten wool slacks (in various colors); ten cotton slacks (in various colors); twenty sweaters, some long, some short; fourteen blouses or shirts; ten pairs of shorts; twenty tee-shirts; five pairs of sneakers; five pairs of casual shoes; five pairs of dress shoes; five pairs of sandals. That should do it for the basics. Then you make your lists for extras and underwear.

Stop. Why would you pack all those clothes, assuming you even owned them, for a two-week trip to one place where the weather won't change much? Most of that clothing would never

Part III: Chapter 12

be worn; it might get rumpled and tattered in the traveling, or, most likely, it would be left behind or sent home to lighten the load. After all, who wants to carry five trunks of stuff around with them when they will use the stuff in only half a trunk?

Who wants to—or will—carry through life all the stuff they read, heard, and saw in school when they will use only a minute portion?

What do you still remember from your twelve years as a captive in the public education system? Of all that information that bombarded your ears and eyes for 180 days a year for 12 years—a total of 2,160 days, and 15,120 hours—what do you still remember? What do you still use? What has been truly helpful as you have worked your way through adult life?

What would the curriculum standards for public education look like if they were based on the answers to these questions? Perhaps a look at the mythical community of Smartplace, USA, can shed some light.

First, the community leaders, like the leaders of all the other communities in the state, compiled a short list of "Guiding Principles" about what, based on their own lifetime experiences, they knew their children would need to know and be able to do in order to prosper emotionally, socially, and economically as an adult. They derived their list from discussions during a series of town hall meetings they held for a period of six months. Their list looked like this:

To communicate effectively, a graduate must be able to 1. read and understand a purchase contract for real property, a credit-card contract, an automobile purchase agreement, and a loan agreement; 2. read and understand an editorial commentary in our local newspaper;
3. read and understand our voter information pamphlet; 4. read and understand a pre-nuptial agreement, divorce document, and last will and testament; 5. use word processing programs on any computer; 6. use e-mail and internet functions; 7. write a convincing letter of complaint to a major company; 8. write, with

Set Up for Failure

complete accuracy, a letter to persuade a politician to take a particular position.

To function with numbers, a graduate must be able to 9. compute price per unit for any item, marked or un-marked, in any kind of retail store; 10. compute price per square foot for any kind of flooring or for any window treatment; 11. compute miles per gallon and commensurate cost; 12. compute income taxes owed or returns due; 13. compute dividends on savings accounts; 14. compute interest cost on any loan for the life of the loan.

To function as a contributing citizen, a graduate must be able to 15. explain the varying causes for the Big Events in United States history: the settlement of America, the treatment of native Americans, the development of democracy, the Revolutionary War, the establishment of the Constitution, the settlement of the Western United States, the development of slavery, the War Between the States, the Reconstruction period, the development of the industrial society, U.S. involvement in World Wars I and II and subsequent wars, the Depression, the Civil Rights movement, and pop culture of the United States; 16. explain and defend their evaluation of the impact of these events; 17. select one person throughout American history that he or she admires, and defend that feeling; 18. read and explain the Constitution of the United States; 19. explain the impact of modern living on various environmental situations; 20. explain the impact of environmental losses on modern living.

To be a healthy citizen, a graduate must be able to 21. explain how the body utilizes food; 22. describe the effects of exercise and various foods, drugs, and medications on the body; 23. develop at least one life sport to an intermediate level; 24. explain how a fetus develops and responds to various potential impacts.

To be a cheerful citizen, a graduate must be able to 25. read and understand a novel of his or her choice; 26. read and understand a novel of the school's choice; 27. explain how an automobile works; 28. drive a car.

Part III: Chapter 12

The leaders checked over their list, and agreed that it was all there: reading, writing, and arithmetic, and a few other essentials like health and computer literacy and good citizenship.

They sent their list, called the Need to Know List, to the state department of education where the list was compiled with other communities' lists into a data bank that sifted and sorted them. Subject-area experts refined and generalized the language of the standards, and delivered a final NTK List which the state adopted as the General Education Standards for Graduates.

The state department of education then developed an exit exam which graduate-candidates would have to take and pass in order to receive that state's Basic Public School Diploma. The exam required the candidate to actually perform the desired outcome. For example, for the standard that she must read and understand an editorial commentary in the local newspaper, the student must read an assigned commentary and explain its thesis and supporting points, and critique its argument. The student may do this orally to a panel or in writing. For the standard that he must explain how the body utilizes food, he must show through the use of visuals (which the candidate would prepare ahead of time) and oral or written explanations just what happens as food enters the mouth and travels through the digestive system. Nowhere on this exam would the student find the traditional multiple-guess section filled with tricky questions about meaningless, disconnected pieces of information.

The exam would be given in parts over the period of a week. It would be scheduled four times each year, and a candidate would be allowed to attempt the exam at any time. Once the student successfully passed the exam, he or she was free to go.

In Smartplace, a panel of three community members, six teachers, and two parents evaluate the candidate's exam. This guarantees that the pedagogical experts of that community would be in the majority for the final assessment. Generally, the community members and parents on the Smartplace Basic Public

Set Up for Failure

School Diploma Determination Panel tend to be tougher on the candidates than do the teachers.

By providing a state-developed and adopted exit exam, the state could guarantee that all graduates of the public schools would have the same basic skills and knowledge. However, the state left the details of instruction up to the individual schools and communities.

Once the General Education Standards for Graduates had been developed, the state sent them back to the communities and schools and directed them to "make certain all their graduates could do them, any way that works for your students." With the new standards in place—those standards that everyone had helped develop based on real, practical experience—, the Smartplace community members and teachers got to work.

Subject matter expert teachers took pertinent standards for their field and analyzed them carefully to determine what macro- and micro-skills students needed in order to master them. The American history and government teachers took the standard, "Read and explain the Constitution of the United States", and "task-analyzed" it, starting with the question, "What would the student need to know and be able to do in order to explain the Constitution?" The answer to this question provided the extensive list of individual skills and content pieces that would have to be taught and learned in order for the student to master the standard.

Then, they determined in what sequence each macro- and micro-skill should be taught so it logically builds on the previously-taught skill, forming a well-constructed chain of knowledge. This analysis provided them with a plan for when to teach each skill and concept. (In old parlance, the results of these two analyses were called the Scope and Sequence of the curriculum—the "what you teach and in what order".)

This "what and when" constitutes the content part of the curriculum. Next, the teachers developed the "how" component of curriculum. In this discussion, they examined various

Part III: Chapter 12

instructional strategies and materials for best developing the students' understandings.

Benefits of this curriculum standard development process:

Neither top-down nor bottom-up, this process involved equally the executive powers and the end-users in the development and execution of content standards. The executive powers—the state department of education representing the welfare of all the citizens—provided the end-users—the teachers—with the big picture of what the citizens want; the end-users determined how, in their expert opinion, this big picture should be painted—with what brushes, in what order, and with how many details. Without this autonomy, the end-users would become just the messenger. Without the general mandate from the citizens, the end-users would have no idea where to go. The citizens provided the destination, and the teachers provided the detailed road map.

Like the state's other teachers who followed this new process for developing and implementing standards, the teachers in Smartplace schools discovered that their instruction became tightly focused, that everything they and the students did had a clear purpose which was related to meaningful, agreed-upon standards. As the macro- and micro-skills required for one standard showed up in many others, the teachers also integrated all the instruction; reading for comprehension, for example, showed up in every standard, so every teacher taught it. In order to prepare the visuals for the exam's test on the digestive system, the students had to learn some kind of art, painting, drawing, computer graphics, or videography, skills a community artist could teach and all teachers reinforce.

The teachers also discovered that they were teaching better, giving adequate time for practice and application and the all-important but usually ignored component, feedback followed by correction and revision. This serendipity came about because they had eliminated more than 50 percent of the content and

Set Up for Failure

skills they used to teach. The floors around their curriculum development worktables lay strewn (figuratively) with discarded, useless standards; any skill or content standard that did not directly impact the mastery of one of those few and hallowed General Education Standards for Graduates got the ax.

No longer do Smartplace students ask, "Why do we hafta know this stuff?" or proclaim, "This is stupid". Students and teachers both know and understand why they have to learn a particular skill—say, converting unlike fractions to like fractions, a skill used to help them measure and compute square footages of various household spaces.

With reality- and community-driven standards in place, Smartplace students know exactly where they are going, how they are going to get there, and why they have to go. And they go with happy feet.

The mastery of these realistic, rational standards provides Smartplace students with a foundation for advanced, in-depth study of subjects ranging from astrology to business management to Deutsch to modern law to contemporary Black poetry to trigonometry to videography to zoology. While Smartplace students can elect to leave public schools once they have passed the Basic Public School Diploma Exam, they are entitled to continue in the free system until they are 18 or have been accepted into higher education. These Continuing Students may pursue subjects that help prepare them for an occupation, prepare them to meet college requirements, or just plain tickle their fancy.

For these Continuing Students, Smartplace designed courses based on criteria and standards defined by the workplace and by the colleges. The standards for the college prep classes tend to resemble the old detailed, laundry-list-style standards, and rightly so. The college prep students don't complain: for their path of advanced studies, they can see the relevance of the required minutia.

Part III: Chapter 12

Community business people help determine the standards for the workplace courses, relying on their own experience and current national and state trends. Many members of the local business environment actually teach or co-teach the subjects, and, usually, the classes take place outside the school campus. The instruction, happening in real situations utilizing fresh, new equipment and applying the very latest theories, genuinely prepares students to effectively compete for jobs.

We leave this visit to Smartplace and return to reality, a reality which aches for a curriculum which has genuine meaning for someone besides the subject-area mavens who have studied for decades to master the standards they decree young teens should master in a few years. Logic cries out for finely-tuned, relevant standards that dictate in-depth understanding rather than the shallow once-over "coverage" allowed for by the current standards.

When challenged with curriculum which has direct applications to real lives, students respond with delightfully surprising curiosity and enthusiasm. Which high school classes have the most consistent attendance and the greatest success rates? The elective classes, of course, those which the students choose based on their own interests and needs.

Students will study and they will learn and succeed when they perceive a good reason; when they don't, they just get by.

Part III:
Stop the Failure

Chapter 13:

Create Small Schools

Few students =
more attention per student, more adult contact,
and less peer contact which =
more mature behavior, higher self-esteem,
and deeper learning.

"We've gotta build a consolidated comprehensive high school so all the kids can have the facilities and choices of courses that they deserve," shouted Ryan Hodges, the new school board member, at the first public forum about the construction of a new school. He slammed his fist on the table, knocking over the full coffee cup.

"How will you put together a football team, or a band? If you break the school into three or four small schools, we'll have

Part III: Chapter 13

to build three or four gymnasiums and cafeterias and auditoriums. How will we pay for that?"

"Mr. Hodges," old Ruth Dillingham, a school board veteran, began in her salty, gruff voice, "sit down." She deliberately straightened the stack of papers in front of her, pursed her lips, then folded her hands neatly on the table. "Why are we here?" she asked, her steely gaze piercing his red-faced expression.

Why, indeed.

Have we built public schools to train a farm club for college athletics, or to provide entertainment for the community? Have we built the public schools to provide jobs for local clerical and maintenance workers? Have we built the public schools to provide a market for text book publishers and distributors? Have we built the public schools to provide a market for soft drink bottlers and fast food outlets? Are these the true purposes of public schools? If so, we are serving our purposes well, for the mega-schools with one thousand, two thousand, three thousand and more students do all of the above.

They house enough students so athletic coaches can pick and choose truly talented candidates to fill their team rosters while lack-luster athletes never get the opportunity to play at all; but, hey, the school deserves top-notch teams so the community will buy tickets to the games. Furthermore, colleges and universities need to be able to find the gifted players they want for their schools. They couldn't be bothered by traveling to a bunch of small schools spread out over the countryside.

The enormous facilities require constant maintenance and support, and the strong unions for classified personnel negotiate to guarantee that only union employees can do the work. Lost are any opportunities for students and staff to learn construction and maintenance services by helping to preserve and protect the buildings and grounds where they spend a third of their days, or to learn fiscal responsibility and communication skills by ordering and monitoring supplies themselves, using a budget they had prepared.

At the mega-schools, administrators and teachers generally order more books than they have students so they can keep class sets in each room while students take books home to use for homework, an unlikely occurrence. The text book publishers love it.

Soft drink manufacturers establish lucrative accounts with the mega-schools where they install multiple soda dispensers. Schools buy into this because the manufacturers offer a substantial kick-back to the school, a kick-back which funds activities that otherwise would not happen. The fast-food companies also have made the happy discovery of a captive audience for their goods; if they don't actually build a mini-restaurant on the campus, they send the food daily at lunch time from a local facility. The school gets more money, the fast-food companies get more money, and the kids get their junk food. Everyone wins, unless one believes the students might be better off if they prepared their own food from produce they picked at the gardens they tended on the campus.

Did I just hear a small voice in protest? Did someone cry out for a different purpose for the public schools? The public schools, the voice seems to say, exist to benefit students, not big business, unions, or college athletics.

Schools should exist to serve each and every student, to prepare them to function effectively as adults in a democracy, making informed decisions about their local and national communities and about their own lives. Schools should encourage each student to realize his or her gifts. Schools should nurture each student's curiosity and nourish each student's mind. Schools should instill in each student a sense of responsibility for the good of the order. Public schools should do all of this.

As they do this, if they happen to entertain the community, or provide a few jobs, or enrich local businesses, all

Part III: Chapter 13

the better. But public schools' sole purpose must be to teach people.

"Well?" Ruth Dillingham asked of Ryan Hodges, who sat down in a huff.

"You know damn well why we're here," he shouted at her. "We're trying to make the right decisions for our kids, and I'll tell ya, the bigger the better." He leaned forward across the table and pointed his right index finger at Ruth. "At the bigger schools, kids have more choices of teachers and classes, they get to have more activities, they have better facilities because we can put all our money into one big science lab and one big cafeteria and one big library and one big computer room and one big auditorium and one big sports complex instead of having to give a bunch of little schools each a little bit of money which won't buy anything."

With barely a breath, he rushed on. "For those brainy kids, the bigger schools can give them more advanced classes because we can afford to pay for the teachers, whereas, if the schools were small, there wouldn't be enough kids in any one class to hire a teacher for it." He settled back in his chair. "Now, Dillingham, isn't that what we're here for?" He seemed especially satisfied.

"You're so filled up with misconceptions, Mr. Hodges, that there's no room in you for one more sip of coffee," Ruth Dillingham spoke softly and slowly. "Let me tell you a little story."

"Once upon a time," she began in a genuine tone of voice, "a fourteen-year-old girl prepared for her first day in ninth grade. She was excited mostly because she was terrified. She had heard stories from her older brother about how the upper classmen treated the newbees for the first couple of months. Tradition, they said. It's tradition that we give the ninth graders a little hell. They'll get to do the same thing when they get older.

"Nora—that was her name—bought a new back pack and filled it with school stuff, like the good student she had always been. She had usually earned Bs at the middle school and she really did well in science classes.

"She took the bus to school because she lived eighteen miles away. The bus ride took almost an hour each way, and, because the bus left right after the last bell of the day, she wouldn't be able to stay after school for any extracurricular activities, not even tutoring if she would happen to need any help.

"Like the other eleven-hundred freshmen on the first day, Nora picked up her schedule at the attendance window where she had waited in line for a half hour. She had been assigned her classes by a computer that figured out what she would need based on a survey she and her mom had filled out the previous spring. She didn't know any of the teachers.

"Nora went to seven different classes that day for 45 minutes each with eight-minute passing periods—the school's academic buildings alone covered 50 acres of the campus—and a twenty-five minute lunch, during which she actually had only seven minutes to eat because the lines for food were so long. Her smallest class had 33 students in it, and her science class had 38 students, so many kids that each student would be limited to one fifteen-minute lab per week.

"Her P.E. class had 125 students, both boys and girls. They took ten minutes to dress and ten minutes to undress which left twenty-five minutes to do P.E. If they were on the tennis courts, they would each get five minutes to play on any given day.

"She only got harassed three times the first day—two big girls snatched her back pack at lunch and threw it in the fountain, a twelfth grade boy told her to pull the top of her shirt down farther, and a group of juniors ordered her to walk backwards all the way from one class to another. They followed her the whole way—it made them late to their own class, but they didn't care.

"Four of her seven teachers lectured all period, the science teacher showed a film, and the P.E. teacher stacked the

Part III: Chapter 13

kids into the gym and passed out the P.E. rules for them to read. Only one teacher, her math teacher, invited the kids to talk about their expectations. In that class, Nora and the other 35 students shared what they liked, disliked, understood, and misunderstood about math. The teacher listened, and together they wrote a plan for learning about the first set of curriculum standards.

"At the end of the day, Nora had sore feet, a sore back, a head ache, and she had homework in only one class—the math class. They were assigned to keep track of every instance when they or someone they observed used any kind of math in real life. The other teachers had promised they would be assigning at least an hour's worth of homework each night.

"Nora went to sleep early that night, and when she awoke the next day, she found herself back in the day before, only she was getting ready to go to a different school. This school was one of five high schools in a cohort that handled the district's 4,000 secondary students. Her school would have 750 students, not more than 200 in each grade level.

"She walked to school, only a half mile away. It's the same school she and the neighbor kids went to every afternoon to play on the fields and basketball courts. She and her brother and her mom went there on Wednesday nights to an art class for families.

"When she got there, she took out the schedule she had received the week before at the reception for ninth-graders and parents. The upper classmen had planned the reception and each one took charge of a ninth grader to mentor them for the first semester. They had to do this for partial fulfillment of their graduation requirements.

"She had met all of her five teachers at the reception, and she got to hear the drum line and the pep band perform. She learned that, of the 750 students in the school, more than 300 students played some kind of instrument. They had a jazz band, a pep band, a concert band, a marching band, a beginning orchestra, a chamber orchestra, and a symphony orchestra.

Set Up for Failure

"On her first day, she went to only three classes; the others were scheduled for other days. The classes lasted about 80 to 90 minutes each—the times were flexible in case the students and teacher were too deeply involved to just quit instantly with a bell. That's why the school allowed fifteen-minute passing periods. Her largest class had 22 students in it, and her science class had only 15 students; every student was expected to spend at least thirty minutes a day in the lab, even on the days when the student didn't have the class.

"Since the school had so few students, it had only one administrator—the principal, and the money that would have paid for two or three other administrators went to pay for more teachers.

"Her English teacher took the class outside to practice descriptive adjectives. The kids felt leaves and grass and dirt and tree bark—all with their eyes closed, and described textures and smells and temperatures. Then they wrote the descriptions, and put it all together in a communal poem about the school's garden.

"Her math teacher, working with only 18 students, started the students on setting up a business in the classroom. The students would learn to plan a budget and manage the income and expenses of the business as part of their math experiences.

"She would do P.E. everyday, but she would fit it into her own schedule and go to the workout room which was across the street—it actually was a commercial fitness center that worked with the school district to provide facilities. Other kids would choose to do physical labor on the school grounds, maintaining the lawns and trees and gardens. Others could count their physical activities at home, like bicycle riding or horseback riding, for credit. Still others could be part of the athletic teams which had to take any kid who signed up. That way the school managed to field most of the competitive teams. Since all the schools in the cohort ran the same way, the quality of the playing was equitable. All students were required to keep a log of their physical activities.

Part III: Chapter 13

"Students worked lunch around their schedules, and usually managed 30 to 45 minutes to eat. Nora brought her own lunch, and ate in the patio or at the student restaurant where a couple of classes of students prepared and served the food. For the first semester, only upper classmen who had had the class before could cook and serve, since the first-timers would just be learning. The food was made with ingredients that came from local markets, small nearby farms, and the school's own garden, so it was fresh and tasted pretty good.

"Nora didn't leave school that day until almost 4:30. She had stayed late to work in the science lab where a senior from a local college helped after hours to earn some money by supervising students. She did most of her background work—that school didn't call it homework, since the teachers didn't care where the student did the work, just as long as they had the background work done for the next class's activities—before she left school. As she left school, she stopped at the library, which was still open because it served as the public library for that part of town, to pick up a novel to read for English. On her way home, her feet barely touched the ground."

Ruth Dillingham stopped and looked around the room full of townspeople, hushed and focused. She stopped her gaze at Ryan Hodges.

"Now, Mr. Hodges, tell me: where will she learn the best?" she asked quietly.

Ryan Hodges shifted his butt to the other side of his chair. "That's a fairy tale. It can't happen that way, and you know it."

Oh, but it can happen that way, and it does.

Statistics on the worth of small schools

At the Metropolitan Career and Technical Center in Providence, Rhode Island—an even smaller school than Nora's little school—individually, the students plan how they will make progress towards the school's learning goals. This happens each quarter at a meeting with a team which includes the teacher-

Set Up for Failure

advisor and at least one parent. They design independent projects which focus on their personal interests and strengths while meeting the school's requirements. Each quarter, they display exhibitions of their work rather than take tests. They don't meet with several different teachers and groups of students each day; instead, they work with one advisor and a group of 13 to 14 peers. The adults in the community mentor them in different areas of expertise.

The class of 2000 graduated 43 young adults. Of these students, 52 percent qualified for free lunch; 22 percent were African American, 38 percent were Hispanic, and 38 percent were white. The class included gifted students and students who had repeated or failed grades. When they first came to that school, many were two or three years behind grade level skills, and most students fell into the lower end of the achievement scale. Seventy percent of the students came from families whose parents' education ended at high school. At graduation time, every one of the students applied for and was accepted to at least one college.

At Central Park East Secondary School in East Harlem, 80 percent finish high school, and more than 90 percent of the graduates go to college. The Metropolitan Learning Center, a small 30 year-old high school in Portland, Oregon, accepts any student who wants to focus on the arts. It reports a dropout rate of 2 percent while the rest of the district has a 30 percent dropout rate. Of the graduates at Nova, a 135-student high school in Seattle, 85 percent go to college. In 1997, 62 percent of Nova's juniors rated as proficient on the city's writing assessment while only 28 percent of the district's other students earned that rating.

The statistics supporting the notion of small schools have begun to pour in, and they overwhelm any argument of small versus large school. Whether measuring dropout rates, absenteeism, graduation rates, or cost per graduate, the numbers prove that the small school movement constitutes far more than a blip on the screen.

Part III: Chapter 13

Using 1999 statistics from the U.S. Department of Education, the document "Dollars & Sense, the Cost Effectiveness of Small Schools" reported that, when comparing schools with less than 300 students to schools with more than 1,000 students, the **big schools** have
- 825 percent more violent crime;
- 270 percent more vandalism;
- 378 percent more theft and larceny;
- 394 percent more physical fights or attacks;
- 3,200 percent more robberies; and
- 1,000 percent more weapons incidents."

"While 38 percent of small schools reported any incidents, 60 percent of medium-sized
schools and 89 percent of large schools reported criminal incidents." ("Dollars & Sense", p. 9)

The authors of "Dollars & Sense", copyrighted by Knowledge Works Foundation, discovered interesting revelations about the actual fiscal cost of small schools. Under the same assumption as was (fictitious board member) Ryan Hodges, big school proponents believe that, while small schools have some advantages with regards to student services, they cost far more than they are worth. The statistics show the opposite. In "Dollars & Sense", the authors cited researchers at New York University's Institute for Education and Social Policy as reporting that while small schools (600 students or less) cost $7,628 per student annually and large schools (2,000 and more students) spent $6,218 per student, the actual cost per **graduate**—that student who actually finishes high school—was slightly lower at small schools: $49,553 as compared to $49,578 at big schools. This real cost difference reflects the disparity of dropout rates between small and large schools: schools with 600 and less students had a five percent dropout rate and large schools had a 13 percent dropout rate.

Nebraska schools reported similar differences in dropout or graduation rates. In 1999, researchers reported that districts

Set Up for Failure

with fewer than 100 students had a graduation rate of 97 percent while districts with 600-999 students had a graduation rate of only 80 percent. *With significantly fewer students graduating, the cost per student who spends all four years in the classrooms and uses the facilities actually increases.*

Big schools cost more than small schools in terms of administrative expenses. Remember that 89 percent of the big schools (compared to 38 percent of the small schools) report criminal—not to mention mere anti-social—behavior problems. This means the big schools require added administrators, security personnel, and police presence to manage the discipline and security issues. In most cases, the job of the assistant principal primarily involves meting out the discipline to recalcitrant students. These are students who feel alienated socially and educationally from the school, who have been discounted and devalued by the public education process since their early years. They have little interest in being part of the structure they hate so vehemently, so they act like jerks. These are not students who get overlooked by the big schools: no, indeed. In fact, they take up 90 percent of the administrators' time as the assistant principal tries valiantly to force the kids to fit into the neat public education box created especially for students. Not only do the big schools require more expensive administrators, but that expense generally falls on fallow ground—it's wasted.

How do students get to their schools? In the case of small schools located close to the students' neighborhoods, students walk, ride bikes, or get rides from parents. In the case of big schools which draw students from an enormous geographical area, students must be bussed. According to "Dollars & Sense", transporting students—a cost born by the school district—to big schools costs twice as much as transporting them to small schools.

Besides the obvious and painful fiscal expense, busing has other costs. Time spent on buses—sometimes an hour or more for students going to and from big schools—means less

Part III: Chapter 13

time spent working on homework, handling chores at home, visiting with family, or participating in community activities. Students who ride buses cannot stay after school to participate in extracurricular events or to get help from teachers and tutors.

When push comes to shove, informed people agree to the benefits of small schools in terms of the students. The tremendous potential for individual attention for the students means more responsive instructional strategies; the close proximity of the school to the students and their families means more parental and community involvement in the goings-on of the school; the small, intimate staff means more involvement of teachers in all the processes of the school. But, people will argue, they're just too expensive to construct. So goes the standard thinking.

The authors of "Dollars & Sense" discovered that small schools actually cost only five dollars ($5) more per square foot to build than did large schools. For their research, a small high school held less than 680 total students and a large high school held more than 1,500 students. The small school cost $109 per square foot to build while the large school cost $104 per square foot. Architects, builders, and real estate agents generally prefer this calculation, while school boards prefer to view the cost per student. In the latter case, small schools cost $15,709 per student to build while large schools cost $12,977 per student or approximately 17.5 percent less than for small schools. At those costs per student, a small school with 500 students cost $7,854,500 to build while a large school with 2,000 students costs $25,954,000, more than three times as much as does a small school.

Of course, you could argue that a district with 2,000 students must build four small schools at a total cost of $31,418,000, still 17.5 percent, or $5,464,000 more than the cost of one large school. True. And the expense of four principals for the small schools comes out slightly greater than the cost of one principal and three assistants for the large school. However, the added security personnel, busing expenses, and maintenance and repair costs elevate the real fiscal cost of the large schools.

And have we forgotten the fiscal cost of the dropouts, most of whom come from the large schools? Of the heads of households receiving public assistance, over half are dropouts. ("Dollars & Sense", p. 12) According to the Urban Institute, USDA Food and Nutrition Services, in 1999, the 2.7 million families on welfare received $4,344 per year for a cost of $11,728,800,000. Dropouts are ". . . three-and-one-half times as likely as high school graduates to be arrested, and 82 percent of inmates in the adult criminal justice system are dropouts", this according to the Coalition for Juvenile Justice 2001 report. In 1996, the average annual expense for the almost 1.4 million inmates cost $28,140,000,000, or $20,100 per inmate (U.S. Department of Justice) compared with $5,923 spent in 1996-97 per student (U.S. Department of Education, 1999).

Enough of numbers. What about students?

"No child left behind," proclaimed President George W. Bush in 2002, as he unveiled his proposals for improving education. He had better look to the small school as the primary educational improvement because that's where the student at risk of getting left behind thrives. According to studies reported in Education Leadership, December 1997, at-risk students are ". . . much more likely to become involved, to make an effort, and to achieve. . . ." in the small school.

This involvement and effort and increased achievement result from a simple numbers game. In a school with 400 middle school students, all of the staff, including clerks and custodians and principal, know all of the students. In a school with 1,500 young teen-aged kids, the administrators know only the ones that sit outside their doors every day, waiting for their usual punishment. The administrators would like to know the rest of the kids, but the huge numbers of kids prevent this. Imagine being one of 400 kids who walk from class to class instead of

Part III: Chapter 13

one of 1,500 kids. Imagine the attention—or scrutiny, if you prefer—you would get.

With personal knowledge often comes personal care. At the small school, everyone will know when the student comes to school smelling like cigarette smoke, or sporting a severe bruise on her arm, or bearing a sad expression. Teachers, closely involved in developing the curriculum and assessing the students' progress, know by face and name who is succeeding and who is not, and they can tell you why, and they can tell you what they will try to do about it.

When teachers bear the privilege and responsibility of developing and monitoring curriculum and instructional practices, they become deeply interested in whether or not their work makes a difference. And they work harder and smarter. With their names closely and visibly attached to the curriculum product and the student successes and failures, they have a personal stake in what happens to their kids. Their ownership in the school with 20 teachers and one principal far exceeds that of a teacher at a school with three administrators and 80 teachers ensconced in one of ten or twelve departments far removed from each other.

Resistance to establishing and building small schools stems largely from a misunderstanding of cause-effect relationships in education. In a 2001 survey of parents and teachers, Public Agenda, a nonpartisan, nonprofit research and public opinion organization, discovered that, while parents and teachers saw the benefits to students at small schools, they viewed other reforms as more important. For example, they saw stronger discipline as more important than school size for improving education. This, however, gets the cart before the horse; at the large schools, the discipline is as strong as it can get without bringing in the National Guard, hopefully an unlikely situation. Badly-disciplined-young-people happen naturally at large schools, but not at small schools where curriculum better fits the individual student, and a problem with one in 400 students can be spotted and interrupted more quickly than a problem with one in 2,000. If the parents and teachers want better discipline—and who wouldn't?—they must start looking to small schools.

The survey also found that parents and teachers saw more benefit to small class sizes than to small schools. Research has shown, however, that in small schools where class sizes were large, the students still out-performed large schools' students. According to the 2001 *Report Card on American Education*, students performed better in situations where the principal knew their name, clearly possible at only small schools. Their 1994 study showed that, even with class sizes larger than the national average, schools with 300 students or less showed the best performance on standardized tests, such as the SAT and the ACT, (notwithstanding those tests' poor capability for demonstrating actual learning). Apparently, if one had to choose between small schools and small classes, the former should take precedence.

The parents and teachers also believed that better teacher pay was more important for improving schools than small school size. That implies that teachers will work harder only if they receive more pay. Hogwash! With a handful of exceptions at each site, teachers already work painfully hard in situations that only other completely-dedicated professionals would tolerate. Increased paychecks will not improve teachers' work; decreased paychecks, however, will drive them out of the field.

What does a small school look like?

Perhaps those people who have misgivings about small schools would like to see one so they could understand what goes on there.

The small elementary school would have a student-to-teacher ratio of no more than 20: 1. Students would remain with one team of teachers for two or three years to enable those

Part III: Chapter 13

teachers to work in depth to build or enhance a student's skills and understandings.

For the academic subjects, it would assign its students to teachers or teams in ungraded—that means not determined by age—learning environments, so a student might be with one teacher for the mathematics curricula and another for language curricula, depending entirely on the student's skill and/or concept-attainment level. He might be with older students for one subject and younger students for another. In other words, where he is cognitively determines where he is instructionally. For the non-academic subjects, he would mix with students of all ages for instruction that emphasized exploration, creation, and recreation. He would learn from the older students and help the younger students, learning collaboration and helping rather than competition.

All students, regardless of age or competency, complete at least one interdisciplinary project each year. The project is based entirely on that student's capabilities and interests. With parents and teachers, the student plans the goals and processes for the project. If parents and teachers agree, the student may even propose the project. Each project must involve a community member as mentor.

For each academic subject area, students advance to the next level as they show mastery of the skills and concepts essential to succeed at the next level. They show their mastery through a series of culminating activities which include producing a portfolio of the work they have completed during the time spent studying the subject; the completed interdisciplinary project; and an interview with a panel of adults selected by the student at which student, teacher, and community mentor explain the project, including the student's explanation of what the student did well, what the student would do differently, what the student learned from the project and experience, and how the student is prepared for the next level. Such a culminating event allows the student to do metacognition: the process of understanding what you have done by thinking and talking about it. This NEVER happens in assessments currently in use, but it is precisely this process that causes a learner to develop knowledge networks in the brain, networks the student will use to begin to learn the next concept.

At least one day each week, students and teachers leave the campus for excursions to the community to build their understanding of how their studies fit into real life. The community members—business people, retired people, public employees, and stay-at-home parents—come to school at least once each week to volunteer to tutor, to offer their expertise for student interdisciplinary projects, or give demonstrations and presentations.

All students may qualify for their own e-mail address at school where they will receive communications from fellow students, teachers, the principal, the support staff, or the community mentor.

The site has large rooms and small rooms, libraries in each room and libraries at the core. The libraries don't have to be expensive, because teachers, parents, community mentors, and students buy many of the books at swap meets and garage sales and bring them to their classes. The large and small rooms allow for differing activities, so a teacher may one day use two small rooms for small group work and another day join another class in a large room for a presentation. Every wall, hall, and communal area are filled with student and faculty art.

Students eat lunch at prescribed times, but never more than 40 at a time. Teachers sign up a week in advance if they have a preference for lunch times, otherwise, they fit in the lunch as their students need it and/or as the activities permit. Students bring their lunches, or make them together in the school kitchen, with the help of the school chef—perhaps a local restaurant chef—first thing in the morning. The students use the ingredients they grow in their gardens or they buy at the local grocery store where they go once a week on an excursion.

Part III: Chapter 13

The small elementary school has at least one produce garden where students from various disciplines work together to grow food for their kitchen or to sell as a business venture. The school probably has at least one flower garden as students from the different academic disciplines prepare for the twice-yearly flower show.

Teachers at the small elementary school meet up to ten hours each week with their colleagues to compare students' completed work and progress. They meet bi-weekly with every parent; every parent has signed an agreement to be on site at least that often to help, so the meetings get arranged easily.

The small elementary school has a principal who assists the teachers in finding instructional support, who guides the collaborative discussions to focus on what helps the kids learn, who knows every student and parent by name, and who has a lizard, a bunny, and an aquarium in the office. The office staff manages the budget, school district communications, and the press contacts.

The small middle school might not even exist, especially if the small elementary school held students through age 14. If it did, according to "Dollars & Sense", the small middle school should hold 50 students per grade level for a total enrollment of 200; (The middle school where I taught held 1,500 students. Argh!). The small high schools should hold 75 students per grade level for a total enrollment of 300 total students. .

"How will those upper grade levels offer all the advanced courses?" ask traditional thinkers.

A high school in a community with a college could send its advanced math and science students to the college for classes, or call in local retired engineers to "coach" the few students who sought advanced guidance. English literature students could meet once a week at a local bookstore to discuss a particular book, under the guidance of one of the college professors or a local retired teacher, maybe even an actual author: what a concept! Writing students could work as apprentices with local

Set Up for Failure

journalists. For particularly esoteric courses, students could utilize the programs available on the Internet. Kids interested in music—in the unlikely event that only a few of the 300 students qualified—could work with local music teachers for instruction and local radio stations for performance opportunities. Speaking of which, those thespians at the schools could be assigned to work with the neighborhood theater group. Physical education—as in the case of Nora's second school—could happen through community team sports or local commercial gyms.

If we can believe that learning happens in places other than a classroom where, once a day, the information-supplier pumps facts and figures into the students' heads like a cement mixer pumps liquid cement into a form, then we will see the infinite possibilities. Involving the community business people and the retirement community in the education of the community young people gives everyone a stake in whether or not the students succeed. Teaching a concept or skill in a real, practical situation gives legitimacy to the requirement for the standard.

Many small high schools offer excellent real-life examples of offering complex curricula to the students. At Grove Public Charter High School in Redlands, California, students are developing a demonstration farm on land they purchased adjacent to the school. There, they will build a working dairy farm, much like the one that existed on the property one hundred years earlier. They will learn horticulture and livestock agriculture (which necessarily involve chemistry, geology, anatomy, and biology), farm management, budgeting, and business planning. Their farm will become part of the local historical heritage park.

A small public high school in New York City offers another example. What had been a seriously failing comprehensive high school with 2,400 students and housed in an aging, multi-story brown city building, became a site for six schools, including four high schools, a middle school, and a K-8 school. From the very first year in 1993 when the average

Part III: Chapter 13

attendance rate of 9th graders rose to 88.5 percent from 66 percent the year before, the small school concept of the Julia Richman Educational Complex has yielded phenomenal results. One of the high schools there, the Urban Academy, serves mostly low-income and minority students; 90 percent of the graduates, who at one time had been at serious risks of dropping out, are accepted to college.

The school's 140 students face schedules, course work, and assessments unlike anything they had ever known. Students even have a say in the hiring of new teachers; they make their recommendations after they attend demonstration lessons presented by the teacher candidates. They provide input for schoolwide issues by sending student representatives elected by members of each advisory.

In 1995, a large public high school in Oakland, California decided to make the school relevant and valuable to all students—not just the few students who joined the teams and sat on the student council. They broke up the 1,695 students into five "learning communities", each with a slightly different focus. The Center for Technology, Environment, and Communications, for example, asked students to pursue their studies by working with ongoing scientific investigations in the community and at nearby universities. In the other "schools", students fulfilled weekly volunteer service requirements by exploring new fields in the community, which, not incidentally, provided more than 100 mentors. In order to pass an activity or a class, students needed to earn at least a C letter grade. The school boasted the lowest dropout rate in the school district.

A composite of existing small high schools might look like this.

Before the school year starts, each of the 300 students meets with a team of teachers, the parents, and a community mentor. Together, with the student's most recent portfolio in hand, they plan the students' course of study for at least a year, more if the student feels certain about the future. The student is placed in academic courses that fit his or her skill level and will help him or her reach the short- or long-term goal. The student also works with the team to develop a community service plan—every student is required to spend two hours each week helping in the community or apprenticing at a business.

If the school has no teacher who can provide the necessary instruction for a particular student, either in a class or in private tutoring, the school connects the student with appropriate private tutors, college courses, or internet connections.

Every class connects to another class, so students receive no instruction that is isolated from everything else. Every culminating activity bears an interdisciplinary stamp as the student must connect each academic subject to at least one other. So an American History student might discuss the Civil War in the context of the songs produced during that era, then write a short story in the style of the time, with reference to Stephen Crane's <u>Red Badge of Courage</u>. Or the science student might predict the economic impact of an insect infestation on a cash crop in a third world country. In fact, no academic subject gets taught in isolation.

Students might meet part of the day in academic classes, but not the same classes every day; this way, they don't burn-out on the same 'ol, same 'ol, day after day. Also, the classes meet for one-and-a-half to two-hour blocks so teachers and students can work in depth on any given activity. A student might meet one class one day and three classes the next day. During those hours when the student is not in class, he or she might work on the projects independently or with the community mentor, or the student might perform the community service, or he or she might complete the physical fitness requirements at the local commercial gym, or maybe go home.

Students move into academic classes as they are ready; they must show through their portfolios, teacher recommendations, or oral arguments that they can be successful

Part III: Chapter 13

in a class they wish to take. Parents must agree to any course assignments. This requirement presumes the student understands the course requirements and the contribution of that course to the student's goal.

Every student participates in school-wide performing arts productions, as a writer/composer/choreographer, a performer, a lighting or sound technician, a costume or make-up artist, a promoter, or a support staff. The productions happen at least two times a year, and the staff and community mentors participate, too.

Like at the elementary school, students bring their lunches or make them themselves at the school kitchen using ingredients they order through the head chef in the kitchen. Students eat lunch as it fits into their schedule, but they must maintain a diet journal to monitor their food consumption.

Since the community has its own business-sponsored competitive sports teams for teen-agers, the school does not sponsor athletic teams. But it does provide coaching for individual life-sports like tennis, golf, volleyball, snow-skiing, water-skiing, skating, jazzercise, bowling, and bicycling. The coaches often come from the community as the golf-pro at the local country club works with several students or the local bowling alley owner mentors a few students. If the student already is involved in physical activities such as horseback riding or skate-boarding, he can count that as credit toward his graduation requirements.

The faculty at the small high school meets weekly during half-day release periods or periodically during staff retreats to develop curriculum delivery systems and assessment procedures; to practice new instructional techniques; to consult on student progress; and to plan for and order supplies and materials. As a group, they decide on school-wide productions and interdisciplinary project proposals. Of course the high school will have only fifteen full-time teachers. Each teacher serves as an advisor to 20 students, meeting weekly for at least 15 minutes with each student to help with misunderstandings, to encourage their efforts, and to guide them toward their goals.

Twice yearly, parents, faculty, and elected representatives of the students meet for a two-day session—or for however long they decide—to discuss curriculum standards and assessment practices. Students offer opinions and suggestions about existing and possible activities. Parents offer ways they can help. Teachers present and discuss the possibilities for everyone's involvement in helping the students get where they need to go. In fact, before the school opens each year, the same group meets to discuss curriculum standards, and attempts to determine which are relevant and which are not—they will focus on the standards that make sense for their students.

Using this same process, the group several years earlier had established exact and specific criteria which students must meet in order to receive a diploma from that high school. Before the adults asked the students to meet the requirements, *the teachers and administrators had to take and pass their own standards-based assessment.*

Every student completes a project each year, much like they did in elementary school. The project must show the student has mastered particular academic skills and concepts in the context of a real-life setting. For example, a student may observe a hospital emergency room in action, interview the E. R. personnel about their work, gather statistics about E. R. services and patients' use of the emergency rooms, write a "creative" guide to working in the emergency rooms, and write a valuable pamphlet for "non-emergency" patients to help them make better choices about when to use the E. R. This project uses interpersonal skills, math, creative writing, and consumer writing. It requires the student to use analysis, synthesis, and evaluation, all higher-level thinking skills.

Whenever the student finishes the project, he or she schedules and presents the project to a review team which listens to the presentation of the findings, asks questions about any

Part III: Chapter 13

relevant information—in the case of the E.R. report, they might ask about various occupations involved in the E.R., or the types of technical equipment used there, or what percentage of different ethnic groups use the E. R. the most. With the community mentor and teacher mentor present, the student explains everything he or she has learned through the project.

The small high school views the student-as-worker and the teacher-as-coach. The student is not a passive receptacle of knowledge into which the teacher pours brilliance. Rather, the student actively seeks knowledge, and the teacher actively guides the student.

When the student demonstrates acceptable capability in all required skills and concepts, he or she is finished. Whether this happens at age 14 or 19, the student leaves the high school. But that's another discussion.

The small high school buildings remain open from 6:00 a.m. until 10:00 p.m. as many of the rooms and facilities get used by parents for classes on how to help their kids with studying, or by parents and kids for family classes in various art media, or to allow students to study with computers in the evening. The school library serves as one branch of the community library, and the meeting hall is used by various organizations that need a large space to meet.

Buses don't come to the small high school; students walk, ride bikes, drive their cars, or get rides from fellow students or their parents. Students are always welcomed on the campus to use the library, meeting hall, or other facilities, no matter what time of day, until the campus closes at 10:00 p.m. Since adults are always there, (and for many other reasons), students seldom cause trouble.

Students also are required to maintain the buildings and grounds, and the work they do counts toward apprenticeship credit and/or physical fitness credit for graduation. At these small high schools, students have an uncanny interest in making sure the place looks terrific and works great.

Set Up for Failure

The small schools described here illustrate a composite of activities and techniques in place in small schools throughout the nation. Not all schools have all these characteristics, but they successfully demonstrate some of them. These constitute the ideal small school, the one where parents and teachers and community members believe one hundred percent that the student is the reason for the school's existence and commit one hundred percent to doing their part to make that happen.

The small school constitutes the sports car for the champion team of teacher, student, parent, and mentor to drive to victory in the education race of life. Without the small school and its creatively logical curriculum delivery systems, the teacher, no matter how skilled and committed, will never see the checkered flag waving; the teacher will be sitting in a broken-down jalopy, trying to figure out how to make it work. Without the small school, the teacher can't win. If the teacher doesn't win, the student loses.

Part III: Chapter 14

Part III: Stop the Failure

Chapter 14:

Create Rational, Research-Backed School Structures and Curriculum

Question #1: What do we know about how dogs learn?

Answer: We know that, on their own, dogs learn through trial and error, and perhaps from observing their mother and siblings.

For things *we* want them to learn, we know that they learn through a system of rewards and corrections. If the dog (accidentally) sits when we manipulate his body into that position, the handler gives it a biscuit. Biscuits are good; dogs like biscuits. Yummy biscuit. Oooo—he's pushing on me again. I'll just sit down again. Wow! Another biscuit. Another push. Oh, boy, another biscuit! Maybe if I sit again he will give me another biscuit. Yeah! It worked! Watch this! I'm gonna make him give me another biscuit. Boy, this guy is good. I sit; he gives me a biscuit.

Set Up for Failure

Because we know that dogs learn our curriculum according to this system, expert dog trainers teach them according to this system. Can you imagine the effectiveness of making a dog watch a video or sit through a lecture? Do you think they would respond to a balloon for a reward?

Question #2: What does this have to do with teaching people?

Answer: What we do about helping dogs learn is almost the antithesis of what we do about helping people learn: *we teach dogs according to how they learn; we teach people according to "how it was when I was in school", or the way we think they ought to learn*, which, for 70 percent of the students 100 percent of the time, ignores how they really do learn.

Question #3: What do we know about how people learn?

Answer: We know that people learn first, by taking in information through their senses. Since our brain is a pattern-seeking device, the second step is to look for patterns in our mental storage system (called short-term memory) to see if the new information looks similar to anything already there. Think of this storage system as a wall full of post office mail boxes, or "cubbyholes", each with a slightly different label for the type of information it stores. If the new information fits any cubbyhole, it gets stored there. If it doesn't fit and is otherwise meaningless or inadaptable, it gets dumped. If it has meaning to the person, it will be re-organized into a new cubbyhole which is custom-built using materials from various relevant existing cubbyholes.

Third, people store information in long term memory for future use; like mail at the post office waiting for its claimant, if the information doesn't get picked up (in this case, moved into long-term memory) or used, it gets dumped.

There's more.

We know people vary regarding which sense they prefer to use to take in information.

We know that people's cubbyhole systems vary from person to person, organized according to what we now know as

Part III: Chapter 14

their various intelligences as researched in the 1970s and 80s by cognitive scientist Howard Gardner. Some may come with many built-in cubbyholes in what Gardner has labeled as the mathematical/logical intelligence, while others come with more bodily/kinesthetic cubbyholes; those people must custom-make their mathematical/logical cubbyholes to handle numbers and formulas. Gardner actually has identified at least eight distinct "intelligences", strong ways that people perceive and present information and ideas.

We know that people's cubbyholes may be mostly in one or the other hemisphere of their brain. This issue of hemisphericity determines which information they will organize and how they will organize it and use it. Predominantly left-brained people prefer to sort information into lists, use words and dialogue, and work in a step-by-step, one-task-at-a-time mode; to get to a new destination, this person would prefer to use written directions. Right-brained people handle multiple tasks at once, and perceive and present information in shapes and spaces; they would use a map or descriptions of landmarks to find their way to a new destination.

We know that people will sift and sort new information as they try to make it fit old cubbyholes, or as they fit it into newly created cubbyholes.

We know that people will easily sift information (into existing cubbyholes or build new ones) when the information is connected to other subjects and not isolated.

We know that people will sift and organize information more efficiently or create new cubbyholes more quickly when they learn collaboratively, listening to and teaching each other.

We know that most people will not spontaneously sift information: this process must be explicitly directed and taught.

We know that people will store into long term memory information that is meaningful to them—meaningful in the sense of useful (in their mind) for living, doing, believing, deciding, or moving on to the next step.

Set Up for Failure

We know that people will store into long term memory information they explicitly state as being there.

All this we know through cognitive science research of the past thirty years.

Question #4: How does this information about how people learn translate into teaching practices?

Answer: At the moment, not very well. The primary method of instruction in elementary and secondary schools—teacher talk about subjects isolated from each other, as described in another chapter—violates almost all we know about what makes learning happen.

If research indicates that people learn when information

- is presented to all senses;
- accesses several intelligences;
- is meaningful to them;
- is related to other subjects and skills;
- involves them in the discovering, sorting, and organizing of information;
- is attacked collaboratively;
- and requires them to think about how, what, and why they are learning,

then teaching must

- use many teaching techniques and delivery systems;
- use the visual and performing arts to access all the intelligences;
- hook new learning onto old;
- integrate subjects;
- insist that students question and think critically;
- allow students to work together in mixed groups;
- and direct students through metacognitive activities at the close of each lesson.

Part III: Chapter 14

Teaching must be far more than teacher talk and student worksheets. In fact, teacher talk does not equal student learning at all: it never has and it never will.

Question #5: What does a "learning classroom" look like?

Answer: A "learning classroom"—which may not be a room at all--, one where students' time is consumed with the joyful and purposeful quest for knowledge, would look like
- an archaeological dig,
- an orchestra rehearsal,
- a seminar discussion,
- a science experiment,
- a house restoration project,
- an auto mechanic's shop,
- an artist's studio,
- an aerobics class,
- a vegetable farm,
- a cathedral tour,
- a sail boat race, ...

These are places and activities in which knowledge
- has a purpose;
- is sought after;
- is based on prior knowledge;
- is manipulated and adjusted;
- is approached collaboratively;
- uses both sides of the brain, all the senses, and all the intelligences;
- is used in conjunction with other knowledge:

in short, where the curriculum and the techniques reflect what we know about how people learn. Duh.

To comprehend what a learning classroom looks like, take an imaginary journey into two classrooms. Listen to what the teachers say, watch what they do, study the environment, and especially listen to and watch the students. Take a check-list

Set Up for Failure

with you, if you must, to help you make certain that all the criteria listed above are being met. Above all, be a learner.

The Elementary Classroom

As you approach the open door of the classroom, you see three students, apparently different ages, sitting in a small circle on chairs they dragged from the room to just outside the open door. They are sitting on the edge of their chairs, leaning in to the center, obviously studying an old looking map spread out on the hallway floor.

"We can't go that way," says the biggest of the three students. "See? (pointing to some mountain-like markings on the map) Mountains. They didn't have any highways then. We couldn't get through, especially not this time of year."

"But the other wagon trains are going through the mountains?" suggests the smallest student.

"Yeah, but they're going way north," says the third student. "Look at the way these markings are. See? They aren't as close together. That means that the mountains are more spread out, like a table top."

"And," offers the first student, "see these numbers? What do they say?"

The smallest student studies for a moment. "Three thousand, six hundred and fifty," she says hesitantly. "Four thousand, one hundred and ten, four thousand, five hundred and fifty . . . "

"What's the difference between the first two numbers?" asks the first student.

The small student thinks for a moment, whispering as she worked the subtraction problem. The third student wrote the problem on a scrap piece of paper. "Four hundred and sixty," she says.

"What's the difference between the next two numbers?"

"Four hundred and forty," she says more quickly.

Part III: Chapter 14

"See how far apart the numbers are on the lines? The numbers tell you how high the mountains are—like way high here (pointing to Mount Evans) to way low over here, like the mountains at the part in Livingsville: those are really low, so would they have a big number or a little number?

"Little," said the little student quickly. "I know those mountains—they aren't very high at all. I saw a really high one when we went on vacation this year."

"OK," says the first student. "That's the idea. Now, when the lines are close together, that means that the mountains are steep—they go high really fast. When they are far apart, like these up north, they seem more like hills. Which ones would be easier to climb?"

And so they go on, studying the map and its markings and their meanings, and trying to imagine themselves figuring out how to get to their destination in a safe and timely manner.

The third student looks up at you. "Good morning. Are you coming to help?" he asks matter-of-factly.

Inside the classroom with its high ceilings and its windows taking up one long wall, you see what looks like a workshop. Under the windows are book shelves stuffed with books. The wall opposite from the windows is empty, and spread on the floor in front of it is a piece of butcher paper running the entire length. Four students (again, of varying sizes) busily paint and construct some work of art with fragments of torn construction paper all around. The wall between the windows and the art work and farthest from you is lined with study carrels; two students sit separately there, with books and papers stacked and spread around them. The wall closest to you is divided into cubicle-type areas, with what appears to be a teacher's desk in one, a large table covered with art supplies in another, three comfy chairs, and a stereo in the other.

Close to the window wall, a student stands at the portable white board, drawing what appears to be a spider web connecting ovals which contain words. Eight students and what must be the

Set Up for Failure

teacher, sitting at the table arranged in a "u" shape, listen to him explain how he wants to organize his research.

"I don't get it that way," says one student, possibly nine years old. "All those lines and ovals confuse me. You know I think in lists: I have to put my stuff into neat lists. That's left-brained thinking, isn't it?" she asks the teacher for confirmation.

"Good recall," replies the teacher. "So, if you're a left-brained thinker and you organize information into lists, and if Pete organizes his research information into diagrams, what kind of a thinker is he?"

"Right-brained," she responds quickly. "He organizes stuff by shapes and placings."

"It looks more lame-brained to me," offers another student with a giggle.

"And you should be so lucky to be that lame-brained," quips the teacher. "So which way is best for organizing all your research before you start writing it?"

"It depends on how you think," answers yet another student, peering intently at the chart.

"And what does that mean?"

"Either way of organizing your ideas is OK. Just as long . . . ."

". . . As you organize before you write," they all say in unison.

"Well done, my good and faithful students." The teacher looks toward you and smiles. "Now, let's see some organizing." She gets up from the work session and comes toward you.

"Welcome to the Westward Movement Workshop," she says as she extends her hand.

"Are these students all the same age?" you ask.

"Oh, no, not at all. I believe the youngest is eight and the oldest is twelve."

"Isn't this supposed to be elementary school?"

"Well, yes and no. It's elementary in the sense that the students here are generally of the age for the traditional

Part III: Chapter 14

elementary school—five through eleven and twelve. That's probably where the similarities end."

"I don't understand." You are genuinely puzzled.

"In order to progress through the school's curriculum," the teacher explains, "students must meet benchmark criteria, established in chunks according to learning patterns. As they meet those criteria, they move to another set of workshops—we don't call them classes here. It's a terminology thing: the idea of "class" connotes isolated subject matter, which in no way describes what goes on in the workshop."

"Well, what does go on?"

"Every workshop is theme-based—some on science, some on literature, some on math, some on social studies--, and every workshop contains some of the subject matter curriculum students must know in order to progress to the next set of workshops. Math, reading, writing, and reasoning skills are constantly reinforced through application in every workshop. This particular workshop is the social studies based theme for this level."

"Is a level like a grade?"

"Only in the sense that the levels—there are four of them for the eight years here—are sequenced. However, a student may move to the next level in math but may not be ready to move in social studies. That's why we can have a wide range of ages in one workshop."

"Isn't it hard to teach kids of different ages in one class, uh, pardon me, workshop?" you ask.

"Why should it be? They're all at essentially the same developmental level of concept formation for that subject and skill area, so they should all be able to learn together. Actually, in any given workshop, the students are much more homogeneously grouped by skill level—for that concept—than in a traditional classroom."

"How long do they stay in the workshop? And does it take up their whole day?"

Set Up for Failure

"Their stay in this workshop lasts for twelve weeks. That time limit is still in flex: we're not certain we want to stay with that. At the moment, it seems to be enough time for students to become experts in the subjects and to take their learning into the community. We find that, by having a time limit, students—and teachers—are forced to set goals and plan time, valuable skills in the real world, which, incidentally, we try to make this as much as possible. And, yes, they are in the workshop the whole school day, and often hours before and after."

"So how does this workshop work?" you ask, as you scan the gently buzzing room with its eighteen students.

The teacher walks you around the room as she explains the instructional philosophy and processes. When the school was first conceived, she says teachers at the school who were subject matter specialists met to determine the content and skill criteria that graduates should master, basing their discussions on established state and district standards and their own expertise. They involved interested parents and community members in some of their discussions. The ideas from the business community provided truly interesting fodder for the curriculum development.

They then determined a variety of products students could generate that would show what they understood and could apply: oral exams, written exams, community projects with evaluative reports, self assessments, group projects, a course proposal with a narrative description and detailed outline, a television show written and produced by the students, a book written by the students—the list seemed endless.

Next, they analyzed the tasks required to help the students master the concepts and produce the final project, and used this analysis as their road map for establishing benchmark criteria that could be reached in various subject-matter workshops. If a student's final project required some skills not taught at the school—photography, for example—, the student would ask his

Part III: Chapter 14

or her community mentor to find an expert who would coach the student.

Every workshop begins with a problem which the students must solve by the end of the session. In the Westward Movement Workshop, students must answer the question, "Did the frontier experience change the pioneers, or did the pioneers change the frontier?" (Those of you who have studied the West will recognize that question as one historian Frederick Jackson Turner raised more than one hundred years ago. It is argued still.) Furthermore, they must explain why it is important to explore that problem.

To answer this question, students must know how to research, including what types of resources to use, where to find resources, and how to use resources. They are required to research literature, visual arts, music, and dance; they must study social structures and ethnic diversity; they must examine geography and geology; they must compute distance, supply needs, work effort compared to results, average speed needed to cover a specified distance within a limited time period. They work in groups, pairs, and by themselves. They each work with a community mentor, a person from outside the school who helps them find and use resources from real life. The teacher guides them through specific lessons that provide them with foundational information and skills, as in a new research skill or new writing skills.

In order to enroll in all but the first level of workshops, students must have "passed" previous workshops with at least 80 percent accuracy on prerequisite knowledge and skills, and must show the ability to apply both. The teacher uses assessments from that previous workshop to determine what reading, writing, math, and reasoning lessons the students will need, in addition to the subject matter lessons. Furthermore, parent, student, and future teacher confer about placement in specific workshops.

Some students petition to move more quickly through the workshop problem. At any time they satisfactorily meet the criteria, they move to next workshop. That's why this class has several different ages represented. If a student comes in during the middle of the workshop, he or she will work independently and with the community mentor to fill in the learning gaps, assuming there are any.

The teacher explains that you walked in on a fifteen minute lesson on resource analysis: a system for sorting and organizing research information before writing. The students that were not at that lesson had already shown their competence in using that pre-write system, and were working on pieces of their "problem project"—either the research end or the production end. (Students may have learned pre-writing organization in another workshop, from their community mentor, or from home—who knows?)

For the writing lesson, students were practicing—either by themselves or in pairs—sorting and organizing several groups of information: one in geology of the Sierra Nevada, one in word problems, one in American art history, one in nineteenth-century American literature, and one on the Hand-Cart Brigade. After they finish their practice in sorting and organizing information, they will be required to write a brief paper (one to two pages at the most) about any two of those subjects, showing that they understood how to convert a pre-write system into a formal essay. Next, they would have to evaluate their work according to agreed-upon criteria, explaining and defending their evaluation to the other students and the teacher who would prescribe corrections and adjustments. Finally, they would write their final draft and submit it for assessment and inclusion in their portfolios.

"It's quite a luxury to be able to have only eighteen students in your class," you remark as you look about the room, noting the total engagement of every student, no matter what activity.

The teacher stares at you in amazement. "It is not a luxury: it is an essential component of effective teaching. How

Part III: Chapter 14

else would I be able to offer the one-on-one instruction that has to happen in order for each child to learn? How else would I and the students be able to take the time assessing and refining essays? And research—my heavens: do you have any idea how long it takes to research a simple notion like life on a wagon train on the Oregon Trail? But," the teacher continues, becoming more and more animated, "do you have any idea what incredible amounts of information students take in as they research that one concept? Part of their final assessment involves them sharing what we call "side-bar" information—stuff they learned and found interesting but did not use to help them solve the problem. All that research time is well-spent, but it couldn't happen if there were thirty-five students vying for the same resources and teacher-time and space." She looks to the students on the floor constructing the mural, and one of them gestures to her to come over.

"Look," says the student, maybe about nine years old, pointing to the middle section, "this is the Rocky Mountains. We're showing a cross-section of the landscape the pioneers would have crossed in about 1850. Tracey is doing small water-color paintings showing the various problems the pioneers had to deal with, like crossing a big river. See? They had to unhitch the oxen—they used oxen because they were cheaper and would eat anything, which the horses wouldn't do--, then pull the wagons across with ropes. Sometimes the wagons didn't make it; they got washed down, and everything the family brought with them went down the river. It was a big mess. Aren't these great pictures Tracey has painted? She learned about water-color in the North American Geography Workshop: she had to use it to illustrate plants in her science journal. I want to take that workshop next."

"Joseph," the teacher begins, "how are you going to show how the people on the wagon trains made rules and kept order?"

"Oh," he responds enthusiastically, "we're going to re-enact a camp meeting where we elect officers after the first guys mess up . . . ." And the student goes on explaining the lives and struggles of people who lived one hundred and fifty years ago.

Does this elementary classroom meet the research-based criteria? Is information presented to all senses? Does it access all intelligences? Is it meaningful to them? Is it related to other subjects and skills? Does it directly involve the students in the discovering, sorting, and organizing of information? Is it attacked collaboratively? Does it require them to think about how, what, and why they are learning?

Is it possible?

Absolutely! In fact, this kind of a classroom is happening in many successfully restructured schools in the United States. Linda Darling-Hammond, author of The Right to Learn, has researched many successfully restructured schools and reported on them in her book. One school, Keels Elementary School in Columbia, South Carolina, had been scheduled for closing because its student performance had declined. With fewer than half of the students meeting the state's "readiness" standards for kindergarten, after only four years of restructuring, 90 percent of the students met state standards in reading and mathematics after first grade. Darling-Hammond reports that PTA meetings are standing room only, and families outside the attendance zone wait on a list to receive transfers to the school. She describes the classes there:

Teachers initiated the use of
"cooperative learning in heterogeneous classes, whole language instruction and hands-on work in mathematics and science, social studies projects such as studies of the stock market, computer-based learning applied to such programs as Writing to Read and Reading Recovery, parent education workshops and home visits, and after-school programs including tutoring and supervised homework sessions. Students are involved in peer teaching and in decision-making about school discipline and extracurricular events. Faculty are now developing performance assessments and portfolios in science." (p. 100-101)

Part III: Chapter 14

Darling-Hammond goes on to quote from a case study of Keels:

"A sign proclaims: 'This is a Risk-Free Environment.' In one corner of the room, a group of students were working a lab experiment where traits of plants were being investigated and students were classifying, sorting, and measuring. These students were finishing up a 3-week unit on seeds, stems, and leaves.... [They] wore visors with the word "scientist" inscribed on top.... Other students were writing about what they were learning. Those students wore visors with the word "author" inscribed on top. [The teacher] deftly reads and critiques Constance's work and says to her in a resonant voice, "You just about have a science book written." Constance joyously responds with a "YES!" In other corners of the room, a child reads sitting on a bean bag chair and next to him another child "meets an author" on audio-tape. Across the room there are three computers where students brush up on phonemes. [The teacher] noted 'the more they write the more they learn'." [Berry, 1995, p. 122] (As cited in Darling-Hammond, p. 101)

Does this room environment resemble that in the Westward Movement Workshop?

Other evidence abounds. The New American Schools is a coalition of seven education improvement design teams whose purpose is to "dramatically improve American education". Its partners include the New American Development Corporation, the Education Commission of the States, RAND Corporation, and ten cities and states where the New American Schools' effort is currently focused.

Individual school designs differ because the coalition recognizes that no one approach to reform is fool-proof. However, the designs have several essential components in common:

1) The schools are places where students "are active, responsible and respected learners . . . [they] work independently and in groups, in classrooms and in their

community to master basic and advanced skills and complete projects that connect their studies to real-life situations. [They] work toward high academic standards . . . linked to state and national standards . . . . Learning and progress toward meeting the standards are measured regularly through a variety of means, including . . . portfolios of student work, public displays of student projects and standardized tests."

2) "Teachers plan and work together with their peers, parents and other community members to make key school decisions geared to the specific strengths of their students."

3) Teachers, principals, and administrators are provided numerous opportunities to "develop new skills in assessment, standards, child development, leadership, interdisciplinary instruction, uses of advanced technology. . . ."

4) The community and parents are involved regularly in activities such as "providing support at home, serving on decision-making committees, and offering their individual expertise in the classroom."

(All quotes in paragraphs 1-4 are taken from A Guide to New American Schools, 1996.)

All of these elements are supported by research; all spell success for students.

The Coalition of Essential Schools (CES), whose small-schools advocacy was described in a previous chapter, provides another source for evidence of restructured schools that legitimately address teaching kids the way they learn, not the way that's most convenient. Like the New American Schools, the CES drives restructuring according to principles rather than prescribed one-fits-all formula.

Their schools break large schools into several small schools. According to CES, schools must be small in order to hold to their non-negotiable principle that all students must be well-known by the staff. Another principle directs that the school's routines, including student schedules and staffing patterns, must be flexible. So, they may use teaching teams that

Part III: Chapter 14

share a small group of students, or they may keep students with the same teacher for several years. Because CES schools believe that the school's design must be based on the assumption that all students can and will demonstrate serious and useful intellectual work, students are grouped in multi-age, heterogeneous ways. Since CES maintains that family and community involvement must be expected and cultivated, they take learning, especially for high school students, into the community; at School Without Walls in Rochester, New York, high school students come and go as they need, in order to attend classes at the local college, attend to the community service commitments, or serve their internships. (Cushman, 1999)

Across the United States, you can find evidence of elementary school reforms that result in genuine learning for students. Generally, the reforms involve a complete reaming-out of the structure of a school. This happens more easily in the elementary schools than in the secondary schools where subjects are isolated from each other literally and figuratively, as if teachers and administrators feared that they might contaminate each other. Is it possible to apply research to practice in existing secondary school structures? Let's step into an imaginary high school class to examine the situation.

The Secondary Classroom

As you walk through the door of the eleventh-grade United States history class, you see students sitting in groups of five, six, or seven.

"What's happening in your group?" you ask the students nearest the door.

The young woman on the other side of the group stands up and offers her hand to you. "Welcome to U.S. History in the Making," she says with a flair and a smile. "It's our own name for this class."

You return her remarkably confident handshake. "Thanks. Who named it?"

Set Up for Failure

"We did, of course," declares the African-American boy on the left. "After all, it's our class."

"Is it a required class?" you ask. "Just curious."

"Oh, yeah," he responds. "Actually, it's not a class. What we're studying here is tied into everything else we study, whether it's how American history influenced literature and art, or how the geology of the land determined how our history would develop." He hesitates. "Mr. Bowers can explain it better."

"I see," you respond. "Can you tell me about your groups?"

"Well," the young woman begins, "we are grouped according to the types of intelligences we have or most frequently and easily use. That's according to a cognitive scientist, Howard Gardner. We all take surveys and tests to determine our basic intelligences—that's not how smart we are, but the ways we think--, and then our teacher lets us organize our groups, but we must have every one of the eight intelligences represented in each group." She stops and looks side-ways at you to see if you're understanding. You nod.

"Well," she goes on, "what we realized is that we're all mixtures of these basic intelligences, so when we know that, it's a lot easier to work with each other. We try to access their intelligences that we have, too. Now, in this group—which we stay in for the whole unit of study, and that may be three weeks or a whole term—we work on both group and individual activities and research projects. Whenever we have a group activity, like this one, we each contribute in our own special way."

She describes some of their activities. "Today, we're making a crossword puzzle, but we've also made collages, written poems, journals, made a maze. . . ." She points to the walls. "See? We put our work all over the walls."

As you look around you see original posters, song lyrics, and comic strips, what appears to be a neatly curated exhibit of

Part III: Chapter 14

water color paintings depicting Native-Americans in various encounters with white people.

"We are the BORG," the teacher announces from the side of the room. The students stop their work and look up. You look up, too, not knowing what to expect.

"We are the BORG," he yells again. "Prepare to be assimilated. Resistance is futile."

Students scoot their chairs around to face the front of the room; some get up off the floor where they had been sitting and go to chairs. You sneak into an empty chair off to the side.

Silence falls on the groups of students. The teacher, a tall, late-middle-aged man with a gray pony-tail, works the remote to turn on the television where students watch a five minute film clip from a "Star Trek" movie which showed unarmed human-like figures with distinctive facial features, attempting to escape what appears to be an army of beings bearing weapons.

"What's the BORG?" you whisper to the student near you; the student looks at you and rolls his eyes slightly. "I'll tell you later," he whispers back.

After the clip, the teacher calls out to the student near me, "What's the BORG?"

The student jumps up at attention, and replies, "The BORG are a super species, half organic, half technological in nature, whose goal is absolute perfection. They reach their goal by absorbing all cultures with which they come in contact."

"Well said," the teacher says. "Sit down, and thank you." He looks at you. "Did that answer your question?"

Startled, you stammer, "Uh, yes, thank you." How did he know you had asked that, you wondered.

"What does assimilate mean?" he asks a Hispanic student in the front.

"The student slowly stands up, bows to the teacher, turns to the class, and says grandly, "Assimilate: to absorb into the system, to make similar; to alter by assimilation."

211

Set Up for Failure

The teacher looks at him with a knowing smile. "You looked that one up for homework, didn't you. Well done, my good and studious young man."

The student bows again, and sits, just as grandly as he had stood.

"Who did the BORGs want to assimilate?" the teacher barks at two students on the other side.

"Anyone," one student replies. "Anyone who didn't look, think, or act like them."

"Why did they do that?"

"Because they thought they were perfect."

"And were they?"

"No," a Korean student answers, "but that didn't matter." He hesitates, then goes on. "I think they were afraid of different people, so they wanted to get rid of them."

"And was this a good idea?" the teacher presses.

Eight, nine, twelve students – more than half the class—put their hands up. One says, "May I?"

"Go ahead," the teacher replies.

"It depends." He waits. No one says a word for maybe five seconds. The teacher gestures to proceed.

"Well, if the assimilation process doesn't hurt anyone, or maybe actually helps them get healthier or smarter or richer, then maybe the BORGs are doing them a favor."

The teacher doesn't have to wait for students to respond. "Do you agree with that?" he asks a petite girl.

"No way, man," she blurts out. "That's like sayin' we should all be white, or black, or Asian." She stops and laughs. "On second thought, maybe we should all be like the Asians; they're a lot better students than we are." The teacher and the other students laugh.

"I see," says the teacher. "Well, that's just what you're going to tinker with now." He turns to write on a transparency projected onto the board—keeping his face and voice toward the

Part III: Chapter 14

students. "To assimilate or not to assimilate: that is your question!" he declares with a sweep of the hand and a huge bow.

He proceeds to explain and write at the same time, telling them that they will work on this project as a group, with the task being to describe and give examples of both the benefits and problems with assimilation of one culture by another before they must present and defend a thesis statement about the value of assimilation.

"What's the first step!" he calls out.
"Be helpful!" they call out in return.
"The second step."
"Task analyze."
"Then what!"
"Divide up the jobs."
"And lastly?"
"Create the final product."
"Good job. Now, on your mark, get set, ..."
"WORK!" they holler in return, and swiftly turn back to their groups to begin to work.

Clearly, you think, they have done this before. They are well-versed in the group process and the procedures of the class. You ask the teacher about the students' willingness to start work.

"You know," he begins to explain, "they didn't learn these procedures in a day. We spent two months practicing each step in what you see here before we could put it all together and the students did it automatically. Because I didn't throw it all at them at once, they could take the baby steps in this essentially independent process, have good successes, and still want to do it again. Now, they have a tremendous amount of autonomy and choice because they learned the basics. And, you'll see this at the end of the class today, we never leave a discussion or activity without de-briefing. What I mean by that is we always discuss what was easy or hard about the activity and how we can use this process in some other part of their lives." He pauses to reflect. "That metacognitive portion of the learning process is vital to making learning happen. They don't learn just because they did the activity; they have to think and talk about what they learned, and then it starts to stick."

You find out that the teacher lets the students present their findings—in this case, the defended thesis—in any way they want: a round table discussion, a newspaper, a charade, a picture show, a new song they teach to everyone—it doesn't matter, as long as they use at least three of the intelligences in their presentation. They will have a half hour to present their work, and then they will respond to student questions.

"Yes," he says in answer to your question, "repetition of information does occur. But, ya know, that's not a bad thing. Research shows we have to hear or see something at least seven times before it sticks in our existing network or starts to create a new one in our brain. *Repetition mater de memoria est.* Repetition is the mother of memory."

The teacher checks all written work and notes errors and inaccuracies, strengths, and brilliant observations, and then turns it back to the students without a grade: only when the student resubmits it with corrections—and places his or her own grade on it—will the teacher place a mark on it.

You happen to note three students in the back of the room who seem to be rather disengaged, slumping in their seats, and not talking very much during the work time. (In this class, talking is not a problem behavior.)

You ask the teacher about them. "Well," he says, "they weren't very active today, were they. Let me show you something." He goes to the cupboard and pulls out a story board a student submitted two days ago. It is a cartoon drawing of two trains about to collide. One train flies an American Flag, the other a British flag. The cars are labeled "Tea Tax", "Stamp Act", and "Boston Tea party", etc. It is titled "The American Revolution, The Great Collision."

Part III: Chapter 14

"One of the 'slumpers' turned that in early. It just shows you that you can't always tell what's going in until you see what comes out."

You learn that students come to this class three times a week and spend anywhere from two to three hours each session working on class activities. The Literature teacher shares the same group with this teacher, and meets with them the other two days. They coordinate writing and reading activities so what they learn in one study session applies readily to the next. The teachers also involve physical activities and visual and performing arts instruction into their curriculum, usually bringing in experts from the community to instruct or demonstrate.

In other words, the two classes form the core of the students' instruction for the term and incorporate other subject matter to help students learn the content and skills. As a critical outcome, it illustrates the interconnectedness of all knowledge. Students attend math and science classes during another term when those classes become the core for their instruction. If they choose to earn more credits, they may take mini-courses in any of the subjects at any time, but their absolute requirement is successful completion of the core classes.

"What happens to the students with special needs?" you ask, since you don't seem to notice any of them in this class.

"Oh, they're here," the teacher nods. "You just can't tell because we accept a huge variety of products for the students to show what they know." He looks intently at me.

"What you're seeing here in this class doesn't fix everything. It doesn't eliminate dyslexia or other learning handicaps, nor will it compensate for drug-addicted parents. It won't do squat about a lousy neighborhood. Nobody's complexion will instantly clear up. But, remember, we are focusing on what they can do, not on their handicapping conditions. We cannot do anything about some things. What we can do is to maximize each person's potential, and to value whatever contribution that person can make. Many handicapped

Set Up for Failure

readers are talented artists, draftsmen, or illustrators. Others are very proficient mechanically—remember Thomas Edison? Music seems to be wide open to nearly all ranges of ability. This method of instruction—this school," he gestures all around us, "accepts differences and different capabilities and uses them to everyone's advantage."

What goes on in this class is not a fantasy. It happens daily in some high schools. It has been field-tested and implemented. And it has worked over and over to enable students to learn—to learn how to learn, to learn those things that will benefit their adult lives, and even to learn those things the curriculum makers think they ought to learn.

It's a matter of creating rational research-backed curriculum and school structures. It's a matter of presenting information to the students the way they learn, not the way we think they ought to learn. It's a matter of truly teaching.

James Bowers, teacher, friend, and valued colleague, contributed to portions of this chapter.

Part III: Chapter 15

Part III: Stop the Failure

Chapter 15: Create Every Opportunity to Learn.

Allow young teens to opt-out of school—for a while.

Robert sparkled as a student, pleasing teachers, parents, step-parents, and grandparents alike. He received "A"s in every subject except physical education in which he earned a "B". At thirteen years of age heading into eighth grade, he appeared to be on a fast track to high school stardom.

His first report card in November of his eighth grade reported the first "C" in his career; in fact, it showed three "C"s, two "B"s, and one "A"—in physical education.

"What happened, Robbie?" his step-mom asked him when he came home from school one November afternoon.

Set Up for Failure

"This isn't like you," she said with concern, showing him the report card she had just opened.

He glanced nonchalantly at the damning document. "I dunno," he mumbled with disinterest. The January report card showed straight "F"s.

A disheveled middle-aged woman slumped in the chair on the other side of the round table, rubbing her brow with her nicely-manicured fingers.

"I just don't know what happened to him," she said with a cracking voice. "David did so well in elementary school. Everyone just loved him, and he earned really good grades." She looked at me with a hopeless, helpless expression. "How could he change in just six months? I don't get it."

The principal and I looked at Danielle's cum folder. Her grades through sixth grade told the story of the ideal student: straight "A"s. Her mom had told me that Danielle was really popular, too, making friends with everyone.

"So, why did her grades go in the toilet?" the principal asked me rhetorically. "Her seventh-grade report cards aren't too bad, but, look at this: she failed everything in eighth grade. And her mom expected us to pass her on? What drugs was she on?"

During my last years of teaching, at least three times each year, I held "mandatory" parent conferences with my students' significant adults. (I use the word "mandatory" loosely because, after all, I had no way of making parents come to the school to talk about their child's progress, or lack thereof.) Three times a year, the scene repeated itself, and parent after parent paraded through the conference room with the same story: the child had been a relative genius in elementary school, but when those doors to the middle school opened, another being crossed the threshold. The child that took up space in our classroom for

Part III: Chapter 15

eighth-grade repeaters was not the child that parent had birthed and nurtured.

That child had become a moody, disrespectful, crude, unresponsive, defiant human who held contempt for anyone and anything else. Yet, with very few exceptions, the young teenager had sufficient capabilities to be more than successful in school. In every class of retention students that I taught, at least two students read at twelfth-grade level and several more read at least at eighth grade level.

So, why had these students failed eighth grade?

Aside from the fact that the grading system says more about a teacher's abilities than about a student's capabilities, and the fact that the curriculum is meaningless, and the fact that the rigid, lock-step grade placement and scheduling and the repetitive sameness of the instructional strategies ignore the individual learning styles of each student, and the fact that up to a third of middle school teachers are inadequately prepared—aside from all that, young teen-aged students hate being in class. If it were not for the chance to socialize with friends and play computer games between classes, most young teens would hate school altogether.

So, why make them go?

Research from twenty-five years ago showed that young teens can not learn anything new. They can reinforce old learning, but they cannot add new learning. Assuming this to be true, I can only speculate that their cognitive development rests while their biological development takes off. At any rate, the resulting pubescent young person struggles with comprehending new information just at the time when the state department of education, safely ensconced in its ivory tower, thinks they should be learning challenging new abstract mathematical and literary concepts.

The young teens ache to move, and wiggle, and hit, and run, and throw, and punch their ways through the day. Step onto any middle school campus before school and during passing

Set Up for Failure

periods and lunch times, and you will see a seething mass of small humans hitting, running toward, throwing at, and punching any other human, with or without intent. In fact, much of their ultra-physical behavior appears to be random. They seem to give little thought to their actions; they can't seem to help themselves. Like yearling colts that run and buck and kick across the pasture, the teens simply have to move.

And we, in our infinite wisdom (and blissful forgetfulness of our own youth), lock them up.

Lock up a yearling colt in a small stall for a few days, and you will have on your hands an explosive, anxious, nervous, and potentially dangerous strong, young horse. Lock up young teens in a series of small classrooms every day, and you will have explosive, anxious, nervous, and potentially dangerous young people.

Something peculiar happens to these wild and nasty young teens, however; outside of the classroom, in a one-on-one situation with an adult, they turn into pretty nice people. They volunteer to assist the custodian, they willingly help with the handicapped students, they happily serve as Teaching Assistants for the physical education teachers, and they help set up the auditorium for the assemblies. Once out of the classroom, they say "Yes, ma'am," and "Yes, sir," and they ask, "Can I do anything else?" Once out of the classroom, they become nice people again.

Why make them go to school, confine them to the classroom, and set them up for certain failure?

Because, say the administrator-crats, politicians, and all other all-knowing adults, young people should be in school where they can learn.

But, they don't learn, at least not the things the adults think they should learn. The only things many of them learn is how to be mean to each other, how far they can push the system, and how to get by with doing next to nothing. These are not positive, constructive lessons.

Part III: Chapter 15

Because, say the adults, that's the law.

Perhaps the law should change.

I propose the unthinkable: allow young teens to take time off from public school.

On a return visit to the mythical community of Smartplace, USA, we find just such a program in action. The community leaders, parents, and teachers of Smartplace realized that many of their young teens—maybe even half of them—took a leap into an intellectual black hole during the middle school years.

"You know," observed the Mayor, clearly perplexed after spending half a day at the middle school with its 600 students, "these kids have no business being in a public school. They take up time and space that could better serve those kids who want to learn. They usurp the teachers' time and energy, and they spend a large part of their time in the assistant principal's office." He thought for a moment. "In fact, if these kids weren't at the school, we probably wouldn't even need an assistant principal."

The Mayor's secretary stopped writing, and looked at him from over the top of her glasses, a cautious expression on her face. "Just what are you thinking?" she asked carefully.

"Well," he began, still thinking through his idea, "I think maybe we should let them take some time off from school for a while. You know, like do something else for a few months or a year, until they get their brains back in their cranium."

And thus was hatched the concept of the Alternative Curriculum for Young Teens. Convinced that teens were fully capable of learning if placed in the right environment, the Mayor proposed that young teens be allowed to leave school for one term to two years. According to the plan, however, teens could not just stay at home and watch television and play video games. The teens must exchange the required time in school for time spent in one of three options: an apprenticeship with a community business; volunteer service at one of many local organizations including the hospital, the veterinarian's office, the long-term care homes, or family services organizations; or work.

Any teen was eligible for the Alternative Curriculum for Young Teens. In order to qualify, the teen must present a request and plan to a panel of adults which included the Mayor, two community members, and three teachers. The plan—a description of what the teen would be doing and the proposed duration of the alternative curriculum—must include letters from the business, organization, or workplace where the teen would be spending the time. The teen's significant adult must attend the presentation and verify accountability for the teen's actions. The teen and the adult must be prepared to explain why the teen should be granted the request for alternative curriculum.

The panel would grant requests for six month time periods, at the end of which the teen could request a six-month extension for a total of two years. At the end of the alternative curriculum time, the teen would return to school, and resume his or her instructional program. The teen would be re-placed in school according to results of a re-entry assessment which would determine the teen's reading, writing, computing, and reasoning levels. Conceivably, the teen could have developed considerable skills during the time in the alternative curriculum. Since the Smartplace schools placed students according to competence and not by age, the returning teen would not necessarily be behind his peers.

The first two years of operation for the Alternative Curriculum Program saw lumps and glitches in the process. The Mayor, the community members, the parents, and the teachers, with input from teens, worked continually to revise and adjust the program until it began to fit.

Of the 900 students in the school, 75 teens requested and received waivers during the program's first year. Of those teens, 35 opted for apprenticeships, 28 opted for volunteer service, and the other 12 took jobs with relatives. The local businesses reported monthly to the school about the progress of their

Part III: Chapter 15

apprentices, and the organizations did the same for their volunteers; the employers sent copies of the teens' work records. Allaying their worst fears, not one program-teen was involved in any altercation with the law; they were too busy being productively busy to get into trouble.

At the school, the assistant principal found she had days at a time to spend in classrooms, actually being an instructional leader for the teachers. The number of behavior referrals had dropped by 79 percent once those 75 students had left the school. In class, teachers found they had almost no interruptions from misbehavior. While not all of the usually troublesome teens had left for the Alternative Curriculum Program—in fact, at least a third of the program-teens had been excellent students—, the remaining students had few provocations and incentives to disrupt. Teachers could teach better, and students could learn better.

During the second year, 70 of the original program-teens returned, and after the re-entry assessment, were placed in competence-appropriate workshops; the remaining five teens continued in the program. Forty-one of the re-entry students received placements beyond where they would have been had they stayed and followed the regular instructional program. They immediately delved into their work, and began to thrive. Two students still had difficulty concentrating, so they applied for another waiver.

During that second year, 130 more students requested waivers, and took time off from school. As the program progressed, anywhere from 75 to 150 students at a time sought refuge from the public school classroom, and found challenges and purpose in the Alternative Curriculum Program. More mature and disciplined, they returned to the school with a greater understanding for the power of knowledge and a greater appreciation for what they were learning in school.

At first, the program terrified some community members, certain as they were that the program-teens would run amuck

Set Up for Failure

throughout the community. This never happened. In the words of one of the program-teens who had been in constant trouble in school, "Why would we cause trouble? Man, we're doing something real here, and we're not locked up like zoo animals. And," he added with a little laugh, "we don't have anyone else to get in trouble with. It's great to be around working adults who show us how to behave."

Business people vied for the apprentices. They saw this program as a way to support the entire community, to develop and train potential employees, and to help a young teen learn adult responsibilities. While some had feared that the program-teens would carry a surly attitude, they found that the teens were anxious to please, and, with a sense of importance and accomplishment, grew in their confidence and self-esteem.

After five years, the Alternative Curriculum Program rolled along smoothly, allowing restless young teens to succeed while they developed skills and understandings they never could have known in the public school.

I vividly remember, as a young child, watching the freight trains chugging past my parents' home. In those days, cattle, hogs, and horses were shipped by rail to the slaughter houses. Whenever the trains slowed for the road crossing ahead, I ached to un-bolt the gates of those slatted cars with the frightened and confused horses pressed and pushed against the sides, throw open the gates, and set the horses free.

When I see the classrooms full of young teens, slumped in their chairs and bored to distraction, or sitting with resignation on the bench outside the assistant principal's office, I feel the same ache to set them free. While the fate of the freed horses would inevitably have been as terminal as their trip to the slaughter house, the fate of the "freed" teens, if handled by the mutual agreement of committed adults throughout the community, could unleash a renewed joy of discovery and a

Part III: Chapter 15

sense of worth they could not know in the rigid, lock-step confines of the cattle-car, uh, school.

Allow schools to use place-based learning for students of all ages.

Of all the places where young people might learn, the classroom—that contrived stop on the public education assembly line—offers the least likely environment. While temporary storage of information and skills does occur within the confines of the surreally bland 30' by 30' box, deep and long-term understanding of any concept (once the basics are learned) happens only when the student uses, applies, creates with, and evaluates the information and skills. Partly because of the practically non-stop list of stuff to "cover", students seldom have the opportunity to engage in deep learning. At least, not in the classroom.

The argument follows, then, that we should take children outside of the classroom in order for them to truly learn anything. Yes. Children and teens need to learn in the place where the idea or skill actually gets used. They need to be involved in place-based learning.

Employed for decades by creative, inventive, visionary teachers and schools, place-based learning involves taking the students to some place—any place—where they can learn skills and concepts and apply them to real problems. The resulting deeper understanding of the skills and concepts translates into that hallowed (but vacant) measure of success, higher test scores.

In Alaska, the Alaska Rural Systemic Initiative (AKRSI) has collaborated with 20 school districts to involve students in place-based learning. Students create Cultural Atlases and multimedia presentations on CD-ROM or the Internet as part of their task to systematically document the indigenous knowledge systems of Alaska Native people. The students also participate with Elders in subsistence camps to learn about traditional native subsistence activities. AKRSI has reported that eighth grade

Set Up for Failure

scores on CAT-5 math tests for four years showed gains at schools using place-based education, exceeding scores for those schools that do not.

One school, Russian Mission School, combated the school's problems of students dropping out by developing a curriculum around the subsistence activities of each season that are part of traditional Native culture in rural Alaska. In the fall, they send students out into two-week subsistence camps where they learn about fishing, medicinal plants, hunting, and beaver habitat. One group of students even built a cabin during their two weeks; the cabin remains as a refuge for hunters and trappers. Students documented their work using digital cameras and lap-top computers to create Web pages. Principal Mike Hull reported that, in just five months, some students raised their reading level by more than a year, a trend mirrored by all the third graders who received the highest scores statewide on the Alaska Benchmark Test for third grade, and that, only three years after having the lowest test scores in its district. All six of the seniors passed all three sections of the Alaska High School Graduation Qualifying Exam.

While participating in these learning activities, students learn about geography, weather, the science of plants and animals; they refine their writing and reading skills; they work collaboratively to solve problems; they develop self-esteem and confidence. Russian Mission School students have spoken at the Native Educator's Conference and participated in an international symposium in Japan. That never would have happened with a classroom-locked curriculum.

Eighth graders at Tillamook Junior High School in Tillamook, Oregon, helped the Oregon Department of Forestry survey "snags", or tree stumps, to help monitor the loggers' fulfillment of state requirements. Students counted snags, and recorded and mapped their findings. As they calculated their measurements, they came within a hair's breadth of actual measurements by professional surveyors. For this place-based

Part III: Chapter 15

activity, students learned about state regulations, forest management, and social and economic issues surrounding the logging industry; they learned about the science of forestry; they utilized and refined math and computing skills.

Seniors at Boone Central High School in Albion, Nebraska, discovered a derelict 1911 theater and decided to give it new life. They raised funds and purchased it for $37,000 in January of 2002, and began renovation work; by May of the same year, the students gave the theater its Grand Opening. They continue to operate the theater after school and on weekends. Their ingenuity continued, also: rather than pay hired help, they run the theater themselves or ask for volunteers who then take some of the proceeds to fund their own organizations.

Every facet of this place-based learning over-flowed with learning opportunities. Fundraising taught them about publicity and sensitivity to others' needs; renovation taught them mathematical calculations, budgeting, construction, physics, safety issues, planning ordinances, and city government; Grand Opening taught them about publicity, writing, art, social awareness, and protocol; theater operation taught them math, budgeting, publicity, taxation, and building maintenance. These constitute just a fraction of the skills and ideas these seniors learn as a result of this place-based learning. Again, the depth, variety, and integration of learning could never happen in the context of a classroom. (These examples were reported in "Achieving Academic Goals Through Place-Based Learning", Rural Roots, a publication of the Rural School and Community Trust, February, 2003.)

For years, teachers have attempted to generate pseudo place-based learning with simulation games where either the teacher or a commercial entity sets up a problem—e.g., the pioneers have come to a river and they must decide what items they will leave behind since their wagon cannot survive the crossing fully loaded—and students work in teams to solve the problems. The games usually provide a variety of side-bars that

Set Up for Failure

allow students to explore and evaluate many scenarios. They allow students to work out the solutions themselves; hence, solutions vary from team to team, depending on how students value certain issues. The teacher serves as a coach, a timekeeper, and a source, but never as a provider of solutions.

Simulation games have value. They give an appearance of a real context, they encourage students to collaborate, and they allow diverse and higher-level thinking. If one is confined to the classroom, they are better than nothing.

Students, however, fully recognize the artificiality of the game; depending on the complexity of the game and the basic preparation of required skills, students may buy into the activity and become totally involved, or not.

The reality in place-based learning stimulates a focus not found in simulations. Students experience a thrill in knowing their work will be published, utilized, or enjoyed, and the commensurate increase in confidence can never be duplicated with classroom activities.

Furthermore, place-based learning serves a function beyond teaching students: it gets something done for the community. Students learn, the community benefits, and at little expense. This is education at its best.

Allow students to leave public education when they pass their exit exam, no matter when that happens.

Farmer Peterson's son said it early on: "There's nothin' there for me. Without Mr. Howser or Ms. Ellowitz, that school can't do a thing for me." He knew how to write well enough to get published in the newspaper, he knew math well enough to budget for the farm and maintain his checkbook, he knew how to work the Internet well enough to communicate with professors he had never met, and he knew how to read well-enough to comprehend complicated contracts. He knew about the science of weather, chemistry of pesticides and fertilizers, and geology of

Part III: Chapter 15

the farm land. He probably was 15 years old. Why should he keep going to school?

Think back to your own experience in public school. If you were on a college preparatory track, you enrolled in the high school classes that the colleges and universities prescribed. This should have helped you prepare for the undergraduate work the colleges expect their students to perform. Presumably, every different course would teach you something a little bit different. For the college-bound student, the complex requirements of high school's required and elective courses served a very real purpose.

What about those students who did not and do not go to college? What purpose do those requirements serve for them? At what point does the purported instruction in reading, writing, and mathematics become redundant or unnecessary?

The traditionalist will answer that the teenager needs these courses because she learns how people solved problems throughout history, discovers the power of literature, uncovers the mysteries of science in her daily life, and meets, works, and plays with people with whom she may share her life. The young person, they say, needs all those classes in order to be a well-rounded person, to enjoy life fully, and contribute completely to his community.

As politely and courteously as I can, I will say, "Get real."

Probably 75 percent of the American adults completed American high schools, and the majority of those adults did not complete a college education. I will argue that, if those adults recall anything from high school experience, it is one or more teachers who infused the student with excitement for the subject-matter, one teacher who instilled in the student a passion for the content, someone who lighted that student's fire for learning. I will argue that the adult recalls little or nothing about the oh-so-meticulously crafted curriculum he or she endured. I will argue that most high school graduates could have left public school well before graduation day with absolutely no harm.

Set Up for Failure

"School gets in the way of life," a young teen-ager replied when asked why kids lack motivation. Teachers believe that everything they teach carries tremendous importance. Someone needs to break the news to them that they are the only ones who think that.

Assume, for a moment, that the community develops standards that truly define what a person will need to know and be able to do in order to prosper, should he choose to do so, in the society. The community develops an assessment device, i.e., test, that accurately measures the student's ability to meet the approved standards. If the student successfully completes the assessment, then he or she has done everything the community has said should be done. He or she is finished with public education. He or she may leave school. He or she may go on with life.

Why is that a problem?

Allow the door to public education to always remain open.

The young man, a senior in high school, sat patiently with hands politely folded in his lap, waiting for his school counselor. He had never met with this person in the three years he had attended the school. Now, he had his appointment to plan post high school education.

"I don't think you should try to go to college," the gray-haired man said slowly, furtively looking through the young man's high school records. "Your grades, um, well, they're not quite what a college will expect. No, I don't think you should try to go."

The young man dropped his head and looked away. No, he hadn't been an academic star. He had earned praise and accolades as an athlete, but his grades never impressed anyone.

He left the ten-minute counseling appointment feeling no more and no less unhappy than when he arrived. He had already applied for admission to a state college, and he had been accepted. What did the counselor know about him, anyway.

Part III: Chapter 15

After the first quarter of college, he was on academic probation. He continued to struggle through two more years before he dropped out to marry his pregnant girlfriend. Maybe the counselor had been right: he didn't have the academic stuff to succeed in college.

He was only 20 years old when he dropped out. For the next two years, he worked 60 hours a week, started a family, and dreamed of finishing college.

So he enrolled for his senior year, taking 21 units each quarter, and earning straight "A"s. Finally, he was ready to focus. Finally, he understood what education could do for him, and he believed what he could do. Finally, he was ready to learn.

Take an excursion to your community adult school. Talk to any student there, and ask him why he is there.

"I just wanted to believe I could do it," one might say.

"I didn't really know how important it was to get a good education," another will tell you.

"I didn't have the focus when I was in school. I couldn't have done then what I can do now," the student will explain.

Maybe you know these people. Maybe you are one of them. Maybe you can understand that people cannot be stamped into shape like a cookie or a tract house or a widget on an assembly-line. Maybe you can realize that what is good for one person may not work for another.

The student, like the child to the mother, will return when she is ready to learn what the educators believe has so much value, or when he perceives the power of knowledge. For those students who bolt and run through the open door, always leave that door open so they can return when they are ready.

Public education in the United States remains the most exceptional blessing a government can bestow upon its people. We must make it real, make it wise, and make it mean something.

Part III: Stop the Failure

Chapter 16:

Eviscerate Standardized Test

*"Knowledge must give weight,
but accomplishments give luster,
and many more people see than weigh."*

Lord Chesterfield

THE TEST
Directions: For each item below, select the choice that provides the best response. On your answer sheet, darken the circle that corresponds to the choice you have made. You will have five (5) minutes to complete this exam. Please begin.

1. An "educated" person in the United States is one who
   a) has graduated from high school;
   b) can read, communicate orally and in writing, and can use the four mathematical operations, all to a minimum level;
   c) knows the difference between sine and sign and   sign;
   d) none of the above.

Part III: Chapter 16

2. Of the following groups, which has the highest graduation rate in Arizona?
    a) white young adults;
    b) white teens;
    c) African American adults;
    d) Native American adults.
3. Today's public education system was modeled after the
    a) Japanese management system;
    b) Equation Modification System;
    c) assembly line system;
    d) industrial model.
4. Which group originated the existing high school curriculum?
    a) College professors;
    b) PTA;
    c) state politicians;
    d) the Committee of Ten.
5. Which of the following would be a cause for concern, according to education activist and author Alfie Kohn?
    a) teacher-directed instruction;
    b) student work all over the walls;
    c) parent volunteers in the classroom;
    d) students clustered into centers.
6. Researchers have identified how many different learning styles?
    a) 2;
    b) 3;
    c) 8;
    d) 16.
7. Year-round instruction
    a) supports learning theory;
    b) violates learning theory;
    c) works well for parents;
    d) works poorly for parents.

Set Up for Failure

8. Letter grades
    a) are the most efficient way to express an evaluation of a student's work;
    b) violate learning theory;
    c) are the most inefficient way to express an evaluation of a student's work;
    d) satisfy parents.
9. Small schools are more effective than _____ to promote learning.
    a) one-on-one instruction;
    b) small classes;
    c) home-schooling;
    d) private schools.
10. Norm-referenced standardized tests
    a) help students learn;
    b) designate that an equal number of test-takers must fail as pass;
    c) make lots of money for the test companies;
    d) are easy.

When you have finished the exam, put your pencil down and wait silently for further instructions. The results of your exam will be mailed to you within the next three months.

SO, WHAT'S THE POINT?

Point #1: Did you feel even the slightest twinge of anxiety when you saw this "exam"? Test-anxiety can seriously interfere with a person's performance on a test, causing the person to be unable to focus attention and perform at optimum level.

With absolutely nothing riding on the results of this little multiple-choice test, you should have felt nothing (except, perhaps, curiosity) when you began to read the directions.

Part III: Chapter 16

Nobody knew you were about to take a test. You couldn't pass or fail anything depending on your score on this test. The results mattered not at all.

In fact, you might have felt any number of signals running from your brain into your soon-to-be-sweaty hands or your suddenly palpitating heart. Some of you might have even received an invigorating adrenalin rush at the thought of a test. Students who have mastered the art of taking tests would relish the challenge of facing off this impersonal document with its bland, impartial instructions. Those of you who read quickly, comprehend readily, and analyze easily will take to the test like a kid takes to chocolate. To you, a 100-item test brings out the growl in you and fires you up, maybe even makes you salivate. "Bring it on," you roar, wiping your face with your sleeve, blowing lead-dust off your pencil-tip.

Then there are the others who would rather sit butt-naked on a block of ice than take the test. These people decode letters in reverse order; they might mean to mark "b" but mark "d" instead. They perceive two or even three plausible answers to any given item. "Well, this is true if they meant such and such, but if they meant that, then the answer is the other one." They might have missed reading the one chapter that received the greatest emphasis on these particular test items. They might have poor hand-eye coordination that makes marking the answer sheet a difficulty of its own. They might have had such limited experiences in reading that they cannot comprehend the syntax.

In reality, they might know the subject reasonably well, but be unable to show their comprehension on a paper and pencil, limited-option multiple-choice test, which requires silent reading. For these people, the thought of the test alone can render them dysfunctional.

This is not to say that people should not be "put to the test" just because they have test-anxiety. However, it is to say that standardized tests may provide unreliable assessments of what students actually understand and can do: to place high stakes on the results of one or even a series of tests is unconscionable.

Point #2: Were you tired when you began this test? Did you have a headache? Were you anxious about the argument with your teenager? Did the cat fight outside your window distract you? Were you worried about the bills you can't pay? Did your pet die this morning? Were news stories filled with reports of preparations for war? Did you just learn about your co-workers' illicit relationship, (or did they just learn about yours)? Any one of these factors may have kept you from delivering your optimum performance on the test, as they would keep you from focusing your undivided attention on the questions being asked.

At best, results from any standardized test provide a (one-dimensional) picture of the person at that given moment in time. Had the person taken the test on another day, when she was well-rested, had hugged everyone in her family before she left for the test, received a tax-refund the day before, or just finished making vacation plans to Belize, the person's test results may have been completely different: the person may not have known more about the subject being tested, but the person was free of debilitating distractions and thus able to completely focus thinking on the test items.

Researchers Kane and Staiger, in their paper "Volatility in school test scores: Implications for test-based accountability systems", report that "more than 70 percent of the year-to-year variations in average test scores for a given school or grade can be attributed to external factors, rather than educational factors." (Kober, 2002). Alfie Kohn reports that maybe 90 percent of the variations in test scores among schools or states have nothing to do with the quality of instruction.(Kohn, 2001) Think of your own experiences in test-taking at school: you probably don't need researchers to tell you that any little thing—like the snug-

Part III: Chapter 16

fitting tank top on the girl next to you—can keep you from showing what you really know.

This is not to say that tests can't provide an accurate picture of what a person knows at a given point in time. However, it is to say that standardized tests may provide unreliable assessments of what students actually understand and can do: to place high stakes on the results of one or even a series of tests is unconscionable.

Point #3: Did you happen to know those little fragments of information the test items asked about? Did you know more about the problems with our public education system than the test asked for? Standardized tests with just a few items cannot possibly test all possible information about a given subject. Whether or not you can respond accurately to the test's particular items may be strictly a matter of luck—luck that you happened to study that specific information more carefully that the other stuff.

Standardized test-makers construct an enormous battery of test items for the various subjects they test, then compose each individual test from a small random sampling of those items so the test doesn't ask a thousand questions. The test-makers vary the selected items from year to year for security reasons. (They fear the unscrupulous teacher who would busily hand-copy all the test items while the students are taking the test, then teach those items for the next year's tests. Yeah, right.) The teacher may or may not have happened to "cover" the particular stuff asked about on that year's exam; hence, the students may or may not be lucky enough to have seen that stuff before.

Many standardized tests are purchased by several states which may have inherently different standards. Consequently, the tests may ask questions that students in one state have "covered" while students in another state have not. The latter students can only hope to guess right.

Set Up for Failure

This is not to say that a student will not know everything being tested. However, it is to say that standardized tests may provide unreliable assessments of what students actually understand and can do: to place high stakes on the results of one or even a series of tests is unconscionable.

Point #4: Did you feel like arguing with any of the possible choices? Well, you can't. Multiple-choice tests do not allow measurements of how the test-taker arrived at an answer. They cannot tell you whether the person thought through all the possible ramifications of each choice, whether the person had a perfectly legitimate interpretation of the issue, whether the person looked over someone else's shoulder, or whether he just guessed.

Test-writers pride themselves on being able to force the test-taker to use higher-level thinking skills, to analyze and think critically through the inherent issues. They are wrong: multiple-choice standardized tests cannot do that because they limit the person to one and only one correct response out of four or more prescribed options. In reality, it means the person has no choice; he or she must "choose" exactly as the test-writer would choose since any other choice would be incorrect. The test-taker has no way to explain her reasoning for her choice, and the test-result users have no way of knowing whether she used any reasoning at all.

The best that test-writers can hope for, as they construct their devices, is that the item will force the test-taker to work through multiple levels of recalled facts in order to arrive at the test-writer's choice.

This is not to say that the recollection of facts does not merit assessment. However, it is to say that standardized tests may provide unreliable assessments of what students actually understand and can do: to place high stakes on the results of one or even a series of tests is unconscionable.

Part III: Chapter 16

Point #5: Did you feel even the slightest urge to know the results? Well, you can. After you send your answers to the test headquarters (that's I), you will receive your scored test results within three months.

Results from standardized, mass-administered tests have absolutely no instructional value to the test-taker. Every teacher knows that feedback of results from any work, including tests, becomes a powerful tool ONLY when it comes immediately after the effort. At that point, assessment results can instruct the student in what he did well and should continue doing, and in what he did poorly and should correct.

When test results come back to the student even two days later, however, they might as well not come back at all. By then, it's old news. All the activities and events and ideas that pass through a student's brain over a 48 hour period clog up the cognitive networks. It's like waiting in line for a ride at Disneyland® where so many people take cuts in front of you that you lose your interest and give up.

When results come back two and three months later, as they do with standardized tests, they might as well be recycled into toilet paper.

This is not to say that the results hold no interest to the test-takers who may be waiting to know whether or not they will exit high school. However, it is to say that standardized tests may provide unreliable assessments of what students actually understand and can do: to place high stakes on the results of one or even a series of tests is unconscionable.

Point #6: Did you wonder why you should even care about knowing how many different learning styles had been identified? Were you curious about why you would be expected to know which group has the highest graduation rate in Arizona? Students wonder, too, why test-writers think they should know the minutia and trivia and unrelated bits and pieces of information queried on the exams.

Set Up for Failure

Standardized tests do not measure the knowledge and skills that students will need as an adult. Instead, they measure fragments of information which are unrelated to the other items.

The tests cannot ask the student to evaluate a political candidate's argument, or to critique a job offer, or to analyze the merits of a new car. They cannot ask the student to explain how knowledge of events leading up to the American Civil War could help us avoid another such fiasco. They cannot test the student's ability to make a persuasive case for not going to war.

The math tests ask for skills which the student will never use once she has left the school's hallowed halls. The English/language arts tests pose questions about which conjunction to use, whether to use "lie" or "lay", about which of the four titles is the best choice for the story he just read, and about where to put the comma. These issues have no relevance to an adult who does not intend to work as an engineer or to write for a living. Yet, they are the meat and potatoes of the standardized tests.

Furthermore, these tests demand that students work individually, without collaboration. How many times are you forbidden from collaborating with your co-workers to come up with the best answer? Would you expect your car repair person, or plumber, or accountant, or lawyer, or minister, or policeman to show you how well she can do the job by passing a paper and pencil test?

This is not to say that standardized tests could not be applicable in certain situations—like a contractor applying for a license in electrical engineering. However, it is to say that standardized tests may provide unreliable assessments of what students actually understand and can do: to place high stakes on the results of one or even a series of tests is unconscionable.

Part III: Chapter 16

TESTING YOUNG STUDENTS SERVES NO PURPOSE

During my years as a field supervisor for student teachers and intern teachers, I observed classes during the "spring thing", those several weeks each spring when teachers and students hunker down for the testing season. The testing of elementary students troubled me most.

The second grade test, given to students at grade 2.5 level (second year, fifth month), actually tested skills expected of students through third grade, fifth month. Go figure.

The teachers told me that they spend one hour a day for two weeks before the tests just to prepare students for the test-taking procedures. They did this to relieve some anxiety, hoping that familiarity with the question styles and the procedures of marking the bubbles on the answer sheet would make students comfortable enough that they would be able to better concentrate on the questions. That means they lost at least ten hours that could have been devoted to instructing students in something they actually need to know.

The reading comprehension test—for second graders, no less—asked students to read ten two-to-three paragraph stories with five multiple choice questions each, all within a forty-minute testing period. I observed five children who had stomach aches, and two with heads down, crying.

Part of the math test was to be given orally. Teachers were to read the questions only once. If the student did not happen to perceive auditorily (like only 30 percent of the other students did), he would not understand the question. Most likely, he would guess at the answer.

The reading test required students to read silently through the stories. Unfortunately, they had not yet learned how to read silently. Too bad.

Education activist Alfie Kohn, in his book <u>The Case Against Standardized Testing</u>, maintains that standardized tests pose serious dangers for students under 10 years of age. First, he says, tests cannot show the depth of the young student's

Set Up for Failure

understanding. More importantly, the tests cannot accommodate the vast variations in young students' cognitive developmental paths. ". . . Expecting all second graders to have acquired the same skills or knowledge [at the same time] creates unrealistic expectations. . . ." (Kohn, 2002, p. 13)

Kohn also makes an argument against yearly testing. "It is neither necessary . . . nor desirable . . . to test students year after year after year. [This practice] . . . reflects the assumption that all students must learn at the same pace." (Ibid) This just doesn't happen.

THE DEVIL'S INVENTION: THE NORM-REFERENCED TEST

Standardized tests have still more problems. Didn't you know? They were created by the devil. In the devil's wisdom—and, it is wise—, it created the norm-referenced test to torture thoughtful, creative people who might challenge its position. The norm-referenced test decrees that half the population must perform better than the other half, and that, as Kohn puts it, ". . . exactly ten percent of those who take the test will score in the top ten percent, . . ." (Ibid., p. 14), and that ten percent of those who take the test will score in the bottom ten percent. Regardless of the actual test scores, norm-referenced tests present the results to reflect this curve.

Suppose 100 people took the test at the beginning of this chapter. Let's say that 25 people made seven correct choices (70 percent accuracy), 25 people made eight correct choices (80 percent accuracy), and 50 people made nine correct choices (90 percent accuracy—an A- in most teacher's grade books). (We know most people missed item #10 because it had not yet been taught.) According to norm-referencing—a system which compares one student's performance against other students' performances—ten of the people with 70 percent accuracy will be in the bottom ten percent of the test-takers, and all of the people with eight or fewer correct answers will be in the bottom

Part III: Chapter 16

half of the test-takers. According to this process, a student could answer most of the questions correctly and still be rated below the 50th percentile, depending entirely on how the rest of the students did. You could have made a "B" on the test and still have fallen into the 40th percentile of the test-takers. You would look a lot dumber than you are.

Similarly, test results could make poor performers look pretty smart. On our sample test, if the score results ranged from two to five correct choices—all of which would earn the test-taker an "F" in most classes—ten percent of the test-takers with two correct choices would be in the bottom ten percent, and ten percent of the test-takers with only five correct choices would be in the top ten percent: you could be in the 90th percentile with only 50 percent of the correct choices. According to norm-referencing, no matter how wide the spread between actual scores, the results must fit the specified curve. You see, it's not about how much the student learns: it's about getting a high ranking when compared to all the other students and schools.

Kohn cites Robert Glaser who said norm-referenced tests "provide little or no information about . . . what the individual can do. They tell that one student is more or less proficient than another, but do not tell how proficient either of them is with respect to the subject matter tasks involved." (Ibid., p. 14). And they do not tell whether or not the students are proficient at anything that matters.

The following well-used, and very expensive tests, among others, are norm-referenced: the Iowa Test of Basic Skills (ITBS); the Comprehensive Test of Basic Skills (CTBS); the Stanford Achievement Test (SAT); the Metropolitan Achievement Test (MAT); and the California Achievement Test (CAT). Which one of these devilish devices did your child take this year?

Aside from the obvious result-reporting smoke screens generated by norm-referenced tests, other problems arise. In order to spread out the scores into the desired curve, test-writers must construct some items that only a few students will be able to answer, and some items that most, but not all, test-takers will answer correctly. Because all students have the same access (in theory, at least) to the lessons taught in the classroom, test-writers will look to information gained outside the classroom to separate the test-taking men from the boys. In most cases, the well-to-do children from well-educated families who own a battery of computers will have the greatest access to information not found in schools. Hence, test-writers construct items which only those students could answer, leaving the poor children from uneducated families in the dark.

Why wouldn't they ask questions that only the poor children could answer? Wouldn't that do just as well to separate students according to knowledge gained outside the classroom? True; however, test-writers want to ensure the success of the students who ordinarily do well on all other portions of the test. "A test item on which African-Americans do particularly well but whites do not is likely to be discarded, because of the interaction of two factors: African-Americans are a minority, and African Americans tend to score low." (Neill and Medina, as quoted by Kohn, Ibid., p. 36) The test-writers create a sort of discriminatory self-fulfilling prophecy.

AND, STILL MORE PROBLEMS

The crimes of the standardized test continue. As a student goes through the education system, she becomes a composite of all of her experiences; any test of that student necessarily tests all of her experiences. To hold one teacher accountable—or even one school accountable—for any given student's performance says that teachers and administrators are responsible for years of instruction over which they had no control or impact. That's like saying you are responsible for the stomach aches of all the picnickers who ate your potato salad: your salad was terrific, but the mayonnaise—made by someone else—had spoiled. "Well," the old lady said with indignation,

Part III: Chapter 16

"you shouldn't have used that mayonnaise." Perhaps teachers should refuse to teach students who are not well-prepared. But that's another issue.

Supporters of standardized tests argue that, even with their imperfections, they enable policy-makers (that's politicians and administrators and the media) to assess the achievement levels of a large mass of students at a minimum cost. Similarly, the sale junkie argues that the square wheel, at a 50 percent discount, was a terrific deal! No matter that the square wheel was non-functional and could be used for nothing useful except, perhaps, a planter.

With almost life-and-death stakes attached to results of the yearly standardized tests, and with results published "objectively" in local newspapers and on the Web, teachers feel enormous pressure to make the students do as well as possible on the tests. In California, teachers at schools with gargantuan improvements receive as much as $25,000 each—for beginning teachers, that's two-thirds of a year's salary—as a "reward" for having helped their students learn. Talk about an incentive to cheat!

From March until the end of May, school administrators across the country tremble and shake in the hideous presence of dozens of official packages of tests which arrive with all the importance of a military review team. The hapless assistant principal assigned the distasteful task of ensuring absolute integrity among the test-givers (that's the teachers, who generally view the test like a sweaty, foul-mouthed in-law who shows up uninvited at every family gathering), calls faculty meeting after faculty meeting to detail and review each precious step in the testing process. Schools fly banners and flags on the marquee to proudly announce the testing season. The PTA serves donuts and orange juice to students and teachers for the two weeks of testing. (They would do better to serve Bloody Marys and Screw-Drivers.) Some low-level district administrator makes its yearly appearance at the school to offer moral support. Gardeners and maintenance people are cautioned not to run their heavy equipment during testing hours. (It's OK during instruction hours, however.) Bells and public address system announcements cease. And the school goes into the suspended animation of a testing coma, uneasily maintained on teachers by threats of letters of reprimand, lawsuits by state testing officials, and criminal charges of test fraud. The school administrators stand by helplessly, gnawing at their knuckles, fully aware that their employment fate rests on the desks of the cloud-shrouded teachers and the mostly disinterested but generally agreeable students who know even less about the tested minutia than they care about it.

BUT, HOW WILL WE KNOW WITHOUT THE TESTS?

Still, people will argue, we need to know how the schools are doing; we need to know if they are doing what they're supposed to be doing. Really? Who needs to know?

Parents need to know, that's certain. Parents, the best way to know how your child's school is fulfilling its charge, is to know your child. After all, you don't really care about the school's ranking: your concern is whether or not your child learns what he or she needs to learn in order to succeed in life after school. Therefore, ask your child what he does in class and at school. Don't take her word for it; go to the school and watch your child in class, watch the other children, and watch the teacher. Talk to the principal. Talk to your child's friends. Talk to the other kids in class. Ask them what they do all day, and make them be specific. "We read books and things and do stuff" is not an acceptable answer. Be there at least once a month. If you are happy, and your child is happy, the other children are happy, and the teacher is happy, the chances are that your child's school is doing its job. If you don't like what you see and hear, do something, dammit.

Teachers, too, want to know that the students are learning. They, better than anyone else, should be able to tell the

Part III: Chapter 16

parent, the child, or the principal, exactly what the student knows and can do, and all this without the benefit of any standardized test. Teachers learn this information from a variety of sources, including daily observations of the student's attitudes and efforts; daily work samples; final products; and, occasionally, a test, (although the thoughtful teachers place little significance on the regurgitation of disconnected facts.) If, after all these observations, the teacher does not like the student's progress toward learning, she had better do something, dammit.

Principals should know, too. That's a no-brainer. The principal is at school all day; he or she has no excuse for not knowing what goes on. He must be in the classrooms, watching teachers and students. She must talk to teachers, asking about strategies and curriculum. He must look at student work products, not test results. She must talk to students to ask how they feel, what they like and dislike, why they like or dislike something, what they would do differently, how they feel about being in school. If the principal doesn't like what he hears or sees, he must do something, dammit.

School district administrators want to know, for sure. But, what, exactly, do they want to know? Do they want to know which school's students have the highest scores? Or do they actually want to know that the students are learning what they need to know? In the latter case, they, too, must get out off their office butts and get to the schools. Then, and only then, they can learn what they need to know. They do the same things the principal does: talk to and watch the teachers, talk to and watch the students, look at student work, and they can also talk to the principal. If they don't like what they see and hear, then they had better do something, dammit.

Real estate agents want to know, too. They want the convenient check list of school scores so they can brag about (or cover-up) the virtues of the schools where their client is looking to buy. So what? As we know, the ranking of schools says nothing about the learning of students. While standardized test

Set Up for Failure

scores may provide luscious fodder (or revolting data) for the agents, they do nothing for the schools. We don't need standardized testing for the convenience of real estate agents.

Politicians, also, think they need to know how the schools fare in their constituency. Why? So they can take credit if the schools do well, or point fingers if the schools do badly in the rankings with other districts? If the politician genuinely wants to know whether or not students are learning what they need to know, then the politician must get to the school and look for herself. We don't need standardized testing for the convenience of the politicians.

A norm-referenced, standardized test can tell only that a group of students at a moment in time can or cannot choose correct responses to questions about isolated, disconnected facts that are far removed from reality. They cannot tell if the student has a positive and curious attitude toward learning, or whether she knows how to approach problem-solving, or whether he can assess the worth of an idea, or whether she works well with other people, or whether he respects other cultures, or whether she knows where and how to find information, or whether he makes wise choices about relationships. They cannot tell us anything of any import.

While the important things are by nature qualifiable rather than quantifiable, thereby rendering their assessment impossible to rank, they can be measured. You—the parent, the teacher, the principal, the district administrator, the news reporter, anyone—can know whether the school helps the students learn important things.

First, look at what the students do. Remember the Smartplace Basic Public School Diploma Exam? This exit exam asked students to show what they could do, to produce a product that would prove they had reached the standard of performance expected of them. These final products—a thirty-minute video production about a city's impact on the geology and sociology of the region; a fully staged play the student had written about the

Part III: Chapter 16

suffering of the Iraqi people; a short historical novel about the early efforts in the Civil Rights movement; a science experiment comparing results of different chemical treatments on growth in plants; a staged cooking show about Williamsburg residents in 1760; a new and workable invention to improve sleep patterns for people of all ages—require problem-solving, collaboration, analysis of data, evaluation of possibilities, choices, planning, creative thought, successes and failures, and perseverance. They require all these things we need to be able to do in life after school; therefore, their successful completion offers proof that students have met the standards.

To show what its students can do, a school could hold periodic exhibitions of the students' final products. The exhibitions could be open to the public for two weeks, with an opening reception at which students would be present to explain and demonstrate their product. The press could be there to report what students have really learned, district administrators could attend, as could principals, teachers, students, and parents. Imagine this: it could be a bigger media event than the championship football game. (We would never ask a football player to prove his worth by completing a multiple-choice test about the history and tactics of football.) What better way to discover what students can do? And what better way to connect with the young people, and become thoroughly energized and charged up with the power of the passion for learning?

The "Student Product Exhibition" could become a mainstay for students and schools at all levels, not just for the exit exam. Way beyond any Spring Open House, this event could require students to present demonstrations of their inventions, creations, productions, and inspirations. This event could become the *raison d'etre* for all students throughout the year.

Second, mandate that the schools undergo a performance review every other year. High schools in most states already host periodic accreditation reviews by the state during which the school conducts a self-review, then endures a review by a team of educators—classroom, district, and state levels—who have been trained to observe for specific criteria. This thoughtful process forces teachers, administrators, and parents at a school to examine several areas including curriculum, scheduling, staffing, extracurricular activities, student activities, staff development, and parent and student involvement in decision making. The in-house teams spend up to a year reviewing their own site according to the criteria the state examiners will use. This scrutiny lays all the cards on the table, and forces the school staff to play. They see their strengths, their weaknesses, their vulnerable points, and their paths for the future. When the state accreditation team steps on to the campus, the school staff knows (and has admitted all) that can be known about the school, and they have already begun planning for improvements.

If every school conducted this process of self-review on a regular—say, bi-annual—basis, the habit of looking deeply at what they are doing and why they are doing it would be well-established. They would have no opportunity to relax and languish; their pattern of existence would be one of continuous growth and development into a better and better place for students to learn and become prepared for life after school.

Third, if a school or district or state must quantify the measurement of student achievement—i.e., use standardized tests—, then they had better measure the students against a standard of achievement rather than a comparison to other students and schools. They absolutely must establish a series of scores that reveal how a student compares to an ideal score. If all students scored between 92 and 95 (out of 100) on a test compared to an ideal score of 97, then all students would have been wildly successful. (If that test had been norm-referenced, half of those students scoring more than 90 percent on test would have fallen into the zero- to fiftieth-percentile of students taking the test.)

Part III: Chapter 16

Standardized tests have a place, but only in the pocketbooks and check-accounts of the companies that produce them; for the schools, their place needs to be in the toilet. If you want to know what a student can achieve, look at what he does. Don't look at what he can regurgitate, never to use again.

EPILOGUE

In darkness, people listen.

**The Very Reverend Alan Jones,
Dean of Grace Cathedral, San Francisco**

Teachers' unions organized into a tremendous force in the early 1970s. They said, "If you expect to have better teachers, and keep the good ones you have, pay the teachers more money." So, teachers' salaries rose significantly from my $6,900 annual starting salary in 1969 to the $35,000 starting salary of many of today's new teachers. Still, the graduating students of the United States appear lackluster compared with those of other industrialized nations.

"A Nation at Risk", the famous 1983 report that shattered illusions about the superior quality of public schools in the United States, demanded that the bar on standards and graduation requirements be raised as high as the stiff upper lip of academia. So, most states increased the number of credits needed for high school graduation, and they dictated more and more academically-oriented required courses. Unfortunately, students

Epilogue

greeted the new mandates with curled lips and more-than-one "Yeah, right."

"Excellent teaching is the key to successful learning for our students," cry many of today's serious educators and equally intent politicians. "Our students deserve the very best instructors," they insist. So they do. And, so, state after state increased the number of exams a teacher candidate must pass, and added level after level of requirements for maintaining a credential. Suddenly, the states were having to grant exceptions to allow un-credentialed personnel to teach, because they couldn't find enough qualified people to meet their needs. Consequently, more than a handful of students each year face three, four, and five different short-term teachers in any given class. The students in those classes waste a full year of their precious lives trying to figure out what it is they are supposed to be learning.

Nothing of consequence has changed in a hundred years, and nothing of consequence will change. Not boat-loads of money, not Mensa-level standards nor high stakes testing, nor the finest teachers money can buy will genuinely improve today's outcomes of public education. To expect highly-paid, well-trained expert teachers (armed with black binders filled with standards minutia) to effectively teach young people within our existing public education system would be like expecting Tiger Woods to win the Master's Tournament with a hickory stick for a club, or Earnhart to win the Indy 500 driving a 15-year-old full-sized van, or Calumet farms to win the Kentucky Derby with a miniature horse. It just isn't going to happen: it never has and it never will.

Nothing short of a completely reinvented system of delivering instruction to young people will make any difference in whether or not they learn.

Set Up for Failure

The reinvented system would . . .
- shrink schools and class sizes,
- define high but meaningful standards that relate to real life,
- create authentic means for measuring achievement,
- insist that students move through the curriculum at a pace commensurate with their intellectual progress,
- integrate subject matter,
- take learning outside the classroom,
- flex the time schedules,
- involve every element of the community,
- and allow students to pursue alternative learning situations.

Only when schools get serious about getting real will they begin to prepare young people to thrive in adult life.

Who will make these essential changes happen? You will. Unless, of course, you are a school or district or state administrator, or a member of a university Teacher Education school, in which case, you will fight to the death against any significant systemic changes, as you have for the past 30 years: you will not tolerate changes that would alter your power structure and weaken your mini-domain.

You, parent, are the one who must turn your child's school into a learning habitat for young humanity. You. Maybe single-handedly, like an educational Erin Brockovich. Maybe with a small cadre of fellow parents and local community members. Maybe through highly-organized, intense pressure on your state's legislators. You are the one who will make it happen, if it is to happen.

Any true reinventions of the public schools will have to be generated from the end-user—that's you and your child. The top level won't make the changes because they thrive on the

Epilogue

status quo. The bottom level must demand the changes, the top level must permit the changes, then hand the change engine over to the bottom level who works out the details. Your legislators have the law-making power, and you have the power of the vote. You are their constituent.

Where to start
Begin by contacting any of the reform-oriented organizations listed at the end of this chapter. Ask for help. Perhaps the organization will connect you with a more local group that can guide you, or perhaps they will send you some helpful literature.

Start bending the ears of any other parent you meet, either through PTA or at soccer games or in the grocery store. Give them a copy of this book to read. When you find several like-minded people, organize and write your goals. Be specific about what you want to accomplish and in what order. The information from the national reform organizations will be most helpful with the goal-writing.

Read every article you can about the problems in education: these articles can be found in any journal or newspapers. Cut out the article and make copies to send with letters. Keep the originals in a binder of resources.

Then start writing letters. Write to your district, state, and national legislators. Tell them your concerns and fears, and tell them what changes you want in your public schools. Cite statistics whenever you can. (Statistics don't always mean much, but they carry a big impact.) Include copies of pertinent articles. Ask for a response. Be prepared to follow-up this letter with e-mails and phone calls. Don't let them off the hook from replying to your concerns. And, don't take "no" for an answer; you are right, the status quo is wrong, and you must not settle for anything less than change.

Write letters to the editor of every local newspaper, telling what you know to be true about the problems with public

Set Up for Failure

education. Write to me; I will help you compose your letters. Write the letters often, each with a different point. Write so often that people will begin to say, "Hey, Honey, here's another letter from that nut-case who hates public schools. I wonder what she has to say this time." Make them pay attention to you so they know you by face and name. When they stop you in the store to comment—any comment will do—about your letter, then you know you're making an impact.

Write to the State Department of Education. The personnel there won't help you, because you want to change their power structure. However, they need to hear from you.

Document everything you do in this effort, and keep copies of everything you send and receive. Keep a telephone log recording any calls you make and any you receive, with a brief note as to the content of the conversation.

It won't be easy

Be prepared for a long and lumpy struggle. The massive reinvention of America's public schools would take five to ten years if everyone involved had the same focus; considering that the existing power structure will fight tooth and nail against any change, the struggle could take decades. By then, of course, your child will have successfully (or not) endured the system. Hopefully, you will be able to pass a partially-completed reform package on to the next intelligent and concerned parent.

Where there's a will, there's a way. If you want something badly enough, you will find a way to do it.

"There's a hunger out there," said Theodore Sizer, founder of the Coalition of Essential Schools, "and there are enough families—all kinds of families—who take the time to think hard about what they want. . . ." When asked if parents would be the ones who make the difference in what happens to schools, he replied, "Absolutely. Ultimately they will make the political difference."

Epilogue

If you have ever been involved in some part of a change process, you know how threatening it is to throw out the old and start something new. You know the pain involved, and if you have been successful, you know the absolute exhilaration at seeing progress happen, feeling the winds of change in your face, and experiencing the intellectual and emotional stimulation that comes with new ideas and creative thinking.

Begin now!
The Great Wall of China started with one brick, the Panama Canal with one shovel of dirt, the six-month journey on the Oregon Trail with one step. Your drive to make public schools real and really valuable for your child will start with one phone call; where it ends depends on how much gas you have, and how much help you get along the road. But it has to start somewhere, some time.

"For truth and duty, it is ever the fitting time; who waits until circumstances completely favor his undertaking, will never accomplish anything." Martin Luther.

"It is well to think well; it is divine to act well." Horace Mann.

"A smooth sea never made a skilled mariner." English proverb.

"The risk of trying something new is far less than the risk of standing still." Theodore Sizer.

The big trouble with the present system of free public education in the United States is that it is not even standing still: it is, faster and faster, sliding and sinking into an intellectual black hole.
Truly, we have absolutely nothing to lose by reinventing schools.
Truly, we must try.

Set Up for Failure

Part 4:
Resources and References

Resource List of Education Reform Organizations

The following organizations and associations provide information, guidance, and advocacy for education reform. This list is not complete: other organizations exist for the same purpose. All of this information is available on the Internet.

Inclusion on this list in no way implies endorsement, either the organization's endorsement of this book nor the author's endorsement of the organization.

Annenberg Institute for School Reform
  Brown University, P O Box 1985, Providence RI 02912;
  401.863.7990

California School Redesign Network
  CIRAS building, Room 109-M, 520 Galvez Mall, Stanford, CA 94305;
  650.724.2932
  A clearing house of research and information on small schools and redesigned traditional schools

Center for Collaborative Education
  1 Renaissance Park, 1135 Tremont St., Suite 490, Boston MA 02120
  617.421.0134
  www.ccebos.org

Resources and References

Center on Reinventing Public Education
>Daniel J. Evans Schools of Public Affairs, University of Washington, P O Box 353060, Seattle WA 98195; 206.685.2214

Coalition of Essential Schools
>CES National, 1814 Franklin St., Suite 700, Oakland CA 84612;
>510.433.1451
>www.essentialschools.org

Council of the Great City Schools
>1301 Pennsylvania Ave., NW Suite 702, Washington DC 20004;
>202.393.2427

Institute for Educational Leadership Inc.
>1001 Connecticut Ave. NW Suite 310, Washington DC 20036;
>202.822.8405
>To improve education and the lives of children and their families

Jobs for the Future
>88 Broad Street, 8th Floor, Boston MA 02110;
>617.728.4446
>www.jff.org/Margins/Index.html
>From the Margins to the Mainstream (Effective Learning Environments Inside and Outside High Schools); Reinventing High Schools: Implications for Urban High School

National Coalition of Advocates for Students
>100 Bolyston St. #815, Boston MA 02216;
>617.367.8507
>Addressing real issues for under-served students

Metlife Foundation Family School Connection Project
>P O Box 211915, Royal Palm Beach FL 33421;
>561.383.6227
>Exploring ways to approach under-served students.

Rethinking Schools – An Urban Education Resource
(Longer-format publications on critical topics in school reform)
1001 E. Keefe Avenue, Milwaukee WI 53212;
414.964.9646, 800.669.4192
www.rethinkingschools.org

The Education Trust
www.edtrust.org

Thomas B. Fordham Foundation
1627 K Street, NW, Suite 600, Washington DC 20006;
202.223.5452
www.edexcellence.net
"Advancing sound research and fresh ideas on K-12 education reform"

Resources and References

References

Acheson, Keith A. and John H. Hansen, *Classroom Observations and Conferences with Teachers*, Florida State University, Tallahassee, FL: Teacher Education Projects.

"Action for all: The Public's Responsibility for Public Education", a report from Public Education Network, *Education Week*. Bethesda, MD: Editorial Projects in Education, April 2001.

Adler, Mortimer J., *The Paideia Proposal, An Educational Manifesto*. New York: MacMillan Publishing Co., Inc., 1982.

Allen, Steve, *Vulgarians at the Gate: Trash TV and Raunch Radio*. Promotheus, 2001.

Ayers, William, "Perestroika in Chicago's Schools", *Educational Leadership*. May 1991, 69-71.

Barbe, Walter B. and Raymond H. Swassing, *Teaching Through Modality Strengths: concepts and Practices*, Columbus, Ohio: Zaner-Bloser, Inc., 1979.

Barth, Patte, et. al. eds., *Education Watch 1998*. Washington, D.C.: The Education Trust, 1998.

Bender, Matt, and David James Heiss, "Students failing exit exam", *Redlands Daily Facts*, Redlands, CA, October 1, 2002.

Bishop, John, "Do Curriculum-Based External Exit Exam systems enhance Student Achievement?", Research Report. Philadelphia, PA: Consortium for Policy Research in Education, 1998.

Brandt, Ron, "On Changing Secondary Schools: A Conversation with Ted Sizer", *Educational Leadership*. February 1988, 30-36.

Brandt, Ron, "On Teachers Coaching Teachers: A Conversation with Bruce Joyce", *Educational Leadership*. February 1987, 12-17.

Brandt, Ron, "On Restructuring Schools: A Conversation with Mike Cohen", *Educational Leadership*. May 1991, 54-58.

Brandt, Ron, "Learning with and from One Another", *Educational Leadership*. February 1987, 3.

Brandt, Ron, "On Learning Styles: A Conversation with Pat Guild", *Educational Leadership*. October 1990, 10-13.

Brownstein, Ronald, "Firms on Economy's Cutting Edge Show government How It can Excel", *Los Angeles Times*. June 30, 1997.

Bruer, John T., *Schools for Thought, A Science of Learning in the Classroom*, Cambridge, Massachusetts: A Bradford Book, The MIT Press, 1995.

Brunner, Carolyn E. and Walter S. Majewski, "Mildly Handicapped Students Can Succeed with Learning Styles", *Educational Leadership*. October 1990, 21-23.

Butterfield, Fox, "Why They Excel", *Parade Magazine*. January 21, 1990.

Caine, Renate Nummela and Geoffrey Caine, "Understanding a Brain Based Approach to Learning and Teaching", *Educational Leadership*. October 1990, 66-70.

Caine, Renate Nummela and Geoffrey Caine, *Making Connections: Teaching and the Human Brain*. Alexandria, VA.: Association for Supervision and Curriculum Development, 1991.

Canfield, Jack, "Self Esteem for Dealing with Success and Failure", Audio Tape. Alexandria, VA: Association for Supervision and Curriculum Development, 1987.

Resources and References

Carden, Gwen Yount, "'Seeing Red' 'Feeling Blue'? Color really does affect our moods", *The San Bernardino Sun*. San Bernardino, CA: The Sun Company of San Bernardino, California, 1988.

Carpo, Raymond F., "Face to Face Management", *Engineering Manager*. January 30, 1989.

Chaplin, Duncan, "Tassels on the Cheap", *Education Next*. Leland Stanford Junior University, Stanford, CA: Hoover Institution, Fall 2002.

Coaching Teachers to Higher Levels of Effectiveness. Nevada City, CA: Performance Learning systems, Inc., 1986.

Cohen, David K., and Heather C. Hill, "State Policy and Classroom Performance: Mathematics Reform in California", *Policy Briefs*. Philadelphia, PA: Consortium for Policy Research in Education, January 1998.

Colfax, J. David and Micki Colfax, *Homeschooling for Excellence*. Warner Books, 1988.Combs, Arthur W., "New Assumptions for Educational Reform", *Educational Leadership*. February 1988, 38-40.

"Common Problems Facing the Nation's Schools and New American Schools' Solutions". Arlington, VA: New American Schools.

"Common Sense About SAT Score differences and Test Validity", Research Notes by The College Board, New York, June 1997.

Costa, Arthur, ed., *Developing Minds: A Resource Book for Teaching Thinking*. Alexandria, VA: Association for Supervision and Curriculum Development, 1985.

Costa, Arthur and Robert Barmston, *The Art of Cognitive Coaching: Supervision for Intelligent Teaching.* (An Awareness Workshop). Carmichael, CA: The Institute for Intelligent Behavior.

Curry, Lynn, "A Critique of the Research on Learning Styles", *Educational Leadership*. October 1990, 50-54.

Curwin, Richard L. and Allen N. Mendler, *Discipline with Dignity*, Alexandria, VA: Association for Supervision and Curriculum Development, 1989.

Cushman, Kathleen, "Essential School Structure and Design: boldest Moves Get the Best Results", *Horace*, June 1991.

Darling-Hammond, Linda, *The Right To Learn*. San Francisco, CA: Jossey-Bass Publishers, 1997.

Darling-Hammond, Linda, and Deborah Loewenberg Ball, "Teaching for High Standards: What Policymakers Need to Know and Be Able to Do", National Commission on Teaching & America's Future, and Consortium for Policy Research in Education, 1997.

Downs, Andreae, "Successful School Reform Efforts Share Common Features", *Harvard Education Letter*. Cambridge, MA: Harvard Graduate School of Education, March/April 2000.

Dunn, Rita, "Rita Dunn Answers Questions on Learning Styles", *Educational Leadership*. October 1990, 15-19.

Dunn, Rita and Kenneth Dunn, *Educator's Self-Guide to Individualizing Instructional Programs*. New York: Parker Publishing Company, 1975a.

Dykema, Ravi, "How Schools Fail Kids and How they Could Be Better, An Interview with Ted Sizer", *Nexus*, nexuspub.com, May/June 2002.

"Education: People's Chief Concerns", statistics from PublicAgenda. www.publicagenda.org/issues/images/education/pc c13empprof.gif.

Resources and References

Education Writers Association, Washington, D.C.: "Education Reform, Class Size", June 1999; "Education Reform, Dropouts", March 2001; "Education Reform, Social Promotion", April 1999; "Education Reform, Small Schools", August 1999; "Education Reform, Special Education", February 2003.

Elmore, Richard F., "Investing in Teacher Learning: Staff Development and Instructional Improvement in Community School District #2, New York City", New York: National Commission on Teacher & America's Future and Consortium for Policy Research in Education, August 1997.

"English-Language Arts Content Standards", California State Department of Education. www.cde.ca.gov/standards/englishlanguagearts/

"Fast Facts About Dropout and Completion Rates", Phi Delta Kappa International, Bloomington, Indiana, February 1998.

Fischer, Bill, ed., "Back to School Means Starting Over", *NEA Today*. Washington, D.C.: National Education Association of the United States, September 1990, 4-5.

Fischer, Bill, ed., "Kentucky Overhauls Its Schools", *NEA Today*. Washington, D.C.: National Education Association of the United States, October 1990, 4-5.

Foglia, Ed., "Á Key to Success in Schools", *Teacher Views*. Los Angeles: California Teachers Association, 1990.

Foster, Alice G., hen Teachers Initiate Restructuring", *Educational Leadership*. May 1991, 27-30.

"Gap widened by unintended conspiracy", *Education Reporter*. Washington, D.C.: Education writers Association, July/August 2000.

Gardner, Howard, *Extraordinary Minds*, New York: Basic Books, a division of Harper Collins Publishers, 1997.

Set Up for Failure

Gardner, Howard, *Frames of Mind: The Theory of Multiple Intelligences*. New York: Basic books, 1983.

Gardner, Howard, *The Unschooled Mind, How children Think & How Schools Should Teach*, New York: Basic Books, a division of Harper Collins Publishers, 1991.

Garger, Stephen, "Is There a Link Between Learning Style and Neurophysiology?" *Educational Leadership*. October 1990, 63-65.

Garmston, Robert J., "How Administrators Support Peer Coaching", *Educational Leadership*. February 1987, 18-26.

Gatto, John, "An Award-Winning Teacher Speaks Out", *Utne Reader*, Minneapolis, MN: LENS Publishing Co., September/October 1990, 73-77.

Gibboney, Richard A., "A Critique of Madeline Hunter's Teaching Model from Dewey's Perspective", *Educational Leadership*. February 1987, 46-50.

Glickman, Carl, "Pretending Not to Know What We Know", *Educational Leadership*. May 1991, 4-9.

Goodlad, John T., *Place Called School, Prospects for the future*. New York: McGraw-Hill Book Company, 1984.

Greene, Robert, "Focus on classroom discipline", *The Press-Enterprise*. Riverside, CA, July 1, 1998.

"Guide to National Board Certification:, National Board of Professional Teaching Standards, 1998-99.

Guild, Pat Burke and Stephen Garger, *Marching to Different Drummers*. Alexandria, VA: Association for Supervision and Curriculum Development, 1985.

Hall, Stephen S., "Test-Tube Moms", *The New York Times Magazine*. April 5, 1998.

Halsted, Alice L., "A Bridge to Adulthood: Service Learning at the Middle Level", *Midpoints Occasional Papers*. Columbus, Ohio: National Middle School Association, Spring 1997.

Resources and References

Hand, Kathi L., "Style is a Tool for Students, Too!" *Educational Leadership*. October 1990, 13-14.

Hasenstab, Joseph K., and Connie Corcoran Wilson, *Training the Teacher as a Champion*. Nevada City, CA: Performance Learning Systems, 1989.

Hord, Shirley M., William L. Rutherford, Leslie Huling-Austin, and Gene E. Hall, *Taking Charge of Change*. Alexandria, VA: Association for Supervision and Curriculum Development, 1987.

Hotz, Robert Lee, "In Art of Language, the Brain Matters", *Los Angeles Times*. The Times Mirror Company, October 18, 1998.

Hunter, Madeline C., "Beyond Rereading Dewey. . . What's next? A Response to Gibboney", *Educational Leadership*. February 1987, 51-53.

Hunter Madeline C., *Mastery Teaching*. El Segundo, CA: TIP Publications, 1982.

Ismael, Katie, "'Sow crisis' unites", *The Press-Enterprise*. Riverside, California, November 8, 2002.

"Johnny can't write either, tests show", *The San Bernardino Sun*, San Bernardino, CA: The Sun Company of San Bernardino, California, May, 1990.

"Joint Statement on the Impact of entertainment Violence on Children", Congressional Public Health Summit, July 26, 2002.

Joyce, Bruce and Marsha Weil, *Models of Teaching*. Englewood Cliffs, New Jersey: Prentice-Hall, Inc., 1980.

Joyce, Bruce, ed., *Changing School Culture Through Staff Development*. 1990 Yearbook, Alexandria, VA: Association for supervision and Curriculum Development.

Kiersey, David and Marilyn Bates, *Please Understand Me, Character and Temperament Types*. Del Mar, CA: Prometheus, Nemesis, 1987.

Kelly, Dennis, "U.S. schools consider longer school year", *The San Bernardino Sun*. San Bernardino, CA, October 2, 1990.

Knight, J. Pat, Cheryl S. Knight, and Arthur Quickenton, "Education in Rural Schools", *The Educational Forum*, Fall 1996.

Kober, Nancy, "What Tests Can and Cannot Tell Us", *TestTalk for Leaders*. Washington, D.C.: Center on Education Policy, October 2002.

Kohn, Alfie, *The Schools Our children Deserve*. Boston, MA: Houghton Mifflin Company, 1999.

Kohn, Alfie, *The Case Against Standardized Testing*, Portsmouth, New Hampshire, 2000.

Koppich, Julia E., Charles Taylor Kerchner, and Joseph G. Weeres, "The 'New Teacher Unions'", *Education Week*. Editorial Projects in Education, April 9, 1997.

Kotzsch Ronald, "Waldorf Schools: Education for the Head, Hands, and Heart", *Utne Reader*. Minneapolis, MN: LENS Publishing Co., September/October 1990, 84-90.

Lawrence, Barbara Kent, et. al., *Dollars & Sense: The Cost Effectiveness of Small Schools*. Cincinnati, OH: Knowledge works Foundation, 2002.

Lewis, Anne C., *Figuring It Out: Standards-Based Reforms in Urban Middle Grades*. New York: The Edna McConnell Clark Foundation.

Lewis, Catherine, and Ineko Tsuchida, "The Basics in Japan: The Three C's", *Educational Leadership*. March 1998.

Lieberman, Ann, Linda Darling-Hammond and David Zuckerman, *Early Lessons in Restructuring Schools*. New York: National Center for Restructuring Education, Schools, and Teaching, 1991.

Resources and References

Lieberman, Ann and Lynn Miller, "Restructuring Schools: What Matters and What Works", *Phi Delta Kappan.* June 1990, 759-764.

Link, Frances R., ed., *Essays on the Intellect,* Alexandria, VA: Association for Supervision and Curriculum Development, 1985.

Loveland, Elaina, "Achieving Academic goals Through Place-Based Learning", *Rural Roots.* Washington, D.C.: Rural School and Community Trust, February 2003.

MacDuff, Cassie, "A generation, and the future, may be lost", *The Press-Enterprise.* Riverside, CA, July 27, 2000.

Manzo, Kathleen Kennedy, "Finding Their Voices", *Education Week.* October 4, 2000.

Mason, Robert E., *Contemporary Educational Theory.* New York: Longman, 1972

Mathematics Content Standards", California State Department of Education. www.cde.ca.gov/standards/math/.

May, Frank B., *Reading as Communication,*, fifth edition. Upper Saddle River, New Jersey: Merrill, an imprint of Prentice Hall, 1998.

McRobbie, Joan, Jeremy D. Finn, and Patrick Harman, "Class Size Reduction: Lessons Learned from Experience", Policy Brief. San Francisco, CA: WestEd., August 1998.

Measuring Up 2002: The State-by-State Report Card for Higher Education. The National Center for Public Policy and higher Education.

Miles, Karen Hawley, and Linda Darling-Hammond, "Rethinking the allocation of Teaching Resources: Some Lessons from high Performing Schools", Research Report. Philadelphia, PA: Consortium for Policy Research in Education, 1997.

"Model Standards for Beginning Teacher Licensing and Development: A Resource for State Dialogue", Interstate New Teacher Assessment and Support Consortium, A Project of the Council of Chief State School Officers, September 1992.

Moffett, Kenneth L., Jan St. John, and Jo Ann Isken, "Training and Coaching Beginning Teachers: An Antidote to Reality Shock", *Educational Leadership.* February 1987, 34-46.

Mollison, Andrew, "In their own world", *The Press-Enterprise.* Riverside, CA, November 21, 2002.

Morris, A.J., et. al., "Examining the Impact of the Chinese Educational system", *Education.* Winter 1997.

Mueller, Daniel J., Clinton I. Chase, and James D. Walden, "Effects of Reduced Class Size in Primary Classes", *Educational Leadership.* February 1988, 48-50.

Murfee, Elizabeth, "Eloquent Evidence: Arts at the core of Learning", pamphlet. President's Committee on the Arts and the Humanities, April 1996.

"The Neglected 'R': The Need for a Writing Revolution", The National Commission on Writing, 2003.

Neubert, Gloria A. and Elizabeth C. Bratton, "Team Coaching: Staff Development Side by Side", *Educational Leadership.* February 1987, 29-32.

Nocera Joseph, "How the Middle Class Has Helped Ruin the Public Schools", *Utne Reader.* Minneapolis, MN: LENS Publishing Co., September/October 1990, 66-72.

Obsatz, Sharyn, "Exploring causes of Latino clashes", *The Press-Enterprise.* Riverside, CA, April 30, 2001.

Olsen, Karen D., *The Mentor Teacher Role: Owner's Manual, Fifth Edition.* Oak Creek, AZ: Books for Educators, 1989.

Resources and References

O'Neil, John, ed., "Literature Survey Reveals Few Changes in School Reading Lists", *ASCD Update*. Alexandria, VA: Association for Supervision and Curriculum Development, November 1989, 3.

O'Neil John, ed., "What Do Our 17-year-olds Know?! *ASCD Curriculum Update*. Alexandria, VA: Association for Supervision and Curriculum Development, September, 1990, 4-5.

O'Neil, John, "Making Sense of Style", *Educational Leadership*. October 1990, 4-9.

Ornstein, Allan C., and Daniel U. Levine, *Foundations of Education*, 6th edition. Boston, MA: Houghton Mifflin Company, 1997.

Perrin Janet, "The Learning Styles Project for Potential Dropouts", *Educational Leadership*. October 1990, 23-24.

Project Pride. Nevada City, CA: Performance Learning systems.

"Public Support for School Improvement", press release from Phi Delta Kappa International, Bloomington, IN, August 26, 1997.

Raywid, Mary Anne, "Small Schools: A Reform That Works", *Educational Leadership*. December 1997/January 1998.

Resnick, Lauren B. and Leopold E. Klopfer, eds., *Toward a Thinking Curriculum: Current Cognitive Research*. 1989 Yearbook, Alexandria, VA: Association for Supervision and Curriculum Development.

Roberts, Arthur D. and Gordon Cawelti, *Redefining General Education in the American High School*. Alexandria, VA: Association for Supervision and Curriculum Development, 1984.

Rolfe, Dick, Column for The Dove Foundation. October 2000.

Rothstein, Richard, "Where do school dollars go?", Scripps-McClatchy Western Service, June 2, 1996.

Russo, Alexander, "Political Educator, Paul Vallas pays the price of leadership", *Education Next*. Stanford, CA: Hoover Institution, Leland Stanford Junior University, Winter, 2003.

Santoli, Al, "First Lesson: Believe In Yourself", *Parade Magazine,* February 14, 1990, 18.

Satin, Mark, "Nine Ideas to Improve the Schools", *Utne Reader*. Minneapolis, MN: LENS Publishing Co., September/October 1990, 78-83.

Shanker, Albert, "The End of the Traditional Model of Schooling, and a Proposal for Using Incentives to Restructure Our Public Schools", *Phi Delta Kappan*, January, 1990, 345-357.

Silberman, Charles E., *Crisis in the Classroom: The Remaking of American Education*. New York: Vintage books (A division of Random House), 1970.

Sizer, Theodore R., *Horace's compromise, The Dilemma of the American High School*. Boston: Houghton Mifflen Company, 1984.

Sizer, Theodore, "No Pain, No Gain," *Educational Leadership*. Alexandria, VA: Association for Supervision and Curriculum Development, May 1991, 32-34.

"State High School Exit Exams, A Baseline Report", Action Summary for State and National Leaders. Washington, D.C.: Center on Education Policy, August 2002.

Stevenson, Harold W., "A Study of Three Cultures", *Phi Delta Kappan*. Bloomington, IN, March 1998.

"Student Effort and Educational Progress", National Center for Education Statistics. www.nces.ed.gov/programs/coe/2002.

"Study finds TV-watching teens more prone to violence", *Redlands Daily Facts*. Redlands, CA, March 27, 2002.

"Study sees increase in time parents, kids spend together", *The Press-Enterprise*. Riverside, CA, May 10, 2001.

Resources and References

"Talent Development High School with Career Academies" Tools for Schools. www.ed.gov/pubs/ToolsforSchools/tdhs.html.

"Teachers, Parents Find Smaller Schools Appealing, but See Other Education Reforms As More Pressing", press release from Public Agenda, New York, September 26, 2001.

"Teaching Reading, A Balanced, Comprehensive Approach to Teaching Reading in Prekindergarten through Grade Three", Sacramento, CA: Reading Program Advisory, 1996.

Toch, Thomas, "The New Education Bazaar", *U.S. News & World Report*, April 27, 1998.

"Using School-Community Partnerships to Bolster Student Learning", Policy Brief from WestEd, San Francisco, CA, December 2002.

Walsh, Mark, "Columbus to Try Site-Based management, 'Houses'", *Education Week*. March 1, 1989.

Westerberg, Tim R. and Dan Brickley, "Restructuring a Comprehensive High School", *Educational Leadership*. Alexandria, VA: Association for Supervision and Curriculum Development, May 1991, 23-26.

"What Kids Watch Can Make them Aggressive", www.dove.org/research/what_kids_watch.htm, April 25, 2001.

"What Matters Most: Teaching for America's Future", Report of the National Commission on Teaching & America's future, New York, September 1996.

Wildman, Terry M. and Jerry A. Niles, "Essentials of Professional Growth", *Educational Leadership*. Alexandria, VA: Association for Supervision and Curriculum Development, February 1987, 4-10

Williams, Anne, *Effective Teaching/Supervision: A Staff Development Training Program That Makes a Difference*. Office of Riverside County Superintendent of Schools, Riverside, California, 1981-82.

Wingfield, Arthur, *Human Learning and Memory: An Introduction.* New York: Harper and Row, 1979.

Wohlstetter, Priscilla, and Noelle Griffin, "Creating and Sustaining Learning Communities: Early Lessons from Charter Schools", *Occasional Paper*. Philadelphia, PA: Consortium for Policy Research in Education, 1998.

Woodring, Paul, *The Persistent Problems of Education*. Bloomington, Indiana: Phi Delta Kappa Educational Foundation, 1983.

Wyland, Jessica, "Students RISE and shine", *Redlands Daily Facts*, Redlands, CA, December 14, 1999.

www.ingramcontent.com/pod-product-compliance
Lightning Source LLC
Chambersburg PA
CBHW022106150426
43195CB00008B/295